Also available at all good book stores

9781801500630

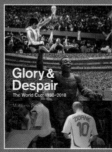

9781801501248

9781785316470

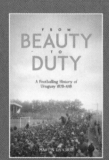

9781801501491

9781801500968

9781801503709

9781801503723

9781801501682

9781801501668

JOHN McNICOLL

An Ode to the

CHOSEN FEW

Football's Piano Players

First published by Pitch Publishing, 2022

Pitch Publishing
9 Donnington Park,
85 Birdham Road,
Chichester,
West Sussex,
PO20 7AJ
www.pitchpublishing.co.uk
info@pitchpublishing.co.uk

A CIP catalogue record is available for this book
from the British Library.

ISBN 978 1 8015 015 5

Typesetting and origination by Pitch Publishing
Printed and bound in India by Replika Press Pvt. Ltd.

Contents

Acknowledgements 9

Introduction. 11

1. Ferenc Puskás 13

2. Diego Maradona 27

3. Eric Cantona 44

4. Steven Gerrard 72

5. Johan Cruyff 95

6. Lionel Messi. 119

7. Cristiano Ronaldo. 151

8. Ronaldo – Il Fenomeno 183

9. Thierry Henry. 212

10. Francesco Totti 234

11. The Nearly Men. 248

12. The Pretenders 282

13. The Final Whistle –
    The Man In The Middle 314

For Edward Christopher McNicoll –

AKA Ted ... The Boss

Acknowledgements

FIRSTLY I would like to thank Pitch Publishing for giving me the chance to share my thoughts on the game we all love. It has been the most interesting but surreal experience of my life. To all the people who helped me along the way, however big or small their contribution, for that I'm eternally grateful. Thanks to friends and family for listening to me going on about it for the last ten months – you know you love it really. Thanks to former referee Keith Hackett for his musings on the game, Tom Pheby for his comments on Thierry Henry, and Alan Tongue for his golden review of ex-Manchester United skipper, Bryan Robson.

Introduction

FOOTBALL TEAMS consist of 11 men on the pitch but, as Bill Shankly once noted, while some will be your more functional members of the team, you need some to play the piano. This book examines how, although the footballing world has been littered with superstar footballers, some have taken it upon themselves to drag their respective teams to glory. Both domestically and on the world stage, these stars have brought joy to fans around the globe by playing the sweetest of tunes for their club and countries. From Lionel Messi to Maradona, Cristiano Ronaldo to the original Ronaldo, Il Fenomeno. This is their story. Enjoy, and all the best.

'A football team is like a piano. You need eight men to carry it and three who can play the damn thing.' – **Bill Shankly**

1

Ferenc Puskás

'Ferenc truly was just a wonderful player. He had a roly-poly physique, but a wonderful left foot and he was a brilliant finisher. I would put Puskás in any list of all-time greats. A wonderful player and a wonderful person and he really enjoyed playing the game.' – **Sir Tom Finney**

OUR INAUGURAL taste of footballing excellence takes us back to possibly the earliest recording of a world superstar. When football was limited in how widely it was broadcast, it was only through newspaper cuttings and matches on home soil that people in the UK were able to witness the technical prowess of some of the players that lived outside its shores.

Hungarian forward, Ferenc Puskás was possibly the first global name in football. Prior to Puskás bursting on to the scene, a player by the name of Jose Andrade had wowed South Americans by inspiring Uruguay to World Cup success in 1930, with an emphatic 4-2 victory over neighbours Argentina in the final. Andrade has been compared to an olden-day David Beckham, with his scintillating football skills, dashing good looks and he was even rumoured to be working part-time as a gigolo, something I'm sure Posh Spice might have had a bit to say about. The Black Pearl, as he was to be known, was to begin the 'superstar' trend that was to follow.

As war raged across Europe, Ferenc Puskás, still able to play football, signed for his local team Kispest. The forward had grown up living in and around the Kispest area, having played in his younger days for the junior teams, and with the player now coming of age, he signed papers on a professional contract in 1943. The 16-year-old made his debut against Nagyváradi and never looked back. The youngster soon attracted attention from a wider audience, so much so, in fact, that by the time he had turned 18 he was called up for the Hungarian national team to face Austria. The Second World War had ceased and international football was again at the forefront of people's minds. Puskás wasn't to be fazed by this huge occasion and notched on his debut in a 5-2 victory, the first of many in a Hungary shirt.

Puskás was in and out of his club side during the first few campaigns as questions over his size and agility were asked. Puskás senior was the coach of the first team at the time and highlighted the fact that his son, despite his streamline-defying shape, was more than capable of roughing it with the big boys. His early years would see a return of 24 goals in 51 starts. As with all young players, inconsistency can have an effect on numbers and statistics. But the striker had scored a goal every other match, which is certainly not to be questioned at any level of football. It was when the forward entered into his twenties that his shooting boots wbegan firing.

As the 1940s drew to a close, Kispest were taken over by the Hungarian Ministry of Defence. The team were to be known as the 'Hungarian Army Team', changing their name to Budapest Honvéd. With a sudden new influx of financial clout and prestige, Honvéd started to attract players to the club, which began a period of domination domestically. Zoltán Czibor and Sândor Kocsis were the first big names recruited into the squad. The pair had shone in the national team alongside Puskás and were deemed excellent additions to the team. The cream of Hungary was slowly but surely drafted in through the turnstiles and, with Puskás now finding his feet in front of goal, Honvéd, secured the first top-tier title in their history at the end of the 1949/50 season.

I say finding his feet. Puskás had one foot for football, the other was merely for standing on. 'You can only kick with one foot at a time, otherwise you fall on your arse,' said Puskás when once quizzed about the rigidness in his playing style. His left foot, though, was deadly. With his frame being a little portlier than your average footballer, the power he was able to generate once in a shooting position was that of a ball being fired out of a cannon.

The army had insisted that all the players at the club be given rank status. This is where one of Puskás's many nicknames came from as he was to be named the 'Galloping Major'. The major was certainly galloping all over opposition defences as his goal return was starting to reveal pure class. In five consecutive seasons from 1945 to 1950, he scored over 30 goals a campaign, including becoming Europe's top goalscorer in 1947/48 with 50. These were quite phenomenal numbers from a player who was accepted as not being very mobile.

With domestic success becoming a regular occurrence for Puskás, international accolades would soon dovetail wonderfully as a period of footballing domination was about to begin for the men from Hungary. With the Soviet Union still heavily occupying large parts of the country and the communist regime causing the worst period of oppression that the nation had ever lived through, the displays of the footballers wearing the badge had lifted the spirits of the folk at home. The 'Magical Magyars', as they were to be fondly known, were to embark on a near-perfect run towards world football nirvana.

For a period stretching over half a decade, Hungary played football that was out of this world. The tactics and formation that were utilised by the team were like nothing that had ever been seen before on the football pitch. The norm around football during this period was the WM formation, which consisted of a 3-2-2-3 line-up. Hungarian manager Gusztáv Sebes had other ideas. He liked his players to drop into pockets and was possibly the first manager to play a deep-lying forward behind the frontline, in between midfield and attack. His 2-3-3-2 formation was revolutionary, as was the fitness regime he implemented during the team's training camps. Of course, this didn't suit all the players but Puskás knew that, if he wanted to play, he had to toe the line.

Sir Alex Ferguson had witnessed the skill and technical ability of this team with his own eyes. 'The great players do things that you don't expect, so when I dodged school on that Wednesday afternoon in 1953 to watch the England vs Hungary match at a misty Wembley on TV, no one expected what we were about to witness: a new way of playing football. It was nothing short of breath-taking.'

Prior to what was dubbed the 'Match of the Century', Hungary had competed in the summer Olympics in Finland. In July of 1952, they embarked on a run to the Olympic podium, starting with a preliminary-round win over Romania. A 2-1 victory ensured that the Magyars were off and running in the competition. Italy provided their first-round opponents and, although Puskás had been on the periphery of the matches thus far, he was still a danger to the men charged with trying to mark him. Hungary advanced with a 3-0 win. With no goals during the opening two matches, Puskás certainly made up for that in the quarter-final tie with Turkey. Hungary had begun to strut like a peacock as they provided their most dominant performance to date.

Leading 2-0 at half-time, Sebes could sense the confidence beginning to ooze out of his players. Puskás joined the party with two second-half strikes as the Magical Magyars ran riot and finished with a 7-1 rout. The golden touch in front of goal continued as semi-final opponents Sweden were also drummed, 6-0, with Puskás again adding to his tally with another goal. 'It was one of those days,' said Puskás, who opened the scoring. 'Once we'd hit our rhythm, we were virtually irresistible.'

In Jonathan Wilson's book, *The Names Heard Long Ago*, it was rumoured that news had reached Hungary coach Sebes regarding unrest back home. Sebes, on the morning of the final, received a telephone call from Mátyás Rákosi, the leader of Hungary's Communist Party, warning him that defeat wouldn't be tolerated. He needn't have worried. On 2 August 1952, Yugoslavia faced Hungary for the Olympic gold medal at Helsinki's Olympic Stadium. Another clean sheet followed as Hungary were to prove far too strong and claim the centre stand of the podium. Puskás again notched in the final, as well as club-mate Czibor, to end the match with a 2-0 win. The aggregate score for the team during the course of the competition was 20 goals for and only two against, as they took home the gold medal.

'It was during the Olympics that our football first started to flow with real power,' said Puskás when interviewed by reporters years later. The Turkey match was clearly the turning point for the team who, once they could smell blood, would finish the job with the cold, ruthless touch of an assassin. The good times just kept on coming as the following year saw yet more honours, with the Central European Championships also added to the team's growing wealth of achievements. The nations' championships were an early format of what's now known as the Euros, or European Championship in old money. This originally consisted of Hungary, Italy, Switzerland, Austria and Czechoslovakia. Hungary breezed through to the final, where they faced Italy. The Hungarians made light work of the Italians and, with two Puskás strikes, completed a 3-0 win to lift yet more silverware.

But what was to become even more historic in 1953 was the aforementioned 'Match of the Century'. England hosted the Hungarians at Wembley, having never lost on home soil to a foreign nation. The Three Lions had a host of quality players in their ranks, including goalkeeper Gil Merrick, Stan Mortensen, Stanley Mathews, Billy Wright and Alf Ramsey. Wright at the time was considered one of the best defenders in the world. The most notable name in this team, though, was defender Ramsey. The soon-to-be England manager was about to be given a taste of the football future.

England, as predicted, lined up in their WM formation, whereas the mavericks from Hungary were playing in their now much-loved 2-3-3-2. The visitors took the lead within the first minute, a sign there and then that England might well have underestimated their European counterparts. The rigidness of England's formation was about to be their undoing as the Hungarians exploited the space in between the lines of defence and attack by situating players in the pockets. The English players were bamboozled by this and were unsure whether to stick or twist in how they lined up to mark the opposition. This was a particular problem for defender Harry Johnston, who was constantly dragged out of position by Nándor Hidegkuti, who was playing in what today we call the No.10 role. Of course, this was unheard of at that time.

England hit back to equalise before Hidegkuti added to his tally to regain the lead. Puskás began to purr. He struck twice, in the 24th and 27th minutes, to put daylight between the two countries with not even 30 minutes on the clock. Mortensen pulled a goal back before half-time, but it wasn't anywhere near enough for the hosts. Hungary came out after the break and within ten minutes had scored a further two goals. The final score on that day at Wembley was England 3 Hungary 6. Over 100,000 fans had crammed into the twin towers and what unfolded before their eyes was a new footballing dawn. The country that had given the game to the world had been reminded that there was more than one way to skin a cat, well in footballing terms anyway.

Sir Bobby Robson said of the match, 'We saw a style of play, a system of play, that we had never seen before. None of these players meant anything to us. We didn't know about Puskás. All these fantastic players, they were men from Mars as far as we were concerned. They were coming to England; England had never been beaten at Wembley – this would be a 3–0, 4–0 maybe even 5–0 demolition of a small country who were just coming into European football. They called Puskás the "Galloping Major" because he was in the army – how could this guy serving for the Hungarian army come to Wembley and rifle us to defeat? But the way they played, their technical brilliance and expertise – our WM formation was kyboshed in 90 minutes of football. The game had a profound effect, not just on myself but on all of us.'

England were arrogant prior to kick-off. 'We completely underestimated the advances that Hungary had made, and not only tactically,' Billy Wright said. 'When we walked out at Wembley that afternoon, side by side with the visiting team, I looked down and noticed that the Hungarians had on these strange, lightweight boots, cut away like slippers under the ankle bone. I turned to big Stan Mortensen and said, "We should be alright here, Stan, they haven't got the proper kit."'

Their arrogance was to add to the misery that compounded the defeat.

Prior to the commencement of the 1954 World Cup in Switzerland, England, still licking their wounds, travelled to Hungary for a return match with one thing on their mind, revenge. They needn't have bothered leaving Heathrow, as this time it was just plain embarrassing. In the Népstadion, Budapest, England weren't only beaten but were also completely humiliated and outplayed yet again. This time there was to be no mercy shown by Sebes's team as the Magical Magyars thrashed the Three Lions 7-1. England were predictable, whereas the wily Sebes had slightly changed his formation to a 4-2-4. Puskás this time wowed the home fans with two goals in the rout, like a conductor leading his orchestra.

This result against what was considered one of the better teams in the world had put the Hungarians in good stead with the World Cup looming over the horizon. Sebes and co had been on a long run of matches without tasting defeat, dating back to 1950. The team were in prime form as the competition kicked off and boy did they show it. Their first two group matches saw huge victories, with a 9-0 opening win over South Korea and an 8-3 demolition of the West Germans. Puskás was revelling on the big stage again and had struck three times in the opening two matches. Berne was to become a venue of both cheers and tears as first a quarter-final victory over Brazil was marred by two red cards in a bruising encounter with the South Americans. Puskás was struggling through injury and was left out of the team, a trend that was to follow in the semi-final as again Sebes left out his talisman, such was the strength of his squad.

Uruguay provided stern opponents in the last four, but a mammoth effort in extra time saw the Hungarians prosper 4-2. Puskás, looking on, wasn't to be left looking on in the final.

Sebes recalled the striker to face West Germany in Berne. In what would be their 50th match unbeaten, the Hungarians raced into a 2-0 lead, Puskás and club-mate Czibor opening the scoring inside the first ten minutes. The quarter-final against the Brazilians had been heralded the 'Battle of Berne' due to its ferocity. This final, however, was to be branded the 'Miracle of Berne'.

West Germany, who had rested many first-team players in the 8-3 defeat in the group stage, were now at full strength and, despite the early setback, powered back in true 'Vorsprung Durch Technik' style. They battled back, reversing the scoreline to lead 3-2 and were heading for championship glory. The Hungarians fought hard and rallied to try to save not only the final but their proud undefeated record. Puskás struck with a little over a minute to go, but an offside flag cut short the celebrations. Again Hungary poured forward. With time ticking on, they thought that they had a lifeline when Kocsis was brought down in the penalty area, but English referee William Ling waved away the protests and West Germany held on to become world champions. I wonder whether the referee had the 6-3 and 7-1 in his mind at that time? Or maybe that's just the devil in me.

Battered and bruised, Puskás returned to his club Honvéd and again secured them the title, a fifth in six seasons. What was to become significant with this accolade was that little did anyone know the chain of events that was to follow. As with any team winning their domestic league around this time, the following campaign would ensure a tilt at the newly created European Cup and a chance to pit their wits against the cream of other nations. The competition had been born a year previous in 1955, which excited teams across the European landscape. Honvéd travelled to Athletic Bilbao in the first round of the competition. In a topsy-turvy match, Honvéd were beaten 3-2 in the Basque region, but the Hungarians were confident of a victory on home soil despite trailing by a single goal. What they didn't know was that they weren't to play on home soil for a very long time.

The Hungarian Revolution had erupted in the capital while the team were away on international duty and, with fear of the regime reigning strong amongst the squad, the players decided to move their families out of the country. Honvéd still had a home leg to take care of against Bilbao, but, with all the goings on in Hungary, decided to host the Spaniards in the Heysel Stadium in Belgium. Puskás scored in a 3-3 draw, but it wasn't enough for the Hungarians and their European trip was cut short ... for now. With the club in effect being homeless, they decided on a money-making tour of Europe, showcasing the team's talents to parts unknown.

FIFA were furious with the actions of the Hungarian club and, along with UEFA, threatened action if Honvéd failed to return to their homeland to complete their league campaign. They didn't, so, in 1956, Puskás and his team-mates were slapped with a two-year ban from football. As if things weren't tough enough at this time for the players and their families, they were now prevented from doing what they loved and what brought in the money. By the time their bans expired in 1958, Puskás had turned 31. His chances of playing at the highest level were beginning to diminish with every passing month, but his future lay somewhere other than his homeland. 'I swore to myself I would never return,' said Puskás. 'I felt bitter at such treatment, after so many years giving my best for the nation.'

First, in an attempt to find himself a new contract, he headed to Italy, but he was knocked back on multiple occasions for both his size and height, a theme throughout his footballing career. Then, in the wake of the tragic Munich air disaster, Sir Matt Busby's assistant Jimmy Murphy attempted to take Puskás to Old Trafford. Manchester United's team had been decimated in the plane crash and Murphy knew that the Hungarian would add the magic that was now missing after the demise of Duncan Edwards and all, god rest their souls. Unfortunately, due to red tape and reportedly high wage demands, the move never materialised. Real Madrid, the Spanish super club, took a punt on Puskás. They already had the emphatic Argentine forward, Alfredo Di Stéfano, on their books, who was a phenomenal goalscorer in Spain. What was most noticeable was the fact that both strikers were moving into the sunset of their careers at the time that Puskás joined the club.

The Hungarian player put pen to paper in August 1958 and embarked on another enthralling chapter of his career. An article on the website Puskas.com details the contract signed by the forward, despite his advancing years and expanding waistline:

> Many thought the four-year length was too long for a fat, old player such as Puskás and there is no doubt the 150,000 pesetas-a-year signing-on fee was down to the generosity of club president Mr Santiago Bernabéu. This amount, a total of 150,000 dollars, suitably covered the loans which Puskás and his family had taken out over previous months, amongst which was one from their friend and fellow football star László Kubala at FC Barcelona, and additionally, according to the contract signed and witnessed on 16th August 1958, Puskás received 3,000 pesetas per month as his salary.

The natives didn't have long to wait to see their newest Galactico. In only his second match, Puskás took home the match ball, with a stunning hat-trick against Sporting Gijón.

His strike partner Di Stéfano wasn't to be outdone and continued with his own ridiculously high strike rate. The pair became so deadly that during their first campaign playing together they both notched trebles in a 10-1 victory over Las Palmas. Despite their heroics in front of goal, neither quite did enough domestically, as the team finished four points behind eventual winners Barcelona.

What did brighten the end of the campaign was a run to the European Cup Final, a first for Puskás. Fate, though, had other ideas as injury curtailed his season at the semi-final stage, ruling him out of the final in Stuttgart against Reims. The bittersweet end of his first year in Spain was compounded when his pal Di Stéfano scored the second of two in a 2-0 win to ensure that the Hungarian was holding silverware on his maiden voyage in the Spanish capital. There was even more to come. This just fired the belly, excuse the pun, of the forward, whose scoring numbers nearly doubled over the next five campaigns, from the 25 times he had netted in 1958/59 to 47, 44 and 40 over the subsequent three seasons.

As well as achieving team honours, Puskás was now beginning to collect recognition of his own, with the Pichichi Trophy (Spain's golden boot) being won on four occasions in eight years. He was runner-up for the Ballon d'Or in 1960 and was the highest goalscorer in the European Cup on two occasions. His scoring was now becoming so regular that it catapulted Madrid to five consecutive La Liga titles. The team also retained the European Cup the year after Puskás was cruelly denied a place in the final. This time out, though, he was to be on that pitch, unfortunately for their German opponents, Eintracht Frankfurt.

Real Madrid demolished their opponents in a very one-sided match at Hampden Park. Despite Frankfurt taking an 18th-minute lead, Di Stéfano and Puskás took it in turns to toy with their prey, before treating them to a 7-3 defeat. Puskás, making up for lost time, scored only the four, while his mate Di Stéfano followed up with a paltry hat-trick. The pair just loved playing together. The Argentine had already endeared himself to the fans at the Bernabéu prior to the Hungarian's arrival, but in the period of the partnership playing together they notched a staggering 426 goals between them in all competitions. Not bad for a couple of 'over-the-hill', out-of-shape pensioners.

Unfortunately, with time most definitely not on Puskás's side, he did manage to add just one more European Cup to his collection as the curtain came down on his amazing career. One last win, against Partizan Belgrade, although Puskás again was to miss the final through injury, was enough to ensure he was heralded a king in Spain.

A side note to this amazing story is that, despite scoring 84 goals in 85 matches for his native Hungary, due to being granted Spanish citizenship, Puskás also collected four caps for Spain in 1961–62. His four matches for his new-found homeland were fruitless in front of goal but, nevertheless, the Spanish people took him to their hearts.

George Best had particularly fond memories of Puskás, which really is saying something considering the talent that Best himself possessed:

> I was with [Bobby] Charlton, [Denis] Law and Puskás, we were coaching in a football academy in Australia. The youngsters we were coaching did not respect him, including making fun of his weight and age. We decided to let the guys challenge a coach to hit the crossbar 10 times in a row, obviously they picked the old fat one. Law asked the kids how many they thought the old fat coach would get out of 10. Most said less than five. I said 10. The old fat coach

stepped up and hit nine in a row. For the tenth shot he scooped the ball in the air, bounced it off both shoulders and his head, then flicked it over with his heel and cannoned the ball off the crossbar on the volley. They all stood in silence then one kid asked who he was, I replied, "To you, his name is Mr. Puskás."

All in all, Puskás tallied up an impressive 511 goals in 533 matches at club level. His skill was commemorated even further when, in 2009, FIFA named an award after the forward for the best goal scored in the world for each calendar year. The inaugural winner of this prestigious new prize was Cristiano Ronaldo of Manchester United for his 40-yard screamer against FC Porto in the Champions League quarter-final. Puskás would certainly have approved.

2

Diego Maradona

*'When Diego scored that second goal against us,
I felt like applauding. I'd never felt like that
before, but it's true … and not just because it
was such an important game. It was impossible
to score such a beautiful goal. He's the greatest
player of all time, by a long way. A genuine
phenomenon.'* – **Gary Lineker**

ITALIAN FOOTBALL was always heavily loaded in the
northern areas of this famous boot-shaped country. For decades
since the league's inception, title after title had been claimed by
its geographically superior counterparts, with a north and south
divide playing a huge part in both economic and footballing
parlances. Juventus, Milan, Inter, Roma and such were all
taking their share of the wealth both on and off the pitch. That
wasn't to say that there was no money at all in the southern
regions, far from it in fact.

Naples, situated on the south-west corner of this proud
footballing nation, was and still is thought by some of as the
sewer of the country. It has been said that many outside the

city, most notably those that come from its two bigger brothers, Milan and Rome, had prayed that once again Mount Vesuvius would erupt and ravage the area like it had done famously before with Pompeii. No football club south of the capital had ever claimed a top Italian title – that was, of course, until SSC Napoli signed a certain Diego Maradona.

The Argentine playmaker had already broken the world transfer record once when he was lured east from his native Boca Juniors in Argentina to sign for Barcelona. His two seasons in Spain were hit and miss as his Barça team finished third and fourth, respectively, in La Liga. Maradona's record in front of goal was pretty useful as he notched an impressive 38 goals in 58 appearances, although his time in Catalonia was to be cut short.

While playing against Athletic Bilbao in the Copa del Rey Final, Maradona was targeted first with abuse and then with some malicious tackling. Eventually the forward snapped and, with red mist descending, headbutted an opponent. This caused wild scenes of fighting such as had never been seen on a field of play in Spain, let alone in a final. The match was played in front of the then King of Spain, Juan Carlos, who was shocked as he looked on in pure disbelief at what was unfolding in front of his very royal eyes, as were the other 100,000 spectators crammed into the Bernabéu Stadium in the Spanish capital. Barcelona lost 1-0.

One Barcelona executive stated, 'When I saw those scenes of Maradona fighting and the chaos that followed, I realised we couldn't go any further with him.' Cue another world record transfer fee broken again. This time Napoli smashed the £5m that Barcelona had paid Boca Juniors, with a £6.9m fee paid. Originally, the deal was to be around the £6.4m mark, but, as the contract was being closed out, Barcelona president Josep Lluís Núñez, demanded an extra half-a-million quid or the deal was dead. The board at Napoli were shaken. They thought they had landed their man and, with their pockets now seemingly empty, what was to play out was to shock them again. The Neapolitan people began a whip-round. Folk were begging in the streets and looking behind their sofas just to make up the shortfall, with fans doing everything in their power to find any spare cash that they could lay their hands on until, eventually, through sheer determination, the city had bundled together the money to land their man.

On 5 July 1984, 75,000 fans scurried into the Stadio San Paolo to see their new hero. One local media outlet wrote, 'Despite the lack of a mayor, houses, schools, buses, employment and sanitation, none of this matters now because we have Maradona!' The city's new messiah then took to the pitch and wowed them with a cameo of ball juggling; before curling a shot into the top-left corner of the net. The place erupted, nearly enough to wake up the local volcano. 'I felt that they loved me, that they really and truly loved me,' said Diego in his autobiography *Touched by God*. 'Naples was a crazy city – they were as crazy as me – soccer was life itself. A lot of things reminded me of my origins. There had been hunger strikes and people had chained themselves to the fence at San Paolo stadium, begging me to come. How could I let them down?'

During his inaugural campaign, Maradona showed glimpses of his brilliance, but with the team around him lacking in quality, struggled to make the impact that maybe both the fans and he could have wanted. A brace in a 3-2 win over Udinese and a hat-trick in a 4-0 demolition of Lazio were the most notable points in a dismal season in which the Neapolitan club would only muster a mid-table finish. Eighth place was certainly not good enough for the striker, who had struggled to get near any kind of title challenge during his short spell on European soil. Despite finishing as the team's leading scorer with 17 goals, the Argentine demanded more of himself and his team-mates.

The poor league performance was enough for then manager Rino Marchesi to be handed his P45. His replacement was former Napoli player, Ottavio Bianchi. The boss quickly built up a rapport with Maradona, realising that, to make this engine tick, he had to oil the right wheels. The upturn was evident when the club's league position improved dramatically. Napoli had turned the San Paolo stadium into a fortress and the team only fell to a single defeat over the course of the 1985/86 season as Maradona was beginning to pull strings. Again, his goal tally was in the mid-teens as his influence on matches and eye for goal were beginning to become more prominent with each passing appearance.

AC Milan were beaten both home and away, while Inter Milan were only able to take one point from the two meetings as Napoli suddenly became a team that was hard to beat. In fact, they only lost five times that campaign, although draws were their undoing meaning that they ultimately finished in third place, six points behind eventual winners Juventus. They were close but not close enough, as even Maradona couldn't help his team past the first stage of the Coppa Italia. Qualification for the UEFA Cup was an added bonus for the club, looking towards the next season. Little did they know that, by the time the squad reconvened in the July of 1986, their talisman and hero would also be a world champion.

Maradona headed off to Mexico with his Argentina team-mates for the 1986 World Cup, where he led the team out in Mexico City as their captain, a role that he had recently taken up at his club. Argentina began in quite emphatic style with a 3-1 routine win over South Korea. Their next two group matches were pretty straightforward, a 2-0 victory over Bulgaria and a 1-1 draw with Italy, Maradona equalising after an early penalty from the Italians. Into the round of 16, where an all-South American affair against Uruguay was played out in the city of Puebla. Argentina were again miserly in defence, scraping through with a 1-0 win. Diego had been effective in his opening four matches, not amazing, but getting the job done. He was clearly saving the spectacular for the quarter-final tie against England in the Azteca Stadium, Mexico City.

On a boiling hot day, England, who had battered Paraguay in the previous round, were licking their lips at taking on Argentina. The Falklands War was still fresh in the mind of both countries as they lined up in front of over 115,000 fans. The first period was tense and cagey with not a great deal of action on the pitch, but the real drama was about to unfold in the second half. Maradona, dribbling towards England's goal, played a short pass on the edge of the penalty area to his team-mate Valdano. Trying to cut out the pass, an unlucky shank from Steve Hodge's shin meant that the ball looped aimlessly into the air, high above the penalty spot. Maradona managed to continue his run, except England goalkeeper Peter Shilton had spotted this and raced from his goal to punch clear. As the Three Lions stopper leapt to clear his lines, Maradona, reaching the ball a fraction of a second ahead of the England custodian, jumped to meet the ball and glanced it over the keeper's head and into the empty net.

All wasn't as it first seemed, though, as first Shilton and then several England players raced over to the linesman to demand that the goal be chalked off as Maradona had in fact used his hand. The goal stood. To this day, it's remembered as the 'Hand of God' goal, due to Maradona's comments to the press after the match, much to the frustration of England's manager, Bobby Robson. The Three Lions' manager wasn't so impressed with the self-titled tag: 'He was a rascal in one situation with a handball,' said Robson. 'He said it was the hand of God; I said, "It was the hand of a rascal".'

With England trailing and looking to get back into the match, what was to follow was something quite breathtaking. Looking back now, I think it's quite extraordinary that two of football's most infamous moments of the 20th century were captured in exactly the same match, by the same player, against the same team. While there was huge controversy surrounding the opening goal, there was to be no doubt whatsoever about the second for Argentina and Maradona, as it was to be dubbed the 'goal of the century'.

Glen Hoddle received the ball just inside Argentina's half and, as he turned, was absolutely nailed in a challenge by Maradona, no foul. The ball was given back to Maradona, who, facing his own goal, pirouetted past Peter Beardsley and Peter Reid to begin running at the England backline. With plenty of work still to do, Maradona skipped past a further two tackles, from Terry Fenwick and Steve Hodge, before coaxing Shilton out of his goal, rounding him and playing the ball into the empty net, despite a desperate lunge by Terry Butcher to try to rescue the situation. Now I can't even comprehend for one minute that I've done this goal justice in words. It was scored by a man running at full speed with the ball seemingly glued to the end of his toes. If you've never seen this before, I fully recommend using your favourite search engine and watching it for yourself because, quite frankly, it's a thing of sheer beauty.

England captain, Peter Shilton, declared that 'it left a bitter taste' after the defeat, despite Gary Lineker pulling a goal back for the Three Lions in the 2-1 win for Argentina. In his book on Argentinian football, *Angels with Dirty Faces*, Jonathan Wilson claims that the goal was 'dazzling'. Maradona and co marched on imperiously towards the final. Belgium awaited in the last four and, with the final within touching distance,

Diego again showed his scintillating skills to the watching world. Argentina won 2-0, with the cunning genius scoring a brace. An excerpt from *These Football Times* summed the occasion up beautifully:

> As against England, Argentina's captain scored two fantastical goals against Belgium. Despite being in a World Cup semi-final, the fact that the double came so soon after the Hand of God match has devalued their brilliance and context. It's the Buzz Aldrin syndrome. Except that, in 1986, only Maradona could overshadow Maradona.

Back to the Azteca stadium for the final, a ground where Argentina had been quite fruitful over the course of the competition. Come to think of it, if you reach a final you tend to be quite fruitful wherever you play. West Germany were the opponents and, on 29 June 1986, Maradona and his mates in sky-blue and white were crowned world champions. Argentina had held a two-goal lead before the West Germans managed to claw back level with just ten minutes remaining. With the game edging towards extra time, Maradona played an exquisite through ball, piercing the backline and freeing Jorge Burruchaga. The forward, looking exceedingly leggy, pushed the ball heavily in front of himself and then slotted it under the goalkeeper before crashing to his knees through a mixture of sheer exhaustion and jubilation.

Speaking to Fifa.com in 2008, Burruchaga said:

> The move began when Ruggeri headed a long ball away from near our area. Hector Enrique was first to the clearance and slipped the ball to Maradona, who was near the halfway line. When I saw the

ball going towards Diego, I figured the German defence would try and catch us offside. That's why I came from the opposite side and shouted to Diego, who almost had his back to me at the time. Diego used to play like he had eyes in the back of his head. So, he fed the ball through to me and I took off. Hans-Peter Briegel was marking me, but I never saw him or even sensed he was close to me on that run.

It's incredible how many things people have told me about that goal. They said I knocked the ball on too far in front of me; that I ignored Valdano shouting for it to my left; that Briegel almost caught me. All I was focusing on was the goal in the distance. What I could see clearly, though, was Schumacher, as he was all in yellow, which not only made it easier to see him, it also helped me work out how far I was from goal. It must have been a 40-yard run, which I finished with a right-foot shot. The plan was to chip it over him, but I ended up slotting it through his legs. I didn't see Valdano who was running alongside me through the middle, and nor did I hear Briegel behind me. It felt like the longest, most exhilarating run of my life. To celebrate my goal, I dropped to my knees and raised my arms, and then I saw Batista. He was exhausted and went down on to his knees in front of me.

Maradona headed back to southern Italy on the crest of a wave: A world champion and lauded as the best footballer on the planet. The Argentine linked up with boss Bianchi and the rest of the squad, who applauded him for his efforts in Mexico, but now it was back to business. Napoli began the 1986/87 campaign like a train with seven victories and four draws in their opening 11 matches, including a 3-1 win away at champions Juventus in Turin. Maradona and his team-mates were turning last season's draws into wins and were now sitting pretty at the top of the table.

The winter break, however, seemed to disturb Bianchi's team's rhythm as a defeat in Florence in January 1987 was to be the first blot on their copybook for the season. A 3-1 loss to Fiorentina added fuel to the fire, though, as Maradona then led his team on another run of six straight victories. With the campaign beginning to draw to a close, Napoli needed to hold their nerve as the team that couldn't stop winning ... stopped! Nervy draws were now being played out, but having held a commanding lead at the top of Serie A, these were enough to ensure that the Neapolitan club crawled over the finish line. Napoli and Maradona had done it. The club from southern Italy had won its first-ever title. Once again, the Argentine attacker had finished as the team's top scorer, with 17 goals in all competitions.

The celebrations in Naples were intense, with some parties rumoured to have gone on for days. Mock funerals were also held by fans of the club for Juventus, complete with coffins and printed 'death notices' – a sign of just how intense that rivalry was at the time. 'The world had changed. The noisiest, most crowded and most chaotic city in Europe was deserted.' Those were the comments made by Italian anthropologist, Amalia Signorelli, when describing Naples on the afternoon of 10 May 1987. Bianchi's team had held off reigning champions Juventus by just three points to claim their first-ever Scudetto title.

With the club's fortunes seemingly on the up, the boss decided to strike while the iron was hot. Bianchi moved to strengthen his champions and signed another South American striker, Careca. The Brazilian forward was added to an already impressive frontline of Diego Maradona and Bruno Giordano, and quickly the trio would soon become known as 'Magica', due to the combination of Ma-Gi-Ca. They were to be the most feared in Serie A.

The start of the 1987/88 campaign mirrored the previous year, with Napoli speeding off like a runaway train and, in a weird twist of fate, again never tasting defeat until the first match following the Christmas break, when they were hammered at the San Siro by AC Milan, who themselves were in fine fettle as the season began to take shape. Even Napoli's three amigos were powerless to stop a rampant Milan team, who themselves were emerging as title challengers. The European Cup had already been put to bed as a 3-1 aggregate defeat to Real Madrid in round one cut short any hope of a cup run.

Again, Napoli embarked on an impressive run of straight wins, including a 6-0 victory over Pescara and a 4-0 drubbing of Fiorentina, who coincidentally would take revenge in the sweetest of fashion as the season concluded. With Milan hot on the tail of Napoli, four straight defeats at the business end of the season were enough for the Milanese club to sneak over the line as the Neapolitans fell at the final fence. A 3-2 defeat in Florence in the penultimate fixture of the season signalled the end of the title push. Despite Maradona scoring an impressive 22 goals, it wasn't enough, as a wily Milan team claimed the Scudetto through impressive defensive displays. New signing Careca had chipped in with 13 goals, but, alas, it wasn't to be as Napoli tasted disappointment on the final day of the season. Milan took the crown by three points as Napoli lost to Sampdoria.

A team that was four points clear with five matches remaining had completely fallen apart. Rumours of black-market betting were afoot as the Camorra (a mafia-like organisation) had laid big money on Napoli NOT claiming a second title. Nearly every Neapolitan resident had put money on a championship retention, which would have bankrupted the Camorra. Of course, these allegations were never proved, although Maradona proved he had links with the organisation after being spotted in the city partying with clan leaders, and there were rumours about his drug addiction also. When you're the hot ticket in town, everyone wants to come to the show.

James Jackson, in an article for the *Football Pink*, wrote:

> The summer of 1988, it was like the whole city was in mourning, almost like a wake, with locals remembering this summer just as vividly as the summer before it. At the end of the season, four players were sacked by Napoli after writing an open letter of protest against their manager. The ugly fallout from the title-winning season had clearly spread through the team. If we want to avoid all the sinister routes to explain Napoli's capitulation in the 1987/88 season, then we have to address the fact that some of the team hated their head coach. Maybe they themselves felt like the only way to get rid of him was to make him fail.

Maradona had also fallen foul of the club president, Corrado Ferlaino. The pair had butted heads amid the collapse at the tail of the season and, with Maradona deciding his future lay elsewhere, he tried engineering a move to Marseille. As the 1988/89 campaign got under way, Maradona had made himself unavailable for the team's opening four fixtures. The transfer to Marseille, though, would never materialise and Maradona had to issue a public apology to both the president and the fans before returning to first-team action.

The stop-go start to the campaign hung heavy on the No. 10, who registered his worst goal return since joining Napoli, failing to reach double figures, as again the team from southern Italy were runners-up to their northern counterparts. Maradona only managed nine goals domestically and, despite Careca knocking in 19, it wasn't to be enough, as Inter Milan were runaway winners of the title. The campaign witnessed an 8-2 victory over Pescara, as well as 4-1 wins over Ascoli, Torino and AC Milan but these dovetailed with defeats by minnows of the league, which ultimately derailed a title bid. Ascoli, Pescara, Pisa and Verona all took points from Maradona and co.

While domestically the shortfall was there for all to see, on the European scene Maradona thrived as Napoli set off on a run in the UEFA Cup. First, they dispatched PAOK of Greece in a 2-1 aggregate win, with Maradona scoring a penalty and Careca finishing off the job in Thessaloniki. Next on their adventure was a trip to Germany to face Lokomotive Leipzig. Defender Giovanni Francini scored in a 1-0 win to take back to the San Paolo. There, Francini again provided the ammunition in a 2-1 victory to send Napoli into round three.

Next destination on the European tour was France, as Bordeaux lay in wait, with a tricky away leg up first. Maradona's expertly whipped-in corner was headed home by striker Andrea Carnevale to edge a slender 1-0 lead. Back to the San Paolo and a tense match for the vibrant home support, where neither team looked like breaking the deadlock, with the match being played at a snail's pace, which clearly suited the home team. Napoli held on for a 0-0 draw and progressed to the quarter-final, where a familiar foe lay in wait.

The Old Lady of Turin, Juventus, were their opponents in an all-Italian affair and you would be thinking that this was to be the end of the road for Maradona and his team-mates, as a 2-0 defeat in the Stadio Olympico meant that the boys in sky-blue had it all to do in the second leg. Maradona, though, thrived on such events. The big stage was where he was born to play. The home stadium swelled with supporters, waving their blue flags and flares. Just over 83,000 spectators crammed in to witness a comeback of biblical proportions, and who better to do it against than your arch-rivals?

An early penalty gave the Argentine a chance to pull a goal back and one he took as he coolly slotted it away after ten minutes. Better was to come for Napoli as, on the stroke of half-time, Carnevale restored parity to send the home fans wild. 2-2. The match then became like a basketball match, with both teams surging forward, looking to edge in front. However, it wasn't to be and there were to be an additional 30 minutes played as extra time loomed. The determination was there, but the legs were starting to run on empty as loose passes were replacing possession football. Then, just as the game ticked towards a penalty shoot-out, Napoli defender Alessandro Renica scored with the last kick of extra time to send the stadium into meltdown.

The semi-final pitted Napoli against German giants, Bayern Munich. The Germans had pretty much wrapped up their domestic league and were looking to add more silverware to their Bavarian trophy cabinet. Napoli took the lead in the 40th minute of the first leg through Careca. The second half was even better for the home team, as with only a few minutes remaining, Carnevale nodded in another Maradona corner. A 2-0 win in Naples was a glorious result to take to Germany for the second leg in two weeks' time.

One of the more iconic videos doing the rounds on social media is of Maradona warming up in a rather baggy rain jacket, boot laces strewn across the pitch, just juggling a football like he didn't have a care in the world. Well, that moment took place during the warm-up for the return leg in Munich. While his Napoli team-mates were stretching, going through their warm-up routines, the Argentine was just in his own little world, enjoying flicks and tricks with a ball, looking for all the world a man who was about to appear in a charity match or an exhibition game, not the second leg of a European semi-final. But that was his way. When quizzed about his extravagant routine years later, Maradona quipped, 'It reminded me of when I was a youth player. We would enter at half-time and put on a show for 15 minutes.'

Careca looked to have put the tie out of Bayern's reach as his 62nd-minute goal ensured a three-goal cushion for the Italians. Despite the German team pulling a goal back, Careca notched again for a 4-2 aggregate win and to send Napoli through to the final, where they would again face German opposition, this time in the shape of Stuttgart. As with most of the UEFA Cup finals of yesteryear, this was to be played over two legs, with Napoli awarded home advantage first. Again, a bumper crowd gathered to see whether their heroes could take two final steps to glory.

Maradona was at the centre of everything in front of the fans who worshipped his every move. Stuttgart shocked the home supporters with an early lead, only for Maradona to be at the heart of another controversial handball moment. Only a few metres from goal, he controlled the ball with his left hand. The 'Hand of God' from his infamous goal during the 1986 World Cup against England was back to aid him. The moment, unseen by Greek referee, Gerasimos Germanakos, resulted in Maradona's attempt at goal being stopped by the arm of defender Günther Schäfer. That was seen by Germanakos and Maradona scored from the resulting penalty kick. With three minutes remaining, Maradona's movement and cute pass in the box found Careca, who dispatched his shot into the corner of the goal. Napoli edged through the first leg 2-1, a slender lead to take to Germany but a lead, nonetheless.

Thousands of Napoli fans flocked to the Black Forest area of Germany to urge their team on to victory and were repaid for their support when Alemáo scored in the 18th minute to make it a 3-1 aggregate lead. Jürgen Klinsmann pulled a goal back just eight minutes later with a trademark header, butwith minutes to go before half-time, Ciro Ferrara scored to all but put the result beyond doubt for the Italians. In the 69th minute, Careca again struck, adding to his impressive tally for the season, to give Napoli a 5-2 aggregate lead.

Stuttgart rallied late on to score two goals to bring the final back to a nail-biting 5-4, but Napoli held on to lift their first-ever European trophy. Just when those fans from Naples thought they couldn't love their talisman more, he hoisted aloft the UEFA Cup into the skies of West Germany. Bianchi, once the final whistle blew, retired to the dressing room briefly, while Maradona and his team-mates paraded around the stadium in jubilation. 'I only allowed myself to smile after the match in Stuttgart, not even after eliminating Bayern and certainly not after the night with Juventus,' Bianchi recalled.

That smile on Bianchi's face would be extended for a further 12 months as Napoli again launched an assault on Italy's finest. With two runners-up places achieved since their inaugural title in 1987, Maradona and co were looking to go one step further and again finish on the top of the Serie A mountain. The campaign began with four wins in their opening five matches before a late equaliser from Maradona away at Cremonese scrambled a draw that laid the foundations for a championship push.

Just days later, the Argentine forward produced a masterclass in a 3-0 victory over title challengers Milan. The Neapolitan side just kept on producing results and had extended their unbeaten run to the new year of 1990. A brand-new decade but one that Bianchi was hoping hadn't begun with a sign of the times, as his team suffered a heavy 3-0 defeat at the hands of Lazio in Rome on New Year's Eve. He needn't have worried, though, as again Careca and Maradona weaved their magic. Whether at home or away, the dazzling pair mesmerised opposition defences, most notably in the victories over Genoa, Roma and Atalanta.

As spring sprang in Italy, the change in the seasons seemed to provide a shift in performance from Napoli as not even Maradona could prevent defeats to both Milan clubs in the space of a fortnight. Shaking off their bloody nose, a quick dust down and again Napoli were on the charge. The team always bounced back from adversity with a show of arrogance, as if to say, 'You can keep us down but not for long', and Maradona's influence played a huge part in that. It was just his swagger. It invigorated his team-mates.

A 3-1 victory over arch-rivals Juventus at the San Paolo kick-started the engines that had been recently stalling in the title tilt, with Maradona bagging a brace for the home team. A week later, he again notched in the 3-0 win against Bari and in the 4-2 away victory at Bologna. With just Lazio to play in the final match of the season, Napoli needed to win. It was a tight affair and, with the 3-0 defeat on New Year's Eve still fresh in the memory for Bianchi, he trusted that his charges would get the job done. They did. A 1-0 triumph was enough to clinch Napoli's second Scudetto in four years and only the second in their history.

Maradona had been an integral part of a team that, for nearly half a decade, had tasted success never even dreamed of on the south-west coast of Italy. His 81 goals in 188 appearances outlined his importance in a team built on Italian defensiveness, coupled with South American flair. Maradona's 34 goals in 91 internationals also helped his country to two World Cup finals. He led his country to glory in 1986, but would taste the pain of defeat in 1990 as Argentina were beaten finalists, losing 1-0 to West Germany. His talent was incredible, undeniable in fact, there's no doubt about that. His personality, though, led him to becoming a divisive figure in world football. Ladies and gentlemen, Diego Armando Maradona.

3

Eric Cantona

'It was him who opened the doors in England to the French, in his time at United, Cantona was one of the best French players of all time. I'd give all the champagne I've ever drunk to be playing alongside him in a big European match at Old Trafford.' – **George Best**

SIR ALEX Ferguson was devastated at the news that Eric Cantona was due to retire at the end of the 1996/97 season. The Frenchman had announced to the boss just 24 hours after the team's Champions League semi-final defeat to Borussia Dortmund that he was going to hang up his boots once the campaign had finished at just 30 years of age, Ferguson was both shocked and disappointed but respected the decision bestowed upon him. The pair had tasted success over the course of their five-year love affair, although, like any marriage, it certainly had its ups and downs.

As the beginning of the 1997/98 campaign rolled around, Sir Alex was still numb from the Frenchman's decision, so much so that he wrote an open letter to

Cantona, I guess to maybe get some closure in his own mind. The letter read:

> Dear Eric, some months have passed since we last spoke and I felt that I should write to you as a mark of respect and the esteem in which I hold you. When we restarted training, I kept waiting for you to turn up as normal, but I think that was in hope and not realism and I knew in your eyes when we met at Mottram your time at Manchester United was over. Although, I still feel you should have taken both your father's and my advice and taken a holiday before making such a major decision.

It finished with:

> As I close this letter, I would like to think that we will have a chat, drink or a meal together soon. Eric, you know where I am if you need me and now that you are no longer one of my players, I hope you know that you have a friend. Good luck and God bless.

Ferguson had written from the heart to a player who had clearly captured his. As the Frenchman rode off into the sunset to attempt a new life in stage and film, what had played out before him was pure drama, and how fitting that the stage would be the Theatre of Dreams.

The story of Eric's signing is a little muddied, depending on where you gather your sources from, but I'll try to summarise the best I can. Bill Fotherby, managing director of Leeds United, had made the first move when trying to sign Manchester United full-back, Denis Irwin, that much is true. Speaking to *The Independent*, Fotherby recalls:

We had got Eric on a recommendation from Michel Platini, who told Howard Wilkinson he could be very difficult to handle but had the potential to be a great player. At the time, we didn't have any money. People thought we had won the pools, but we were pot-less. Because of that when we met his advisors to put together a deal, we agreed to pay Eric something like £500,000 if we kept him after an initial period of a few months. Apart from Lee Chapman, no one in the squad spoke fluent French and for Howard it was a bit of a nightmare. Although we won the title, there was just no connection between them.

I rang United about Denis Irwin, who had been at Leeds as a young boy. Martin Edwards said there was no chance, but I asked him to at least speak to [manager] Alex [Ferguson]. Normally, I wouldn't have expected him to ring back. This time he did, offering me a different player I knew Howard would not be interested in. It was then he asked about Eric. I said, 'Absolutely no way and that it was impossible.' But obviously I knew what Howard felt about him, and I knew this additional payment was due. As I had done before, Martin asked if I would talk to Howard.

On that day Howard was out house hunting in Leeds, so the only person I actually spoke to was [coach] Mick Hennigan. I just said, 'I can't believe it. Guess what has come right out of the blue. Howard will absolutely love it.' I left it a couple of hours, rang Martin back and said, 'I can't believe this, but Howard is willing to let the boy go.'

United signed Cantona for around £1.2m in the autumn of 1992, having already splashed out in the summer on a new striker in the shape of Dion Dublin. The centre-forward from Cambridge United had made an immediate impact but was cruelly sidelined after only a handful of matches, suffering a broken leg that would rule him out for the rest of the season. Ferguson was keen on Sheffield Wednesday's David Hirst, and had been watching the striker for some time, but had seen several offers knocked back. Cantona, however, had been part of the Leeds United team that had pipped United to the title in the previous campaign. His goals in the absence of the injured Lee Chapman ensured that the Whites overtook the Red Devils at the business end of the title chase to clinch the championship. He also scored a hat-trick in the Charity Shield at Wembley, the only player ever to achieve the feat in the season's curtain-raiser.

However, despite the accolades that had followed Cantona since his arrival in Yorkshire, his relationship with Leeds manager Howard Wilkinson was indifferent to say the least. 'I had a bad relationship with the manager,' said Cantona speaking to *FourFourTwo*.

> We didn't have the same views on football. At Leeds, football was played the old-fashioned way – I think you say kick then rush. But it was very important to play for Leeds at first because I learnt a lot with this kind of football. And we had success.
>
> If I don't like the environment, then I don't want to be there. It's like with a woman, sometimes you can't find love and sometimes you can, but it's still not right, you want more, you want to give, and you want to receive. I'm not sure that I would like to be with a woman who is like some of the chairmen I meet.

Floundering in eighth position in the newly formed Premier League, United were in urgent need of a kick-start. Cantona's debut in a 2-1 win at home against neighbours Manchester City on 6 December 1992 was to provide the spark that was to ignite United's season. He was introduced to Old Trafford as a second-half substitute, but little did anyone know at the time that the man who had defected from one side of the Roses to the other across the Pennines was about to become their new messiah.

Manchester United had lost four matches from their opening 13, hardly title contender form, but with the emergence of their new forward began a pattern of form that was purely devastating. So much so that by the new year their performances and wins had stormed them to the top of the tree. Cantona had scored his first goal for the club on his third appearance, a 1-1 draw at Stamford Bridge, as United came from behind against Chelsea. He scored again a week later on Boxing Day as United again came from behind, this time a 3-0 deficit at Sheffield Wednesday, Cantona scoring the third to send the travelling fans into ecstasy.

It wasn't just the goals that were beginning to excite the Stretford End, oh no. It was the flicks, the back-heels and the eye-of-the-needle passes that were now being served up on the menu. His pass to Denis Irwin was a particular highlight in a 4-1 demolition of Tottenham Hotspur. Irwin, picking up the ball on the left-hand flank, played a pass inside to Cantona who, with the outside of his right foot, played a first-time chip over the onrushing Spurs defence. The full-back had continued his run, beating the offside trap and, with one touch, dispatched the ball past Erik Thorstvedt with his left foot to round off a beautiful one-two move.

The crowd loved it. Cantona, with collar up, was revelling on his stage in the Theatre of Dreams. His partnership with

Mark Hughes was also beginning to take off. Hughes, more of a target man, would play as the focal point, the furthest advanced of the duo, while Eric would operate in a floating role between defence and midfield. He popped up everywhere. He would occupy the left wing, switching with Giggs or Sharpe, then suddenly he would be alongside Paul Ince. Opposition players hated it. They never knew whether to stick or twist. This enabled the Frenchman to find the space to hurt teams with his incisive passing.

According to Ryan Giggs:

> He had a massive influence on my career as a young player coming into the team. He was an unbelievable talent to play with and watch in games and training. Eric Cantona brought an extra dimension. Plenty of things he tried didn't come off, but you remember the ones that did – the flicks, the outrageous lobs. He made things look easy that weren't easy at all. Before him, we struggled to score as a team, but as soon as he arrived the goals flowed.

Further wins followed over Nottingham Forest, Queens Park Rangers and Sheffield United. A trip to Elland Road proved uninspiring on the pitch as United and Cantona struggled to find any rhythm at all in a 0-0 stalemate. A showdown against title challengers Aston Villa at Old Trafford saw yet another draw as the Red Devils had to come from behind after a worldie of a goal from Steve Staunton had put the visitors ahead. This time, Cantona was the provider for Hughes, whose header midway through the second half restored parity and ensured a point apiece for the teams positioned first and second.

The Manchester derby at Maine Road followed, and when City took an early second-half lead through Niall Quinn,

United looked to be stuttering again. They soon broke into their stride, however, and when Lee Sharpe was sent away down the left flank, the winger crossed superbly for Cantona to glance his header past Tony Coton to make the score 1-1. Draws were becoming more prominent as United dropped plenty of points around March, having drawn four of their last eight matches.

Five days in April cemented United's title ambitions as first the Red Devils travelled to Carrow Road to play third-placed Norwich City. The Canaries had been playing an attacking brand of football under the tutelage of Mike Walker and their league position was well deserved based on their superb performances. Cantona, receiving the ball on the half-turn in the centre of the park, split the Norwich defence with a beautiful through ball into the path of Ryan Giggs, whose touch was equally pristine. The Welsh winger coaxed Bryan Gunn from the Norwich goal and rounded him to put United 1-0 up after 13 minutes.

Six minutes later, a long clearance from Garry Pallister went to Mark Hughes, who set in motion one of the best one-touch-pass goals ever seen. Hughes flicked the ball to Ince, who flicked the ball out to Giggs, who sent it back to Brian McClair. The Scot slid a lovely first-time ball into the channel to free Andrei Kanchelskis. The speedy winger advanced on the Norwich goal, again teasing Gunn off his line before rounding him and scoring from the most acute of angles.

Norwich, absolutely reeling from the sucker punch on the break, were about to be shedding more tears. Ince, breaking through the Norwich midfield and defence, squared to Cantona, who side-footed home to make the score 3-0 after just 21 minutes. It was a blistering exhibition of counter-attacking football. The Canaries pulled a consolation goal back, but United were again on the march and in devastating fashion.

Sheffield Wednesday headed to Old Trafford on Easter weekend and excitement levels were beginning to grow. Ferguson was keen for the match to get under way as he could sense a shift in his team's psyche. Speaking to *The Guardian*, he referenced their encounter earlier in the campaign:

> More than at any time since I was playing, the club is alive. The 3-3 draw at Sheffield Wednesday was magnificent. It's as if the good old days were back and the major factor, as far as I'm concerned, is the Frenchman. Eric is so clever it's untrue and the lovely thing about special players is they're infectious. The things he tries, the others try, and it's the way the team are playing that's got middle-aged fans jumping about like two-year-olds.

All seemed well in the match until a rather odd chain of events began to unfold. Injury to the match referee, Mike Peck, meant that a changeover of officials was required. The man in the middle had injured his Achilles, cutting short his afternoon in charge. His replacement, John Hilditch, had an instant decision to make as Paul Ince's rash tackle on Chris Waddle saw the substitute ref point straight to the spot. John Sheridan duly obliged and dispatched the penalty kick past Peter Schmeichel.

United huffed and puffed until a corner four minutes from time gave Ferguson's men a chance to load the Wednesday box. The delivery was spot on and Steve Bruce's arcing header drew the hosts level. Then came the controversy. The fourth official signalled seven minutes of injury time and, with just one remaining, Bruce again scored from a corner. The stadium erupted. It was the birthplace of 'Fergie Time' for Manchester United. The Red Devils were in touching distance of claiming their first title for 26 years.

Wins over Coventry City, Chelsea and Crystal Palace followed, meaning that Aston Villa were now needing snookers. Oldham Athletic were visitors to Villa Park, with Big Ron Atkinson hoping his charges would continue their title challenge. However, it wasn't to be, as the Latics headed back to Lancashire with the three points, meaning that United were now officially the best team in the country once again. The Blackburn Rovers match at Old Trafford saw United crowned champions of England after over a quarter of a century of falling short, a period that included a relegation to the Second Division following the break-up of the 1968 European Cup-winning team. Cantona had been the catalyst for the upturn in team performances and finished the season on nine goals in 23 appearances. But it wasn't just his goals, it was his awareness of his team-mates on the pitch.

Eric's second season at United was when the Frenchman really came into his own. First a penalty shoot-out victory over Arsenal in the season's curtain-raiser at Wembley meant that another Charity Shield medal was added to the Frenchman's growing collection in England. United stormed to the top of the table, winning five of their opening six matches until a defeat to bogey team Chelsea in mid-September put the brakes on a touch. A Cantona thunderbolt against Arsenal set the team back on track, then the goals again began to flow.

United travelled to City for the derby and, after conceding two Niall Quinn headers, went into half-time trailing. Cantona, though, was going to grab the match by the scruff of the neck and went looking for the ball all over the pitch. The Frenchman latched on to a poor back-pass from Michel Vonk and slotted home past Tony Coton. With ten minutes remaining, Cantona dropped deep to receive the ball and juggled his way towards the City box. The ball went to Hughes, who played it out wide to Giggs, who swept a first-time cross into the area towards

Cantona. Having continued his run to the back post, he swept the ball home. United were level. Then, with just two minutes remaining, Roy Keane arrived at the back post to slot home a late winner, but the comeback was all about Eric.

United had racked up an impressive run of 23 matches without defeat until, yep you guessed it, Chelsea rocked up at Old Trafford and stunned the Stretford End with a 1-0 win. It was the second time in the campaign that the Blues had stunted the Reds' progress when everyone else was being swept aside. United bounced back from the defeat in fine style with a 5-0 hammering of Sheffield Wednesday at Old Trafford before two blots on the Frenchman's copybook threatened to derail both his and United's campaign. More on these in a moment.

With Cantona suspended for the trip to Ewood Park and title challengers Blackburn Rovers making headway in the league, United were hoping that the striker missing from duty wouldn't be too much of disadvantage. They were to be disappointed. Two Alan Shearer goals gave the hosts a 2-0 win in what was deemed a shift in the title race, as the holders misfired in front of goal. United then beat Oldham Athletic before another defeat, this time at Wimbledon, set the wobbles in. Eric returned after his four-match ban for the derby at Old Trafford and, in true Eric style, scored a brace to ensure calm and to steer the Red Devils back on the right path.

United never looked back and, with wins over Leeds, Southampton and Ipswich Town, they secured a second Premier League title in two seasons. There was more to come for United as an FA Cup Final meeting with bogey team Chelsea was also on the horizon. United fans were heading to Wembley with trepidation after the Blues had secured a league double over the Red Devils. The supporters had every right to feel agitated when, in the first half, Gavin Peacock, scorer of both the goals in the two defeats, rattled Peter Schmeichel's crossbar.

The rain was lashing down in London, even more so than on an average day in the north-west. The pitch at the old Wembley was huge and one thing I have learned over the years from players who have had the privilege of playing there is that the grass can sometimes be a little long and a little sticky when trying to play the ball along the floor. Eric looked subdued. He was certainly not the maverick player that we had seen over the previous 36 months in England. Something wasn't quite right.

United began to dominate with passages of passing. One of these led to Giggs beating John Spencer to a tackle, with the ball finding its way inside the box to Denis Irwin, who was absolutely clattered by Eddie Newton. David Elleray pointed to the spot and United had the chance to take the lead. The previous two penalties in an FA Cup Final had both been saved. John Aldridge of Liverpool was foiled by Dave Beasant in 1988 and Gary Lineker of Spurs was thwarted by Nottingham Forrest's Mark Crossley in 1991. Cantona, who hadn't been anywhere near his usual influential self, placed the ball on the spot. Chelsea's captain Dennis Wise saw this as a great opportunity to step in and try to speak to Eric:

> I had used the tactic before when Tony Cottee was about to take a penalty for Everton. As he stood waiting to take it I said, 'I bet you a fiver you miss.' He just said, 'Leave me alone.' Whether it affected him or not I don't know, but I do know that he missed. Having succeeded once, I thought I would try it again with Cantona. 'Come on,' I said, 'let's have a bet. I bet you miss.' I was a bit taken aback when he said, 'Okay, £100.' I was thinking more in terms of another fiver, but I still agreed. He scored. Later in the game United got another penalty. This time he came up to me and said, 'Hey, double or quits

on the £100?' 'No chance,' I said. And, of course, he
put that one away too.

As Wisey has alluded to here, United did receive another spot
kick moments later, which Cantona placed in the same spot
as the first, sending Dimitri Kharine the wrong way to his
left. It was a complete replica of the first. With their tails up,
United went on to score another two goals to clinch a 4-0
victory and a league and cup double. Only after the match was
it revealed that Cantona had sciatica the night before and had
been struggling with his back. This would explain the below-
par performance, but to show nerves of steel when stroking
home those two penalties shows the true mark of the man. The
forward had contributed 25 goals and 15 assists in a glittering
campaign for United, and Alex Ferguson described him as 'the
ideal man for that situation' after his brace. But what seemed to
be a season of champagne and parties was about to be followed
by the hangover of all hangovers.

The 1994/95 season began like any other, with the Charity
Shield showpiece at Wembley. Cantona again added to his
impressive tally with another penalty in the 2-0 win over
Blackburn Rovers. United stalled in their quest for a third
successive title with three defeats in their opening nine matches,
before Eric put on a show in a 4-2 away win over Blackburn.
The Red Devils again found their stride, including a 5-0 derby
day victory over City at Old Trafford, and all was looking rosy
in the garden again, despite a blip at home against Forest in
December.

Ferguson even strengthened the squad. The boss added
firepower from Newcastle United, bringing in Andy Cole
from the Magpies. Cole had been absolutely ripping it up
on Tyneside since the Geordie boys had been promoted two
seasons prior. The forward's 56 goals in 72 matches had shown

Ferguson that, with Hughes starting to advance in years, the squad was needing a little pick-me-up. United shelled out a record British transfer fee of £7m, with Keith Gillespie heading in the opposite direction.

Cole took a little time to adapt to life at Old Trafford despite scoring on his debut against Aston Villa. Cantona was also adapting to a new partner. Hughes was your typical British target man. You could fire the ball at any height into Hughes and he would kill it stone dead before spraying a pass out to one of the wingers to start a move. Andy Cole, however, was a finisher. His build-up play needed work and some even claimed his first touch was poor. Slightly harsh, as any professional footballer will have a level of basic footballing ability, but they were different players, nonetheless.

If you're brave enough to go on a rollercoaster at a theme park, then there's always that part of the build-up, the buzz and excitement of the ride as it slowly pulls you up the steep track towards the peak. You sit there with heart racing as the front of the train edges closer to the pinnacle before eventually you reach the balance point. The front carriage begins to creep over the summit before gravity takes hold and drags the ride hurtling towards the floor at speed, ensuring fear and discombobulation. Eventually, your brain kicks in and the realisation that you're not going to die subsides. By the time you get your bearings, you're being escorted off by a steward via the exit door. Lost? I thought you might be. This is the story of the remainder of both United and Eric's season.

United headed to Bramall Lane Sheffield to take on their United counterparts in the third round of the FA Cup. The holders faced a stern test from not only an in-form Blades but also the gale force wind that was swirling around the stadium. The weather made for a terrible match. Goal kicks were almost returned to the respective takers, as keeping the ball on the

ERIC CANTONA

deck deemed to be a major task. The game was scrappy until the 80th minute when a well-worked United move led to a Mark Hughes goal. Moments later, came the best piece of play of the night. Cantona, receiving the ball on the edge of Sheffield's penalty area, tried an audacious chip over Simon Tracey in goal. The Frenchman looked up and defied the logic of both physics and meteorology to lob the ball over the keeper and in off the underside of the crossbar. It was delightful.

Blackburn Rovers had taken top spot in the league table after Christmas and headed to Old Trafford in fine fettle. A topsy-turvy match looked to be heading for stalemate before Ryan Giggs's pinpoint cross with ten minutes remaining was nodded in at the far post by Cantona to close the gap on the leaders. The Stretford End erupted and United were closing in on their Lancashire rivals. The rollercoaster was edging ever closer to the summit.

The date 25 January 1995 was a red-letter day in both the Frenchman and United's history. Now, as mentioned earlier, Cantona for all his beauty on the pitch, can be renowned for moments of being a beast as well. During his time in his native France, the enigmatic player had been prone to the odd bad tackle, throwing the ball at a referee and also calling the manager of the French national team 'a bag of shit'. In the previous campaign, Cantona had shown flashes of petulance with a double sending-off in the space of a week. His first red card in United's colours was after a stamp on the chest of Swindon Town's John Moncur.

Just a few days later, Eric was again heading for a shower before his team-mates after two yellow cards at Highbury meant that he was going to sit out the next four fixtures. Defending champions United travelled to south-east London in second place, two points behind leaders Blackburn, who they had beaten 1-0 at Old Trafford three days earlier. Victory

57

at lowly Crystal Palace would see United return to the top of the table.

Palace began brightly and disrupted any flow from the visitors as United tried to mount attack after attack. Richard Shaw in particular was giving Cantona 'special attention'. The second half kicked off and, much the same as the first half, Shaw was still going in on Eric. Moments later, Cantona snapped. Shaw had clipped his opponent one time too many and the red mist descended on an already murky evening at Selhurst Park. Cantona, not enjoying his solo treatment, kicked at the back of Shaw's heels, sending him spinning to the turf. The referee immediately pulled the red card from his pocket and United were down to ten men. What followed was quite unbelievable.

Cantona, dismayed and frustrated, made his way along the touchline towards the tunnel in the corner of the stadium. A supporter, if you could call him that, had clearly touched a nerve with the Frenchman, who exploded into a fit of rage and unleashed one of the most infamous kung-fu kicks ever seen on British soil. This was followed up by a volley of punches thrown at the supporter before Cantona was dragged off by his team-mates and out of harm's way. United even took the lead moments later when David May scored his maiden United goal, before Gareth Southgate equalised from a corner to leave the result 1-1.

Ferguson knew that there was trouble brewing, but he would need to keep it in-house, although that didn't stop him tearing into his team. Goalscorer May said:

> The manager is ripping heads off everyone. Big Pete [Schmeichel], Big Pally, myself, Sharpey, Paul Ince. He had a go at me for their equaliser. He said, 'Who the hell was marking Southgate?' I said, 'Eric.' He turned round and said, 'Eric, I am disappointed in you.

You can't be doing those things.' I thought, 'Is that it? Is that it?!' Any other player would have been given the hairdryer. I just got the hairdryer off the gaffer for not marking someone I shouldn't have been marking.

Alan Smith, Crystal Palace's manager, had no sympathy for the actions of the forward: 'If you want to say, "Gave him one", Shawsie certainly went in. I don't have a lot of sympathy with Cantona. He is a big man, carries himself well, and he had given a fair amount out. Shawsie just thought, "It's on the halfway line, it's in front of the dugout – I'll go for it."'

United manager Ferguson wasn't in agreement with his significant other from across the dugout: '[Referee] Alan Wilkie's inability to stamp out the disgraceful tackles from Crystal Palace's two central defenders made subsequent trouble unavoidable.'

What followed after that brutal attack was a hefty nine-month ban from all football activities and a two-week prison sentence, which was overturned on appeal. Cantona was given community service, which he duly repaid at United's training ground, helping and coaching the young kids during their sessions. The press conference that followed the punishment announcement threw up one of the most bizarre and iconic quotes ever heard. With the paparazzi and mainstream media waiting for an account of events from the Frenchman, or even an apology, what slipped from the lips of Cantona was pretty extraordinary. Seated, and with the coolness expected of him taking a penalty in an FA Cup Final, Eric slowly sipped his water before his short but all so very sweet statement. 'When the seagulls follow the trawler, it's because they think sardines will be thrown into the sea. Thank you very much.' Cantona quickly stood up and marched out of the presser. There were scenes of both bemusement and roars of laughter from some sections of the room, with the press all scribbling down their next headline, trying to make head or tail of the outburst.

The fact of the matter was that United were now heading into February without their talisman and, with a double still to fight for, were to set about the task of showing that this team could still function without the Frenchman. Andy Cole notched five goals against Ipswich Town in a 9-0 victory to ease the concerns of the Old Trafford faithful, but the wheels were soon about to fall off in spectacular fashion. Blackburn Rovers had kept pace with United in the title race and saw their chance to capitalise when United could only muster a 0-0 stalemate at home to Chelsea in mid-April.

With the championship being decided on the final day of the season, United needed to win and hope that old foes Liverpool could do a job on Rovers at Anfield. Upton Park has never been a happy hunting ground for the Red Devils over the years and the Hammers were certainly not going to make life easy for the visitors despite having nothing to play for themselves. The side note to this story is that Blackburn manager Kenny Dalglish was once both player and manager at Liverpool just a few years before and was adored by the red side of Merseyside. Surely Liverpool would roll over and allow their old hero a free pass to the title.

Despite the thoughts of skulduggery and against some scousers' better judgement, Liverpool ran out 2-1 victors. At the same time, United just needed a win, so a third title was within their grasp. It wasn't to be, as a 1-1 draw with West Ham curtailed their title bid and ended their 24-month reign as champions of England. The match was a story of missed opportunities for United as both Cole and Hughes wasted glorious efforts to put the game to bed but that's football and if you don't put the ball in the net, you don't win … simple.

Worse was to follow, as a week later at Wembley United were again humbled, this time by Joe Royle's Everton. The Toffees were huge underdogs in a match that many thought was a shoo-in for Ferguson's men, especially having just been denied the title. A Paul Rideout goal was enough for the Blue half of Merseyside to head back to the north-west buoyant, a decade after a superb Norman Whiteside strike had provided the reverse scoreline in United's favour in the final. Ferguson's men had lost both the league and FA Cup in the space of seven days and it hurt. Gary Pallister, who partnered Steve Bruce at the heart of United's defence, later graciously told *BBC Sport*, 'Everton raised their game, we didn't match it and, on the day, they probably deserved to win.'

The loss of Cantona from the team for the final four months of the season was a defining moment in the club's quest for more silverware. No one can say whether the Frenchman's absence resulted in an empty trophy cabinet that summer at Old Trafford but few could argue that, with him, United's chances would have been much more favourable. They had managed to navigate through Eric's four-match suspension previously, but this lengthy layoff had knocked the stuffing out of the team. It was like a firework shooting into the night sky with everyone waiting for a bang, which ultimately doesn't come.

Forward into the summer, and Ferguson had made changes at the club, most noticeably in the first team, with three big players being moved on to pastures new. Paul Ince, Mark Hughes and Andrei Kanchelskis were shipped out to Inter Milan, Chelsea and Everton respectively. Steve Bruce had eyed a move to Birmingham City to begin his coaching career, leaving a hole both in United's back four and, of course, his partnership with Pallister. Dolly and Daisy were no more, as a new breed of youngsters had emerged from the Cliff training ground in Salford.

Cantona would have to watch as his new-look team began a fresh campaign away at Aston Villa, wearing their infamous all-grey kit. With Cantona suspended and United's next generation merging into the squad, the 3-1 defeat on curtain-raising day was certainly not ideal. We mentioned quotes earlier, with Eric's seagull banger making waves in the press. Alan Hansen's post-match comments on *Match of the Day* resulted in merchandise, posters and even a book. As part of the analysis being carried out on United's performance, the former Scotland and Liverpool defender delivered the damning words to the nation: 'Three players have departed. The trick is always buy when you're strong. He needs to buy players. You can't win anything with kids.'

United rallied, winning their next five matches on the bounce. All eyes were on the Liverpool fixture at Old Trafford on 1 October 1995, as this was the first match that Cantona would be available for after his lengthy ban. The Red Devils were in decent form going into the match, but the question was being asked of the manager whether he was going to include the forward who had been lacking so much football. 'In training, he's been magnificent, his preparation as a footballer is first-class. Absolutely no problem,' said Ferguson. The supporters were singing the name of their hero, who had been out of sight for so long. One banner read: 'The seagull has landed, welcome back Eric.'

The noise that erupted when the Frenchman appeared from the tunnel when the teams took to the pitch was deafening. It got even louder as, just two minutes into the match, Cantona found himself in acres of space on the left flank. He took a touch and sent over a cross that just evaded Andy Cole, but coming in behind him was Nicky Butt, who struck in front of the Stretford End to give United the best of starts. Liverpool, mind you, had clearly not come to be bridesmaid at this wedding. Robbie Fowler struck twice to send those from down the East Lancs Road into a 2-1 lead, with his goals coming either side of half-time.

The referee for the match was David Elleray, and just like in the 1994 FA Cup Final against Chelsea, he awarded United a somewhat soft penalty when Jamie Redknapp was adjudged to have bundled over Ryan Giggs in the box. The stage was set. Cantona, sticking out his chest, casually ran up and stuck the ball in the net and the game was Desmond: 2-2. A goal and an assist on his return was certainly not to be sniffed at, even if he did tire towards the end of the match.

Despite Cantona's comeback, United never really clicked into gear until post-Christmas. Defeats to Arsenal, Liverpool, Leeds and Spurs saw Ferguson and his men staring down the barrel of a 12-point gap between themselves and runaway leaders Newcastle United. Kevin Keegan's team had been playing some champagne football at St James' Park, with the onus on attacking flair rather than defensive grit. They had taken over the mantle from Blackburn Rovers as the new wave of title challengers.

United began the hunt. They picked away at the deficit with a collection of 1-0 wins, most of which had Cantona scoring the only goal. Then, in March 1996, when United rocked up at Tyneside, it was billed as the title decider. Newcastle's seemingly unassailable 12-point lead in February had gradually been whittled down to four by the time the referee blew his whistle to begin proceedings.

The Magpies peppered the United defence with wave after wave of attack raining down on Schmeichel's goal. United's backline held strong, they had to. They knew if they could do their job then someone up the other end would do theirs. With Newcastle missing chance after chance, Ferguson could sense that this could well be their day after all. Phil Neville, with the ball on the left flank, hung up a cross to the far post, where Eric volleyed the ball past Pavel Srnicek in the Newcastle goal. United had weathered the storm and had come out into the sunshine.

In the remaining ten matches of the campaign, Cantona scored the winner in six and the equaliser in another. He had almost dragged the team single-handedly towards another title. Keegan, meanwhile, was a man on the edge and, like Hansen before him, erupted in a tirade of words that again would become famous the world over. With Sir Alex hinting to the press that Leeds United only seem to turn up against his team, Keegan blew his fuse live on Sky Sports after his Newcastle had just beaten the Yorkshire outfit:

> No, no ... when you do that with footballers, like he said about Leeds, and when you do things like that about a man like Stuart Pearce ... I've kept really quiet, but I'll tell you something, he went down in my estimation when he said that. We have not resorted to that, but I'll tell you, you can tell him now if you're watching it, we're still fighting for this title, and he's got to go to Middlesbrough and get something, and ... and ... I'll tell you, honestly, I will love it if we beat them, love it!

They didn't beat them. Newcastle could only draw with Forest, while United were 3-0 victors away at Middlesbrough, as another Premier League title found its way back to Old Trafford. The FA Cup Final was still to come, with another meeting against arch-rivals Liverpool looming at the twin towers. History suggests that the two clubs, who have a hatred for each other on the terraces, respect each other on the pitch as being the most successful teams in England.

What will always stand out from that final is those white suits that the Liverpool players wore on the pitch prior to the kick-off. Ferguson commented in the one-off BBC programme *Sir Alex Ferguson: Secrets of Success*:

> I said to [assistant] Brian Kidd '1-0'. I think that's, what would you call it? Arrogance or over-confidence. It was ridiculous. Absolutely ridiculous. Blue shirt, red and white tie and white suit. And a blue flower. Who designed that? They say it was Armani. I bet his sales went down. I mean Jamie Redknapp's got sunglasses on, but you know the most telling part of it is Roy Evans and Ron Moran had black suits on. I think they were embarrassed.

The United boss was clearly not impressed with the Liverpool attire pre-match. To be honest, they were brighter than the action on the pitch as both teams looked to cancel each other out. Even Cantona was having a quiet afternoon in the sweet London sun. Andy Cole was substituted for United and Stan Collymore for Liverpool as both teams tried to freshen up their attack.

With the final edging towards extra time, Phil Babb's sliced clearance was sent behind for a Manchester United corner. David Beckham swung over the cross into a crowded penalty area. Liverpool keeper David James punched away the cross but it was a tame effort that seemed to ricochet off a couple of Liverpool defenders before finding its way to Cantona, who was loitering around the edge of the penalty area. Arching his back, he swivelled and released a volley back through the crowd and into the unguarded net. I say unguarded. How the ball managed to find its way through the pack of players still baffles me to this day. But it did and United had won their second treble in just three seasons. Cantona, who had been made captain now by the boss, hoisted the trophy into the sky. Oh, what could have been had Cantona not been banned for the finale of the previous campaign.

Clive Tyldesley managed to grab a few words with Eric as the Red Devils began to parade the FA Cup around the stadium to the fans that had remained behind. When asked whether this was the best moment of his career, Cantona replied, 'It was important. After winning the double two years ago, it was a great moment. Now we can go on holiday.' When quizzed further about the lows of last season compared to this, Cantona just smiled and quipped, 'That's life.' The striker had not so much made up for lost time, as he would never get that time back, but he more than showed what the people had been missing with him being in the darkness for so long.

When UEFA banished the three-foreigner rule in time for the beginning of the 1996/97 season, it came a little too late for United and Ferguson. His title- and double-winning team of 1994 had all but broken up and, had the rule been instigated five years earlier, they would really have seen the benefit on European soil. As it was, United's European record after having won the Cup Winners' Cup in 1990/91 was poor at best. Even with Cantona on the pitch, the lack of talent around him was even too much for his powers.

Captain Cantona's impressive Wembley run continued as United destroyed Newcastle 4-0 in the Charity Shield showpiece at the start of the following season. The league was the club's bread and butter, but Ferguson was now eyeing a push on the Champions League, with the team now facing no player restrictions. United were unchallenged on the domestic scene as again Newcastle United were their closest rivals; however, this time around, Keegan's charges lacked the sparkle of the previous campaign. Cantona and his crew were firing on all cylinders until a slight blip in form in October 1996 saw a 5-0 hammering at Newcastle, followed by a 6-3 mauling at The Dell by Southampton. Despite the reverse at St James' Park, Ferguson and his men were never really in doubt on English soil.

The period mentioned was described by *Total Football Mag*:

> On 20 October, the last unbeaten record in the Premier League ended and in spectacular fashion. Newcastle United had a day to remember, beating United 5-0, with goals from Darren Peacock, David Ginola, Les Ferdinand, Shearer, and an audacious lob from Philippe Albert. It was the Red Devils worst defeat for 12 years and just six days later, they shipped six at Southampton, losing 6-3 at the Dell. A home defeat to Chelsea the following week and throwing away a two-goal lead at West Ham in December showed signs of serious vulnerability, that hadn't been seen before by the champions.

Manchester United would again hold off the challenge of Newcastle United to claim another Premier League title, albeit this season they hadn't seemed as fluid as in previous campaigns. Cantona's influence on this young emerging team was enormous as, yet again, his 11 goals in 32 appearances cemented United's foothold in the domestic scene. Liverpool had emerged as late title contenders, having led the table for long periods, but a 3-1 win for United in April 1997 ended any hopes of a championship trophy for the Merseyside Reds, who would eventually finish in third place.

Newcastle United managed to finish as runners-up despite Kevin Keegan walking out in the winter of 1997, having stated that he had taken the club as far as he possibly could. No one ever knew the real reason why Keegan decided to leave while

Newcastle were in touching distance of another joust with Ferguson and United. The city of Newcastle entered a period of mourning, as *The Chronicle* reported:

> They called it Black Wednesday on Tyneside. People cried in the streets or stared at each other in stunned silence. Kevin Keegan has quit after five years in charge, having taken the club from the brink of oblivion and the old Third Division to the heights of the Premier League with a style never before seen at St James' Park.
>
> RIP Kevin Keegan, Newcastle United manager – February 1992 to January 8, 1997.

When Keegan quit, the Magpies were fourth in the league with 37 points, having won 11 and drawn four of their 21 matches, scoring 38 goals, putting seven past Spurs and five past Manchester United. Alan Shearer had signed months earlier for a world record £15m. The decision to quit didn't seem to make sense. Kenny Dalglish took over the reins for the remainder of the campaign and managed to steer them above his old club Liverpool into a silver medal berth.

With the aforementioned relaxing of European rules, Ferguson had set his sights on flexing his muscles against the best teams the Continent had to offer. Footballing royalty, such as AC Milan, Juventus, Real Madrid, Barcelona and Bayern Munich, among others, were now the new challenge on the horizon. Let's not make any mistake here, the Premier League is always the bread and butter for any team in the top tier of English football, but there's something quite magical about pitting your wits in a foreign land. The lure of the unknown was just one of the reasons Sir Matt Busby was pushing so hard to enter his Manchester United team into the European arena. Fast forward over 40 years and now there was a level playing field on which United and Ferguson could operate.

The group stages pitted the Red Devils against Juventus, Fenerbahçe and Rapid Vienna. The Old Lady of Turin was a team littered with stars. This proved to be a stumbling block for United as both home and away would yield 1-0 defeats. Cantona wasn't to be deterred, however, scoring in victories over both Fenerbahçe and Vienna to ensure United finished runners-up in the group and head into the quarter-finals, where FC Porto were United's opponents. Old Trafford was in the mood, Eric was in the mood. There's something quite magical about the Theatre of Dreams on a European night. The floodlights, the smells, the excitement.

Porto had the first chance to score but it was smothered by good defensive work from Pallister. Moments later, at the other end, it was Pallister again, this time rising to a high ball into the box, only to see his header parried out by the keeper. David May, alert to the spill, swept in the opening goal and Old Trafford gushed. United could smell blood. Midway through the first half, a slip from a Porto centre-back gifted the ball to Eric on the penalty spot. He swivelled and lashed the ball past the helpless goalkeeper.

Cantona, now in the mood, found himself in the left-back position, played a beautiful ball down the line with the outside of his right foot, taking three Porto players out of the game. Andy Cole, speeding down the wing, cut inside with the ball and played a reverse pass to Giggs, who had made the run on the overlap. Giggs, taking a touch, then lashed the ball into the net to make it three. United weren't finished there, making sure of the job late in the second half when Cantona, again surging forward, played a delightful through ball to Cole, who slotted it under the keeper to round off a 4-0 win.

Just two weeks later, United completed the job in Portugal with a credible 0-0 draw.

The problem for Ferguson and his men was that the demolition job done on Porto in the first leg was to see the last goals scored in the campaign, as semi-final opponents, and eventual winners of the trophy, Borussia Dortmund, kept Cantona and co at bay in both legs. Despite United riding on the crest of a wave, they were unable to score and ultimately were humbled by two 1-0 defeats. The season had been a success after yet another league title, but Cantona knew that he had fallen short of his usual standards when United had needed him most.

The Frenchman hadn't scored in the last six matches of the campaign, with his final goal coming at Blackburn Rovers in mid-April, but there was no concrete evidence that his form and contribution were on the slide. There still looked to be plenty left in the tank for the talismanic forward, but he had taken the Champions League exit at the semi-final stage incredibly hard. It's claimed that he spoke to Ferguson 24 hours after the defeat to Dortmund and made it quite clear that this was how he wanted it to play out. Ferguson told Eric to put a pin in it as United still had business to conclude in the league. Speaking to the press, Ferguson said:

> In the past, I sensed I could persuade him to stay but this time, he was unequivocal. He has been a marvellous servant to us. He is certainly one of the greatest-ever United players. I think we will find a player of his calibre again because that's what happens in football. Great players emerge all the time.

Cantona's statement was as you would imagine, short but poignant.

I have played professional football for 13 years, which is a long time. I now wish to do other things. I always planned to retire when I was at the top and, at Manchester United, I have reached the pinnacle of my career. In the last four-and-a-half years, I have enjoyed my best football and had a wonderful time. I have had a marvellous relationship with the manager, coach, staff, and players, and, not least, the fans. I wish Manchester United even more success in the future.

With Eric's suspension hampering the middle of his United career, I honestly believe that, had he been available for the remainder of that season, United would have claimed another Premier League title and even another FA Cup. His record of winning the top league with three different teams in three years still stands. The fact that he did it in two countries is even more impressive, after claiming titles first in France with Marseille 1991, before moving to England with Leeds United in 1992 and Manchester United in 1993. His tally of 82 goals in five seasons at United isn't record-breaking, nowhere near it in fact, but what Cantona also brought to the table were his assists, his confidence and an air of arrogance to his team.

The man had an aura about him. Puffing out his chest and proudly stating, 'I am not a man ... I am Cantona.' Merci, Eric. Merci.

4

Steven Gerrard

*'I tried to bring him to Chelsea, I tried to bring
him to Inter, I tried to bring him to Real Madrid,
but he was always a dear enemy. I was dreaming
of having Claude Makelele, Gerrard and Frank
Lampard in midfield.'* – **Jose Mourinho**

AS THE countdown continued towards the millennium year
of 2000, 1998 was also heading towards its own conclusion. On
29 November 1998, during a match at Anfield, Liverpool were
also drawing to their own finale as, with just moments left,
manager Gerrard Houllier made the signal to one of his bench
to be ready for action. The referee signalled for the substitution
to be made and off trotted Vegard Heggem, to be replaced with
an academy graduate by the name of Steven Gerrard.

Fans love to see one of their own enter the hallowed turf and
perform in front of their very eyes. It gives everyone that family
feel, like we're all in it together. The replacement was made and
Gerrard slipped into a right-sided full-back berth to see out the
remaining few minutes. Speaking in his autobiography entitled
Gerrard, he said: 'Your heart is pumping. Butterflies. You see

the nod and the feeling you get it's silly … it's f**king scary.'
His dad was a little more pragmatic in his approach to his son
after his late cameo. 'No one can take that away from you now,
you've played for Liverpool's first team.'

Born on Merseyside, Gerrard spent nearly a decade in the
academy under the Liverpool FC umbrella. Moving elegantly
through the age groups, it was only a matter of time before
the local lad turned good on the biggest stage of all and, to
be fair, they don't come much bigger than at Anfield. His
inaugural campaign was that of sporadic appearances, with
Houllier struggling to fit the vibrant youngster in the starting
XI due to the strength of a midfield consisting of Paul Ince,
Jamie Redknapp and Danny Murphy. Redknapp at this time
was struggling with injuries, water is also wet, and he was in
and out of the team.

Gerrard played in his favoured central midfield role as well
as cover for right-back, as per his debut, and even appeared on
the right side of midfield. The constant shift of position would
take its toll on an already nervous young player. Gerrard recalled
in a November 2008 interview with *The Guardian*: 'I was out of
position and out of my depth.' Despite his own concerns, the
backroom staff and, more importantly, the manager himself
knew what a diamond they had at their disposal. There was a
player in there; they just needed to coax him out.

Gerrard managed a dozen appearances from November
1998 to May 1999, bedding in enough to be told he was going
to be thrust into the manager's thoughts from the off for the
coming season. The belief in the youngster was so complete
that Houllier decided that he no longer needed four central
midfield players and sold England international Paul Ince to
Middlesbrough for £1m, meaning that it was left to Gerrard
or Murphy to fight it out for who would partner Redknapp in
the centre of the pitch.

Liverpool had only mustered a seventh-place finish in the previous campaign, which meant that the Reds would face a season with no European football. This was an ideal time for Gerrard Houllier to give his team a shake-up, which ultimately began with the sale of Ince. Jamie Redknapp was handed the captaincy and Robbie Fowler was made his assistant. New players were brought in, with some continental flair added to try to bridge the gap on the teams above them.

First stop was to try to get back through the European door, then begin an assault on the title. Liverpool fans, however, will always fancy their chances in the league from a standing start no matter what their team is looking like. From the days of Shankly and the famed boot room, it's bred into them. We are Liverpool and we will be challenging, no matter what.

Defenders Sami Hyypiä and Stephane Henchoz were signed from Willem II and Blackburn Rovers respectively. Keeper Sander Westerveld was also brought over from the Netherlands to replace the outgoing David James. Vladimir Smicer was signed from Lens, with Dietmar Hamann making a move over from the north-east at Newcastle United. With this new-look squad beginning to take shape, it was critical that Gerrard began the season in impressive form.

Liverpool didn't really got off to the best of starts, with only three wins coming in the opening ten matches. New signings were clearly taking time to bed in, but Gerrard was beginning to enjoy a good run in the team. His crowning glory was on 5 December 1999 when Liverpool battered Sheffield Wednesday 4-1 at Anfield and the young midfielder was on the score sheet. BBC News website reported:

> Liverpool's home-grown youngsters came of age with
> an impressive display in their side's convincing defeat
> of Premiership strugglers Sheffield Wednesday.

Steven Gerrard, Danny Murphy, and David Thompson – average age 21 and all born within a 30-mile radius of Liverpool – swept away Danny Wilson's spirited side with a goal apiece. All three were only in the side because of injuries to Houllier's first-choice midfielders Patrik Berger, Jamie Redknapp and Vladimir Smicer.

Gerrard's opening gambit, a fine solo strike, pleased both the manager and those waving their scarves on the Kop. 'If Patrik Berger and Jamie Redknapp had been fit they would have played but the youngsters filled in very well and showed they are improving,' said a buoyant Houllier to the press post-match. Even more proof, if it was needed, that the gaffer could trust in the qualities of the emerging youngster.

Liverpool sat in fifth place as the turkey was dished up at Christmas, six points behind leaders Manchester United. Back problems and growing pains were to curtail Gerrard's campaign, as niggles and knocks were beginning to hamper his rhythm. As the millennium chimed in, Gerrard's absence began to show as Liverpool's performances faltered during the final furlong of the season. The title challenge slipped away with a loss of form at exactly the wrong time.

They still had something to play for, as the top three places in the Premier League now meant Champions League qualification. Competition for second and third place was still fierce, with Arsenal, Leeds United, Chelsea and Aston Villa all in close contention. Manchester United had opened a healthy lead at the top of the table, which left the spaces in behind to fight for. Gerrard managed to return but only for a few fleeting appearances as he battled to regain full fitness.

Heading to Bradford on the final day of the season, Liverpool had it all in their own hands. Win and Champions

League football beckoned, also relegating Bradford City into the Championship. City were battling it out with Wimbledon to keep alive their Premier League status. An early David Wetherall header defied the script and was enough to sink the Reds as Bradford carried out the great escape, culminating in Liverpool dropping into a UEFA Cup position. More on that shortly.

Bradford's final-day heroics meant that Wimbledon's tenure in the top division was finally over. After years of roughing it with football's establishment, it was time to leave the party. Oddly enough, it was 12 years to the day that Wimbledon had defeated Liverpool in the 1988 FA Cup Final, one of the biggest upsets in English football. How ironic that a defeat for the Reds this time round would cause tears of pain rather than joy for the Wombles.

The year 2000 held new hope for the young midfielder, who was now starting to show maturity in both the way he played and how he carried himself. People were starting to take notice, most notably the England boss, Kevin Keegan, who had himself once graced the Anfield turf. Keegan knew that, despite Gerrard's fledgling career in top-flight football, if you're good enough, then you're old enough, and the 19-year-old was certainly pushing hard for a call-up despite his recent injury issues. The European Championships were only a month away as Gerrard stepped out on to the Wembley pitch in May 2000.

Speaking to thefa.com, Gerrard, who had previously featured for England at Under-21 level, recalled:

> It was such a high, to run out at the old Wembley –
> it was a dream come true. I'd watched many, many
> Cup Finals and international games at Wembley and
> only ever dreamed of running out to play a football
> match. I think I had 30 or 40 tickets in Wembley

that night, people had travelled from the north to support me. To go out there for my England debut against Ukraine and share a pitch with the likes of Tony Adams, Alan Shearer, David Beckham and Paul Scholes – top players in their era – as a young 19-year-old was a phenomenal feeling.

England went on to win 2-0 and, with Gerrard having impressed, the midfielder had played his way into the thoughts of the manager, with the squad for the Euros yet to be named. 'Getting that little taste of the action, what it's about and what is expected at that level, it certainly brought me on in leaps and bounds as a player,' said Gerrard to the press. 'It's certainly one of the highlights of my international career – you always remember your debut.'

That call did arrive and Gerrard was named in the squad to travel to Belgium and the Netherlands for Euro 2000. England flattered to deceive and were eliminated in the group stages despite turning over old foe Germany 1-0. Gerrard's only appearance in the competition came with a substitute appearance in that win. Nevertheless, it was a taste of international football. 'When I was named in that group for Euro 2000, I really didn't think I was worthy or had the right to be there and involved on the pitch,' he told thefa.com. 'But it was a wonderful experience, and a vital experience, and it certainly helped me to grow.'

With the midfielder heading back home to recover before the 2000/01 season was under way, Liverpool had gone about their transfer business. Their most notable bits of trade were three free transfers. In came Gary McAllister, Jari Litmanen and Markus Babbel, signed from Coventry City, Barcelona and Bayern Munich, respectively. With Liverpool now fighting on four fronts, Houllier knew that adding experience and guile to his squad of youngsters was going to be key to competing in the Premier League, FA Cup, League Cup and UEFA Cup.

Steven Gerrard's fitness issues looked to be behind him as he reported back for training during pre-season. The fixture list threw up an interesting opponent on the opening day as last season's tormentors were drawn at Anfield in matchday one. Bradford City, who had defied the odds on the final day of the previous season, were travelling west to Liverpool. This time around, they weren't to be so lucky as a fine Emile Heskey strike gained revenge on the Bantams to kick-start the Reds' campaign.

Defeat to Arsenal a week later, followed by a draw at Southampton, looked like the making of a mid-table slog for Liverpool. Wins over Aston Villa and Manchester City followed, but another defeat, to Chelsea, derailed what looked like an early push for the title. A goal in the draw at Upton Park was the first of Gerrard's ten goals for the season as, again, another two points dropped scuppered Liverpool's momentum. Danny Murphy's left-footed cross found Gerrard unmarked ten yards out, and the England midfielder finished neatly.

December 2000 brought an early gift for all Red men as, in the space of a week, Liverpool won at Old Trafford courtesy of a Danny Murphy goal, followed five days later by putting four past the hapless Gunners, with Gerrard scoring the opener. BBC Sport website reported on the week's proceedings:

> Liverpool completed the perfect week for boss Gérard Houllier – building on victory over Premiership pace-setters Manchester United by thrashing second-placed Arsenal at Anfield. Houllier's rejuvenated Liverpool now stand only two points behind Arsenal after a performance at home which hinted they may still be title dark horses. Arsenal arrived at Anfield

with a wretched record of no wins in eight years, and it did not get any better for Arsène Wenger's side. England midfield man Steven Gerrard, the game's outstanding performer, gave Liverpool an early lead, setting the tone for a comprehensive victory.

Despite the pre-Christmas hype, the manager was certainly not getting carried away with the two performances. Speaking to the press after the match, Houllier said, 'I am not a dreamer. I think we are five points short and cannot see Manchester United dropping ten.' His predictions were to ring true, as Liverpool, who were in third place going into the new year, never climbed any higher, with Arsenal and Manchester United battling it out for the championship. It wasn't all doom and gloom on Merseyside, though, as it was to be cup competitions on both home and European soil that were about to take centre stage.

In the lead-up to the bell striking on the year 2001, Liverpool had already been busy on UEFA Cup and League Cup duties. The pain of missing out on the previous year's Champions League was still raw, but you can only try to win whatever competition you're playing in. In this instance, the younger, more annoying sibling of the European Cup was on offer. Up first, a trip to Romania to face Rapid Bucharest. The UEFA Cup, unlike the group stages of the Champions League, was a two-legged affair, requiring the Reds to travel to the home of Count Dracula first.

A slim 1-0 win in the capital was just what was needed, especially with the away goals in European competition counting double. Nick Barmby's finish had set Liverpool on their way. A clean sheet in a 0-0 draw at Anfield followed to send the Reds into the second round of the competition. Meanwhile, an extra-time win over Chelsea in the League

Cup, followed by an 8-0 mauling of Stoke City, spearheaded the double-pronged attack on silverware.

Slovan Liberec, a relatively unknown outfit from the Czech Republic, despite being one of the most successful clubs in the country's short history, were the next to venture to Anfield, and again Liverpool walked away with a slim 1-0 victory. It was another clean sheet at home, shutting out the double jeopardy of away goals. Then Liverpool scored three times in Prague to secure a 4-2 aggregate win. The great thing about two-legged football is that you can be mediocre in one of the matches and still manage to get the result that you need.

Olympiakos of Greece were waiting for Liverpool in the third round, as Gerrard and his team-mates ventured to the home of Aristotle, Plato and ouzo full of confidence. The game was a topsy-turvy affair, with Liverpool twice taking the lead, only for the Greeks to discover a way back. Gerrard, finding his way on to the score sheet, had given Liverpool the lead with a glancing header from Staunton's corner to make it 2-1, before a late equaliser set up an interesting second leg at Anfield. With a night under the lights waiting, Liverpool turned it on in front of the Kop, running out 2-0 winners to complete another 4-2 aggregate win.

On the domestic front, Fulham provided stern opposition in the quarter-finals of the League Cup, only to run out of steam in extra time after having held Liverpool to a 0-0 draw in the regulation 90 minutes. The Cottagers capitulated in the final 30 minutes to lose 3-0. It was full steam ahead for Liverpool, though. Their league form was on the turn for the better and their cup exploits were just kick-starting into life.

The Reds travelled to Selhurst Park to face Crystal Palace in the first leg of the semi-finals of the League Cup and were sent back up the M6 with their tails between their legs as the Eagles edged a 2-1 win. The return leg at Anfield was a completely different story as Liverpool were on fire in a very convincing 5-0 win to cruise into the League Cup final, where they were surely nailed on to lift the trophy, since they faced a team from a division below them in Birmingham City. Just a few weeks before that final, a trip to the Italian capital to face Roma beckoned in the fourth round of the UEFA Cup. A Michael Owen double secured two vital away goals, which eventually saw Liverpool through 2-1 on aggregate.

Liverpool's FA Cup run had also got under way. They had already dispatched Rotherham United, Leeds United and Manchester City before a tricky quarter-final tie against Tranmere Rovers on the Wirral had all the potential to be a banana skin. John Aldridge's team had become a bit of a cult cup team at the time and weren't going to be a pushover in this local derby. Liverpool sped into a three-goal lead, with Gerrard netting the third, only for Tranmere to rally with two goals in ten minutes, before Robbie Fowler finally put the game to bed. Gary McAllister floated in a corner, headed on by Marcus Babbel, and Gerrard made no mistake from six yards out.

By now it was a three-pronged attack on the cup competitions. The first of three trophies was picked up in Cardiff as Liverpool had to overcome plucky Birmingham City on penalties after a 1-1 draw in 120 minutes. Gerrard had finally tasted success in a Liverpool shirt and he didn't have to wait too long for some more to come along. With semi-final wins coming over Barcelona and Wycombe Wanderers in the UEFA Cup and FA Cup respectively, Gerrard and his teammates found themselves in another two finals.

First was the FA Cup Final in Cardiff. With Arsenal leading by a goal to nil, Owen pounced twice in the space of five minutes to turn the match on its head and land the trophy. Arsenal looked to have won the match but with less than ten minutes remaining, Liverpool had produced a stunning fightback. However, the most crazy of matches was saved for just four days later as the Red men headed for Dortmund to face Alavés in the UEFA Cup Final.

Liverpool sped into an early lead, with Gerrard scoring Liverpool's second on 16 minutes, but the Spanish team pulled one back ten minutes later. Gary McAllister's penalty just before half-time gave Liverpool a 3-1 lead but Alavés weren't done, as Javier Moreno struck twice in 12 minutes to restore parity. Liverpool leapt into action again, with Robbie Fowler notching to make it 4-3, but with just 90 seconds on the clock, Jordi Cruyff levelled the match at 4-4 to send it into extra time.

With both teams tiring, the tackles were beginning to become a little reckless, most notably from the Spaniards, as both teams were desperate to clinch the trophy. As the match headed towards a penalty shoot-out, disaster struck for Alavés, as not only did two of their players carrying yellow cards see red, but an own goal by Delfi Geli with just four minutes remaining gifted Liverpool the UEFA Cup and a hat-trick of trophies. It signalled the end of a quite unforgettable season for Houllier and his team, and it remains a year that will be talked about forever by the red half of Merseyside.

Gerrard returned to kick-start Liverpool's 2001/02 campaign after a well-deserved summer rest and helped them claim another trophy, this time the Charity Shield, which was whisked back to Anfield after a 2-1 win over rivals Manchester United. Then, in September 2001, England travelled to Munich for a crunch match with Germany in the World Cup qualification campaign. Gerrard scored an absolute fizzer from just outside the penalty area, something the midfielder would become accustomed to over the course of his glittering career. England eventually ran out 5-1 winners in one of the greatest performances by an England team in the modern era.

Speaking to the thefa.com Gerrard said:

It was certainly one of the highlights of my career to score against Germany, away from home, and to win the game 5-1. It was a top, top performance from the lads. It was such an important qualifying game and we were underdogs, everyone thought the Germans were going to run all over us, especially with them having home advantage. I remember the starting eleven being named and it was full of top players.

The midfielder waxed lyrical about his goal:

Germany started strongly but we got control pretty quickly. I remember us getting a set-piece, it was cleared, got put back in and was cleared out. I just remember thinking to myself 'just get a good touch on it, try and set it for a strike on goal'. My touch was perfect for once and I got fantastic contact – the pitch was wet and I put enough power on it to slide past a top keeper in Oliver Kahn.

Another trophy soon followed as Liverpool edged a close encounter with Bayern Munich in the European Super Cup to win 3-2 and make it a five-trophy haul in a calendar year. It was quite something for Gerrard, who was still making his way in professional football. His personal goals tally was just beginning to creep up, which was now making him a very important component in this Liverpool team. Opposing teams were absolutely petrified of a loose ball falling to the midfielder outside the penalty area as Germany had just found out to their peril.

With cup success in Gerrard's back pocket, it was now the Premier League title that was needed to complete the domestic puzzle. In 2001/02, Liverpool were runners-up to

Arsenal, finishing seven points behind the Gunners, who had broken Manchester United's run of three consecutive titles. This silver medal position was the closest Gerrard and his team would get for nearly a decade as, year on year, they would fall away in the spring. The next six seasons would herald a final position of fifth, fourth, fifth, third, third and fourth, before they eventually claimed the runners-up spot again in 2008/09.

Despite his failure to secure the top division prize, in 2003 Gerrard scored arguably one of the best goals ever in a League Cup final. The midfielder picked up the ball a full 30 yards from goal and fired an unstoppable bending shot over the head of Fabien Barthez in the Manchester United goal. Liverpool won 2-0 and again tasted victory champagne in Cardiff.

The 2003/04 campaign was barren for Liverpool and, with a fourth-place finish not satisfying the board, Houllier was given his marching orders and a new man was put in his place. Rafael Benítez had won the La Liga and UEFA Cup double with Valencia, but a fallout with the board meant that his contract was terminated after the spat went public. Benítez, clearly not happy with his employers after delivering the holy grail, told the press, 'I was hoping for a sofa [a defender] and they've brought me a lamp [Fabián Canobbio].' Liverpool's hierarchy jumped at the chance to bring the Spaniard to Anfield, a man who clearly knew how to get a team over the line.

On his arrival, Benítez stated, 'It is like a dream to be here. I am very, very proud to be joining one of the most important clubs in the world in one of the best leagues in the world – and I want to win.' This was music to Gerrard's ears, who had tasted plenty of cup success under Benítez's predecessor but not enough league penetration for the midfielder's liking. As mentioned a little earlier, Liverpool's league positions never really improved, despite the change of manager. However, during the next two seasons in particular, Liverpool and, more importantly, Gerrard were about to taste the next best thing.

First the 2004/05 campaign. Liverpool's erratic league form had come back to haunt them and, with three defeats coming in the first seven matches, the writing was already on the wall for the boys from the Anfield Road. Defeats to Bolton Wanderers, Manchester City, Birmingham City and Middlesbrough derailed the inaugural league title push that Benítez had so desperately wanted. One of the benefits of the new boss, for Gerrard in particular, was that the midfielder was played in a more advanced position. Benítez had signed fellow countryman Xavi Alonso, who controlled the midfield beautifully, enabling Gerrard to push forward to help out the attack.

With Liverpool finishing the previous season in fourth, they had to play a qualifier for the Champions League. Grazer AK from Austria proved to be a tricky task, but with a brace from Gerrard in the first leg, the Reds edged through 2-1 on aggregate. The midfielder would also need to be saving his magic for the latter moments of the group stages. Like the team's league form, their European charge wasn't quite going as planned and, with Liverpool looking to be heading out of the competition at the group stage with just four minutes remaining of their final match, Steven Gerrard stepped up against Olympiakos to score one of the most important goals in the club's history. Well, maybe until next season anyway.

A long ball into the penalty area was expertly cushioned down by striker Neil Mellor. With the ball falling beautifully to Gerrard, who was lurking just outside the box, he struck his instep across the ball, sending it hurtling across the goalkeeper and into the far corner of the net. Anfield nearly exploded. Andy Gray, commentating for Sky Sports at the time shouted, 'Ohhhhh, you beauty. What a hit son ... what a hit!' He was right. It was worthy of winning any match in any league in the world.

An FA Cup third round defeat to Burnley meant that Liverpool could concentrate on two fronts. The League Cup was still in full flow and Benítez's men had made it to the final, where they would meet Jose Mourinho and Chelsea. Mourinho, like Benítez, had embarked on his maiden season in the Premier League and was looking for his first taste of silverware. Jose would get the rub of the green as an own goal by the unfortunate Gerrard sent the Blues back to London with a 3-2 win.

Liverpool had bigger fish to fry. By fish, I mean Bayer Leverkusen, Juventus and Chelsea – all battered on the way to the Champions League Final in Istanbul in 2005. I think this final is what epitomises why I decided to write this book. As a Manchester United fan, I could only watch on and marvel at the huge contribution that Gerrard made that night. Rivalry aside, I was lost in admirations at the huge task, of the huge task ahead of the Liverpool skipper that night and the way in which he went about it in a no-nonsense fashion.

AC Milan, like Liverpool, are European Cup heavyweights. When they raced into a three-goal lead in the first half, it looked like the Rossoneri were to be heading back to Milan with 'ol' big ears'. Liverpool looked shell-shocked. Milan had absolutely destroyed them with their devastating attacks and cool finishing. It looked like the heroics against Olympiakos would all be forgotten as the Red men walked off at the interval, weary and discombobulated, like a boxer who was against the ropes and punch drunk.

Djibril Cisse remembers how the changing room was at half-time. The French striker says Benítez was 'really optimistic' and gave a positive talk to the team. However, Cisse has claimed that it was Gerrard's speech that really changed the match. Cisse, who would go on to score a penalty in the shoot-out, told *The Mirror*:

> He [Gerrard] asked nicely to the staff to be alone with the players. He said that he is a Liverpool kid, always been his club, he didn't want to see his club being like this, being humiliated. And he said if we scored in the first 15 minutes we would win the game and he's the guy who scored the first goal.

Gerrard pulled a goal back in the 54th minute with a guided header that found the far corner. Just two minutes later, Smicer arrowed a shot into the far corner of the net. Moments later, Gerrard was fouled in the penalty area and Alonso stepped up to take the kick, scoring on the rebound after a save to make it 3-3. Liverpool had struck three times in six second-half minutes to level the match and do the unthinkable. Well, the easy part was done, now to go for the win. Neither team could manage to find a winner and the inevitable penalty shoot-out ensued.

How on earth were Milan here, standing on the centre circle, waiting for the jeopardy of spot kicks when they had had Liverpool right where they wanted them? By the time Andriy Shevchenko had put the ball straight into the legs of Jerzy Dudek, Gerrard and co were headed off to celebrate with the Liverpool supporters.

The Liverpool Echo reported:

> Gerrard and company have rewritten football 'possibilities' throughout this campaign, but even the heroic efforts of Olympiakos, Juventus and Chelsea were rendered insignificant compared to this. It shouldn't have happened. Some of us aren't convinced

it did. Only the pinch marks confirm it. We thought it was all over. It wasn't.

Gerrard was now the go-to man for Liverpool. When they needed him most, he would often come up trumps. Looking back, he said:

> If you're talking about one individual goal that was so important for the team and the club, that helped us progress to that incredible night in Istanbul, it'd have to be Olympiakos. The timing of the goal and what was needed on the night … in the dressing room afterwards, I realised it was an important goal to help the team progress, but it wasn't until Istanbul had calmed down a couple of weeks later and I reflected on the whole journey of the Champions League triumph, I realised the Olympiakos goal was such a huge goal.

The 2005/06 season would see Liverpool again triumph in the Super Cup, this time with a 3-1 win over CSKA Moscow. Their league form was patchy, and the holders of the Champions League eventually crashed out in the last 16 to unfancied Benfica. Liverpool had made some big moves in the summer market, with Peter Crouch coming for £7m. The striker had taken a while to find his feet, but once he started scoring, the team seemed to gel a lot better.

The FA Cup was proving a nice release for the team and they had navigated their way to the final again in Cardiff by beating Luton Town, Portsmouth, Manchester United, Birmingham City and Chelsea. Gerrard himself had notched a couple of times on the road to the final, where the Reds would face the Hammers as West Ham United swapped the capital of England for that of Wales. The Liverpool skipper was now becoming a bit of a pro at leading his team out in big games, such was the frequency of Liverpool reaching finals from the turn of the millennium. In fact it was their seventh visit to the stadium in just five years, and that was without the UEFA and Champions League finals too.

With the story already writing itself, by the time the clock had ticked to the 28th minute, West Ham's Dean Ashton was wheeling away to score his team's second goal of the match. Another final, another mountain. Cisse managed to pull a goal back for Liverpool on 30 minutes but that was how the half-finished. Liverpool were again behind, although this time the mountain seemed more molehill than the year before in Istanbul. Nevertheless, it was a scoreline that needed overturning and who to turn to than Stevie G?

In the 54th minute, a ball into West Ham's box was nodded down by the dominant Crouch into the path of the onward-rushing Gerrard. Not even breaking stride, the midfielder lashed the ball past Shaka Hislop to make it 2-2. Ten minutes later, the Hammers rallied. Paul Konchesky advanced down the left flank and sent in a deep cross to the back post, which completely fooled everyone and made its way into the far top corner. Complete fluke, unless Konchesky says otherwise, of course.

The match was now running away from Liverpool and, with the fourth official holding up the board to signal just four minutes remaining, a long hopeful ball was hoisted into the West Ham area. The defence, tired and clinging on for dear life, cleared the danger with a solid header. The ball fell into a space around 30–35 yards from goal and, from out of nowhere, Steven Gerrard strode on to it and struck what was probably one of the cleanest hits of a ball you'll ever see. It absolutely flew past Hislop before he could even see it. 3-3. John Motson burst into life, roaring, 'Gerrard ... he's done it! Oh Steven Gerrard, just when he looked injured and out of it, has equalised for Liverpool with 90 minutes gone.'

West Ham were on their arses and somehow managed to cling on for a penalty shoot-out. Unfortunately for them, a host of misses handed the cup to Liverpool and Gerrard. The 2006 final was called the 'Gerrard Final' for the midfielder's heroics. Another example of dragging your team through the mud to get to where you need to be. From Istanbul to Cardiff, Gerrard was the difference in those two finals. 'Chest out, give me the ball and I'll do the rest.' A leader of men, by example and words.

What made the goal all the more remarkable was that Gerrard had been lying on the Cardiff turf just moments earlier, suffering from cramp. But with typical determination, he dragged himself up and then fired Liverpool level. 'When the injury-time board went up we thought our chance had gone,' admitted team-mate Peter Crouch. 'But it is always good to have a player like Steven Gerrard in your team.' The midfielder had finished the campaign with 23 goals in all competitions, his best return so far.

The 2006/07 season again saw Liverpool reach another Champions League Final, but this time, despite their captain's heroics, they were unable to overcome AC Milan, who were on a revenge mission from two years previous. A 2-1 defeat to the Italians was a sore end to an otherwise disappointing campaign. And 2007/08 didn't get any better either, as the club failed to reach a final for the first time in four years. Liverpool finished fourth in the league, absolutely miles away from the title, despite the summer signing of Fernando Torres. His 33 goals in all competitions were still not enough to help them mount a serious charge.

A year on and, with the partnership between Torres and Gerrard seeming to find some traction, the Reds looked to go head to head with Manchester United for the title. The most notable match that season was when Liverpool rocked up at Old Trafford and marched back out of there with three points after a 4-1 demolition of the Red Devils. Both Torres and Gerrard were on the scoresheet that day in what was a monumental shift in the title race.

The problem with Liverpool was that, despite only losing two matches in that campaign, they threw away plenty of points in the form of too many draws. Even if United lost, Liverpool would only draw and, eventually, with those from Old Trafford getting their noses in front in the table, they managed to fight off a very good Liverpool team. I would go as far as to say that this Liverpool team for me were better than the one who nearly won the title in 2013/14, but the difference was that this time it was Manchester United's title to lose as opposed to Liverpool's, as was the case in 2014.

So near but yet so far. Even with Gerrard finding the net on 24 occasions, it still wasn't enough to earn him that first Premier League medal. Rafa Benítez was also still searching for the pinnacle of English football, but it wasn't to be for the Spaniard, who was relieved of his duties at the tail end of the 2009/10 season, with Liverpool again falling short of their domestic target. Roy Hodgson was named as the new boss and Liverpool seemed to enter a period of transition.

Hodgson's appointment never really appealed to those on the Kop, and two league finishes of seventh and sixth never really helped his cause either. The experienced coach was handed his P45 and Liverpool legend Kenny Dalglish was installed as a temporary measure. As the noughties turned into the tens, Gerrard was now beginning to pick up a few more injuries, much to the annoyance of Dalglish, whose team was desperate to keep their talisman on the pitch. An eighth-place finish in 2011/12 highlighted just how big a rebuilding process there was, and even a League Cup win against Cardiff City couldn't sway the board to stick with Kenny.

Brendan Rodgers was brought into the club, a young vibrant coach who had Swansea City playing some mesmerising football. Unfortunately for Rodgers, he was now getting a Gerrard who was heading into his sunset years, but if you could get him off the treatment table, he could still do a job for the team. Rodgers's first season didn't go well at all, but there again this was a Liverpool team who were nearly unrecognisable from the 2006–09 team. Seventh place was nowhere near good enough for those who frequented Anfield, but they could see that Rodgers was setting the building blocks for something pretty special.

Luis Suárez and Daniel Sturridge had been signed from Ajax and Chelsea, respectively, to help bolster the team's firepower. But even with the 23 goals in all competitions from Suárez, it was clear that Liverpool had problems at the other end of the pitch. However, in 2013/14 they clicked. Kolo Touré and Mamadou Sakho were brought in to add some much-needed steel to the backline.

Liverpool were lurking around the top three spots as the year turned to 2014 and, after New Year's Day, they went on a barnstorming run towards the Premier League title. They put six goals past Cardiff, five past Stoke City and Arsenal, as well as four past Everton, Swansea and Tottenham Hotspur. The three of Sturridge, Gerrard and Suárez were absolutely red hot. When Liverpool found a way to win away at Norwich City, the Reds held a five-point advantage over Manchester City with just three matches remaining.

Chelsea headed to Anfield with Jose Mourinho back to try to spoil the party. The game was pretty tight and you could feel the tension in the ground. That feeling became a million times worse as, on the stroke of half-time, an uncharacteristic slip just inside the Liverpool half by Gerrard gave Chelsea forward Ba the freedom of Anfield. He strode forward to slide the ball past the onrushing Mignolet. The Blues struck again, this time through Willian in stoppage time, as the Reds pushed for an equaliser.

Liverpool were down but certainly not out. A week later and with the title still in their grasp, a crunch match with Crystal Palace meant that if they won it was all over. Liverpool were flying at 3-0 to the good until a crazy last ten minutes ended the Reds' title ambitions for another season as Palace scored three times in 11 minutes, handing the title to Manchester City. Gerrard had been close before, but not as close as this. The midfielder had one more season in his locker at Liverpool, but the heartache of missing out in the previous campaign was still there for all to see. He said in an interview with BT Sport:

> The slip happened at a bad time, it was cruel for me personally. There's not a day that goes by that I don't think about if that hadn't happened. Would things have been different? Would it have turned out different? Maybe, I don't know. You've got to be thick-skinned and take a bit of criticism along the way. I'm not scared of any criticism or cruelty.
>
> I understand it and the impact it had it kills me, don't get me wrong. Inside it kills me and it will do for a long time. I think to myself, 'If I'd have got that league, it would have been the icing on the cake.' But what helps me with it is that I've got the cake. I've achieved a lot of dreams with a team that has never been the favourite. I've got memories – good memories – that will live with me forever but that one moment will always hurt me until the day I go

because if I'd have got that moment, I'd have achieved every dream with Liverpool.

Gerrard ended his final campaign on 16 goals, but it wasn't enough for the team to reach any higher than a sixth-place finish. The end was nigh for the midfielder, who had given his absolute all for his hometown club. He may never have achieved Premier League glory but what he did win would be the envy of any modern-day footballer. The Englishman made a fleeting appearance in the MLS with the LA Galaxy before coming back to these shores to begin a coaching career, which to date has included a Scottish Premier League title with Rangers.

His international record with England was one of more disappointment about what could have been, although 21 goals in 114 caps is a sign of longevity on the big stage. Gerrard's record with Liverpool wasn't too bad either, with the local lad scoring 190 times for the famous Reds in 749 matches. Some of those goals are the most important in the club's history, but that was just the kind of man he was. It was a shame that Liverpool lost out on his later years through a team making so many changes at once. Still, he was phenomenal when called upon for so many years. 'Gerrard is for me, in the position he plays, one of the very best in the world. He has a huge impact. For the job he performs, for me, he is one of the greatest.' – Ronaldinho.

5

Johan Cruyff

*'I loved the Dutch in the '70s, they excited me
and Cruyff was the best. He was my childhood
hero; I had a poster of him on my bedroom
wall. He was a creator. He was at the heart of
a revolution with his football. Ajax changed
football and he was the leader of it all. If he
wanted he could be the best player in any
position on the pitch.' – **Eric Cantona***

FOOTBALL HAS been played all over the world now for
well over a century and more. During this time, there have
been players who have graced us with not only their talent
on the pitch but have also managed to leave a legacy off it
as well. Hendrik Johannes Cruijff, born in Amsterdam on
25 April 1947, is just one example of this but, boy oh boy,
what an example he proved to be. False 9s, pivots, double
pivots and even more of the 'FIFA generation' phrases
weren't only coined by Johan Cruyff over 50 years ago,
but he would also have played in all of the positions as
well. As a player, Cruyff wasn't only well ahead of his time

in technical ability but also he was a thinker: a full-time student of the game.

Before the triumph there was devastation as, at a tender age, Cruyff would lose his father who was just 45. Being a child at the time in 1959, 12-year-old Cruyff took the loss hard, as anyone would when losing a loved one and idol. His mother left her job as a grocer and took up a higher-paid cleaning gig at Ajax football club, where she would meet her soon-to-be second husband, Henk Angel. Angel worked at the club as a groundsman and would become a steadying influence on Cruyff as he made waves through his juvenile years.

Ajax football club weren't the behemoth of Dutch football that we all know now. In fact, Dutch football itself was still not represented in a professional way until the 1956/57 season. Prior to this, the Royal Dutch Football Association (KNVB), had rejected any form of payment or salaries for players. This prompted the more talented guys to head out of the Netherlands to look for more financial gain elsewhere on the continent, with France seemingly the country of choice. With this in mind, the KNVB banned all absconding players from ever appearing for the national team if they were only interested in lining their pockets rather than playing for the love of the shirt.

On 31 January 1953, the North Sea flood killed over 2,000 people, damaged tens of thousands of buildings and left nearly 20 per cent of the Netherlands under water. With ocean levels rising nearly six metres above their normal heights, sea defences in England, Belgium, Scotland and the Netherlands were unable to prevent widespread disaster. There were fatalities at sea as well as on land as trawlers in the area were sunk. The devastation was huge and it was estimated to have cost around £50m to restore all the infrastructure, a lot of money now, let alone in the 1950s, post-Second World War. Dutch footballers living in exile decided they should try to arrange a charity match in Paris to help raise money for the relief back home.

Cor van der Hart played football as a professional in France when the dykes broke in Zeeland. 'I heard the news on the radio,' he said in 2003, 'and understood that the Netherlands was in a panic.' He then played in the legendary 'Watersnood' match, which would change Dutch football forever, along with players such as Kees Rijvers, Gerrit Vreken, Bertus de Harder and Rinus Schaap. The interest in the Netherlands showed what could be achieved by professionals, but still the KNVB wasn't moved.

With public interest now riding high, the NBVB (a rebel professional football association) was founded and a professional league was now beginning to form in time for the 1954/55 season. Still the KNVB shunned the idea of the change from amateurism and prolonged the league system that had been in place since the turn of the century. On 3 July 1954, a group of concerned chairmen called the KNVB to discuss their worries and an emergency meeting was held. By the time the delegates had filtered back out of the Terminus Hotel (we will revisit Dutch football's birthplace a little later), the professional league had been agreed and the 18-team Eredivisie was founded. Ajax, incidentally, won the inaugural trophy in the 1956/57 season and embarked on a mesmerising run to modern-day glory.

So now we had a league, a foundation in which Cruyff could set a footing for others, like adding a layer on a cake. Speaking of cakes, on the day that Cruyff was blowing out the candles on his 10th birthday, the ink was just beginning to dry on his youth contract. Jany van der Veen had spotted Cruyff and his mates playing football in a local playground and had asked the youth to come for a trial. 'He always played football with older boys, and he had bossed them. It seemed like he was fused with the ball,' said Van der Veen, who clearly knew a player or two, having spent time around a certain Rinus Michels.

Cruyff was nurtured at the now famous Ajax academy and eventually made his first-team debut on 15 November 1964 in a 3-1 defeat to FC Groningen, at the age of just 17. It was a landmark moment for the attacking midfielder, who also scored the only goal for Ajax in the match. It was a season of struggle for the club from Amsterdam as they finished in a very sorry 13th position, their lowest since the inception of the professional game. This didn't deter the youngster, who by now well and truly had the bit between his teeth. Ahead of the 1965/66 campaign, Cruyff was deployed in a role where he could operate a little more freely. His slight frame still meant that, while technically he was already head and shoulders above most of his opponents, he needed to find half a yard to ensure he wasn't bundled off the ball as, of course, referees were much more lenient in those days.

At any one time in a match, Cruyff would occupy numerous different positions. First, you might see him in a centre-forward role, then moments later he would be picking the ball up from the toes of his own central defender. This made it near on impossible for opposition players to track exactly where he was playing, and how do you stop someone if you have no idea of their next move? 'I always threw the ball in, because then if I got the ball back, I was the only player unmarked,' said Cruyff. Providing another example of a player who wasn't only always on the move on the field but was also always thinking one step ahead.

His new-found freedom yielded fruit for both club and player as a 25-goal haul in 23 matches secured a Dutch league title for Ajax, Cruyff's first taste of trophy champagne. His Ajax team had won the Eredivisie in emphatic style, only losing on two occasions. Defeats to the now defunct Fortuna '54 and

Sparta Rotterdam were soon washed over as a footballing masterclass was served up every other week at the De Meer Stadion. The boys from the Dam finished an impressive seven points clear of their nearest challengers, Feyenoord, at a time when it was still only two points for a win. The title winners had also found the net on many more occasions than the team from Rotterdam.

Having grown up playing the Ajax way, Cruyff embodied everything about the club and how the game of football should be played. Take the modern day, for example. Their academy in the Netherlands is second to none in the players that they craft. It's a conveyor belt of talent that just keeps on rolling, producing players, some of whom eventually outgrow their surroundings and move on to pastures new. This model works for the club and it works for the player. Ajax sell at a price that enables the academy to keep on growing organically. By organically, I mean that they don't need a multibillionaire from some far-eastern oil state who will gainfully splash millions of pounds at the drop of a hat. Horses for courses. The primary objective is simple. Invest in youth, don't sign footballers from outside unless they're exceptionally more talented than your own academy players, believe in possessional football, play attractively, pass, defend forward. This was Cruyff's childhood. This was what it meant to represent the people of Amsterdam in those red-and-white shirts.

With Cruyff's taste of league success still fresh in the mouth, it was now time to widen his footballing palate and explore the delights of football outside the Netherlands in the form of the European Cup. The 1966/67 campaign saw Ajax come up against Turkish opposition in the first round. Beşiktaş were easily put to the sword on this occasion and were beaten 4-1 over the two legs. This then set up a tie against Bill Shankly's Liverpool. Cruyff scored goals in both the home and away legs to ease the de Godenzonen into the quarter-final stages.

Meanwhile, back on Dutch shores, Ajax were still at their brilliant best, and in particular the ever-so-majestic Cruyff. MVV Maastricht, FC Groningen and FC Utrecht were all beaten in emphatic fashion, 8-0, 8-3 and 8-3 respectively. Then there were FC Twente, Fortuna Sittardt and again FC Utrecht, who were thumped 6-1, 6-0 and 7-0 respectively. Even title contenders Feyenoord had five put past them. The goals were flowing at not only the De Meer Stadion but also at the other 17 grounds across the top division. Ajax didn't care who they faced – just turn up, do the business and get back on the bus.

Back to European duty and a tricky tie awaited Cruyff and the gang. Dukla Prague from Czechoslovakia were in town and, due to Ajax stadium not being big enough to host large-scale fixtures, the Olympic stadium was used to help with demand. Over 55,000 spectators watched an exciting 1-1 draw, which meant that the Dutch had it all to do in the second leg, as Prague had managed an equaliser and therefore had an away goal. In that second leg, Ajax scored midway through the second half to hold a 2-1 advantage, but when Dukla equalised the teams were preparing for 30 minutes of extra time. Unfortunately, a last-minute own goal by Frits Soetekouw ended Cruyff's dream of European glory. For now, anyway.

With only the domestic scene to concentrate on, Cruyff and his team-mates set their sights on a domestic double. First up was the Eredivisie. Again, Feyenoord tried with all their might to keep on the tails of the boys from the Dam, but, yet again, they fell just short. Ajax won the title by five points and scored 122 goals in a remarkable campaign. Cruyff had just been crowned the Dutch footballer of the year and was now eyeing the KNVB Cup Final against NAC Breda at the De

Meer Stadion. Despite Ajax trailblazing their way through domestic league opposition, NAC proved to be a tougher nut to crack, even though they were huge underdogs before a ball had even been kicked.

The match began and the 21,000 fans who were expecting to see a show were in for a long afternoon. Neither team created many chances until Cruyff finally broke the deadlock in the 64th minute. This, however, seemed to spur Breda on. They huffed and puffed and eventually got their reward with an 88th-minute equaliser, although their hearts would eventually be broken in extra time as a Klaas Nuninga strike in the 99th minute ensured that Johan Cruyff had won the first of his three league and cup doubles with Ajax.

The 1967/68 season was certainly a comedown after what had happened in the previous crusade. Ajax would again claim the league title, but would flounder in both cup competitions. Real Madrid battled past them in the first round of the European Cup despite Cruyff notching in the first leg. It wasn't enough as his team crashed out early doors, 3-2 on aggregate. And their attempt to retain the KNVB Cup was thwarted in the final by a spirited ADO Den Haag team, who ran out 2-1 victors in a shock result against the holders.

Cruyff was adamant that this was just a bump in the road. He was again named as the Dutch footballer of the year, but he was interested in the team rather than individual success. His 25 goals had nearly secured a second successive double, but it was a case of so near yet so far. 'After you've won something, you're no longer 100 per cent, but 90 per cent. It's like a bottle of carbonated water where the cap is removed for a short while. Afterwards there's a little less gas inside,' said Cruyff.

In the 1968/69 campaign, a bold European adventure took the de Godenzonen all the way to the final in 1969. Ajax easily dismantled both Nürnberg and Fenerbahçe, 4-0 and

5-1, respectively, over two legs. Then came a trickier tie in Lisbon as Benfica provided stern opposition in the quarter-finals. With the Portuguese team leading 3-1 after the first leg, Ajax hit back brilliantly in the second to win on away goals. They then faced the relatively unknown Spartak Trnava from Czechoslovakia. Cruyff scored early in a 3-0 home win, but was left sweating as the Czechs fought back in the home leg fall just short in a 2-0 win.

So, on to Cruyff's first European final, against a Milan team looking for their second European Cup success. Coach Rinus Michels said before the match, 'Our team is in magnificent form and we are coming with hopes of winning.' Milan didn't get the memo. The Dutch team were battered and bruised and were completely outclassed by their Italian counterparts in the Santiago Bernabéu. The Rossoneri were 4-1 winners in a final that Ajax were only ever really on the periphery of after an early goal had clearly knocked the stuffing out of them.

Ajax finished that campaign empty-handed back home as well. Feyenoord finally edged past them in the Eredivisie, although some would point out that Ajax had bigger fish to fry elsewhere in attempting to reach the pinnacle in Europe. Nevertheless, a title had been lost and, for every lesson learned in victory, there's much more to gain from the defeats. Michels, like Cruyff, was a dreamer. His ideology of football was second to none. 'It is an art in itself to compose a starting team, finding the balance between creative players and those with destructive powers, and between defence, construction and attack – never forgetting the quality of the opposition and the specific pressures of each match,' said Michels.

The coach had come so close to reaching European success but at the expense of the bread and butter back home. Football is ever changing and, to adapt to the shifting landscape, Michels would follow suit. After the team had been taken apart by Milan in the final, he decided he would now employ a midfield 'pivot' in front of the back four. This would look and play like a midfield sweeper, with the extra man outnumbering the opponents' two. Sacrificing a forward enabled Michels' teams to dominate the ball in the centre of the field.

The 1969/70 season was the birthplace of 'Total Football' in the Netherlands. The concept had been used previously around the world by the likes of the Austrian Wunderteam of the 1930s, the Magical Magyars of Hungary in the 1950s and even Burnley in the 1960s. Jimmy Hogan, a Lancastrian from Burnley, had taken his ideology on football over the borders to Austria and helped create a fantastic team in the mid-30s. His concept spread until it reached his native town in the mid-century.

For the layman, Total Football is a style and system in which any player can play comfortably in another's position, enabling the fluidity of the formation or system to still function at maximum capacity. It requires quick thinking and expansive play at all times, with players moving around like a carriage at the fairground. In a Champions League final in 2009, Manchester United faced a Barcelona team who were arguably the greatest club side ever to have played the game. Michael Carrick had been warned by his manager of the pitfalls of playing against a team who had the Total Football DNA ingrained in them from an early age. Johan Cruyff had set up Barcelona to be the mirror image of Ajax during his stint in charge. A little more on that soon.

Carrick said, after United lost the match 2-0:

> Sir Alex warned us of Barcelona's 'passing carousel' which could make us dizzy, and I soon saw what he meant in the Champions League Final in Rome in 2009. Xavi, Busquets, Iniesta and Messi circulated

the ball between them, keeping it, hurting us, and punishing mistakes. I was loose with a header and Iniesta was on it in a flash, passing to Messi. Barcelona are ruthless in transition. I was close to Messi but couldn't prevent him passing back to Iniesta who got ahead of me and Anderson. Iniesta slipped the ball to Eto'o, who got away from Vidic. I slid in but only got close enough to Eto'o to see him score.

With the new regime beginning to take shape, Cruyff and co set about reclaiming the Eredivisie. An emphatic 7-1 away win at DHSC, followed by an 8-0 mauling of SVV, meant that Michels' team were on the right track. They were unlucky to be eliminated from the Fairs Cup at the semi-final stage, but eventually held off Feyenoord to claim yet another Dutch league title. The players had bought into the new system and were now about to be rewarded for their efforts, as it began to bear fruit, a lot of fruit.

Having already claimed the title, Ajax marched on to the final of the KNVB Cup, where they faced PSV Eindhoven. Cruyff scored their second goal in the second half to round off an impressive 2-0 victory. European football apart, Michels and his charges had only managed to lose one match on home soil during the 1969/70 campaign, their only defeat coming at the hands of rivals Feyenoord in the De Kuip Stadion. The team from Rotterdam had pushed Cruyff and Ajax hard, only losing once themselves, although too many draws had prevented their title defence. 'We played a kind of football that was not normal at that time in Europe,' Cruyff recalled. 'We played our own style – something you did not see in other countries, and that drew attention in Europe.'

What Cruyff and his team had tasted before was about to become even sweeter in the 1970/71 campaign, as what started off like any other season was soon to turn into a spell of excellence. Cruyff was on fire. He scored six goals in an 8-1 demolition job on AZ Alkmaar, which included two fine solo efforts to crown a rousing victory. They kept on coming. There were goals against NEC Breda, ADO Den Haag, Go Ahead Eagles, Telstar, PSV and Celtic in the 3-0 drubbing in the home leg of the European Cup quarter-final.

Ajax were playing champagne football. They were swatting aside all before them as yet again they were one of the most dominant teams in the Eredivisie. Feyenoord, as usual, were stuck to their tail every step of the way. Cruyff, however, was looking to go one better this time. I think that, in focusing so much of the attention on reaching the 1971 European Cup final, maybe Ajax did take their eye off the ball a little, as a few silly league defeats cost them eventually and Feyenoord swooped to snatch the title out of the grasp of the boys from the Dam.

The KNVB Cup was still up for grabs and what should have been a regulation outing against Sparta Rotterdam was anything but a notmal day at the office. Johan Cruyff needed to muster up all his magic to save the match as he snatched an equaliser with a little under ten minutes remaining. It finished 2-2 and a replay was required, in which Ajax achieved an uninspiring 2-1 win to reclaim the trophy and lighten the mood after the league setback.

While domestic football hadn't quite gone to plan in the shape of the league, Ajax's European Cup adventure had gathered quite a bit of momentum. First, they beat Nentori of Albania, followed by a trip to Switzerland to face Basel. Once they had been taken care of it was on to the quarter-finals where the champions of three years previously were waiting. Celtic were taken apart by an impressive performance, one that showcased Ajax's footballing prowess. Atlético Madrid were a stiffer test in the semi-final and actually led at the halfway stage. However, Ajax were superb in turning around the result in the Spanish capital to head into the European Cup final.

Ajax had to wait a few weeks until the showpiece final, to be played in England, and as the domestic season had already finished, it provided the ideal opportunity for Michels to get to work on his plans on the training pitch. Greek champions Panathinaikos were their opponents in the final at Wembley Stadium on 2 June 1971, where Ajax showed the world and the 83,000 fans packed into the stadium what they were all about.

Cruyff, playing in a slightly deeper role, was like the conductor of an orchestra. Ajax scored early on to settle the nerves with a Dick van Dijk goal after just five minutes. The team from Greece tried as they might but couldn't get any rhythm going against a team that were just dancing all over the Wembley turf. With just three minutes left on the clock, Ajax put the game to bed with a goal from Arie Haan.

Cruyff had done it. He had now felt the success on the biggest stage of them all, well at club level anyway. When quizzed after the title he said, 'Of course, I had my own special qualities, but a team is formed by every player's different qualities – no player can do it on their own. Then, when every player is ready to give their all and use their special quality, then you get the maximum output and results.'

Feyenoord had claimed the first European Cup for a Dutch club the year before, but within just 12 months, Ajax had equalled them. And just when you thought the pinnacle had finally been reached, a bombshell was about to be dropped from a great height on to the club. Michels believed that he could no longer take them any further than he already had, prompting him to accept an offer abroad and leave for Barcelona, saying, 'I have achieved everything that I could – it is impossible to do better.' A bold statement but in football you can always achieve more, something his successor Stefán Kovács was about to prove.

Michels had already lit the spark at Ajax, so it was just up to Kovács to keep the fire burning. Cruyff had scored 22 goals in all competitions during the 1970/71 campaign and was also named the Ballon d'Or winner in 1971, but just when you thought it couldn't get any better, it did. Sit back, grab your popcorn and enjoy. What was produced at the De Meer Stadion over the course of the 1971/72 season was absolute box office. If the fruit that Michels had planted was now ready to be picked, then this footballing year was the ripest of the lot.

Following on from the highs of winning the European Cup, Cruyff put pen to paper on a bumper seven-year contract. The board had already lost their head coach and were clearly starting to get nervous about the movements of one of the key components of the team. Kovács was preparing his charges for another tilt at glory and needed to make sure that all the players were still onside with the methods that had been put in place by Michels; I mean, if it's not broke then surely you don't try to fix it, right?

Ajax were again in imperious form in the 1971/72 Eredivisie league campaign, recording an 8-0 win over MVV and an impressive 7-1 victory against FC Groningen. Cruyff scored three goals in the 6-2 second-round win over Marseille in the European Cup and produced more moments of magic in the quarter-final win over Arsenal to reach the last four of the competition for the second year running. Domestically, Ajax were nearly unplayable at times and won all 17 of their matches at the De Meer Stadion. In fact, the de Godenzonen only lost one match throughout the whole league campaign, with the only bump in the road coming in a 1-0 defeat away to Volendam.

Cruyff had again scored his quota of goals, notching 25 times as Ajax marched to Eredivisie glory. Feyenoord, this time around, were powerless to stop Kovács and his team as they again reclaimed the title from the grasp of the side from Rotterdam. The gap was eight points and Ajax had again breached the 100-goal barrier as they swept aside all in front of them, showing fantastic form, which continued into the KNVB Cup. As it stood, Ajax hadn't lost a cup tie on home soil for nearly three years, and they weren't about to start now either.

The final, held in the De Kuip Stadion, was about to become a home from home for the boys from the Dam. Feyenoord's ground wasn't only host for the 1972 Dutch Cup final, but also the stage for the European Cup final too. In the domestic cup, Cruyff opened the scoring in the 34th minute, then Ajax doubled their lead midway through the second half. ADO Den Haag pulled a goal back with 20 minutes to play, but again Ajax extended their lead, claiming a third successive trophy with a 3-2 win.

In Europe, Ajax fought off a stubborn Benfica to scrape through to the European Cup Final and were again back at the De Kuip. This time they were again facing Italian opponents, in the shape of Inter Milan. Cruyff and his team had come unstuck before against the other Milan outfit and were desperate for history not to repeat itself. After a goalless first half, Cruyff struck early in the second with a fine right-footed shot to put Ajax a goal up, before a header in the 77th minute from the man himself wrapped up proceedings and Ajax had secured a historic treble. They were the kings on the Continent as well as in their native land. *Soccer: The Ultimate Encyclopaedia* said: 'Single-handed, Cruyff not only pulled Internazionale of Italy apart in the 1972 European Cup Final but scored both goals in Ajax's 2–0 win.' Kovács had taken the ingredients and arguably made this team even better than the one left to him by Michels.

The crown didn't slip the following season either, as the only blot on Ajax's copybook was a KNVB Cup defeat in the last 16, which ended their four-year run in the competition. Despite that, a much tighter title race was fought out, but Ajax managed to regain their title by just the one win. Cruyff, who was now playing slightly deeper, seemed to lose his goal touch, but for the second year running the Dutch title was heading back to Amsterdam. The European Super Cup was also added to the club's trophy cabinet, Cruyff scoring twice in a 6-3 aggregate win over Glasgow Rangers.

Ajax had received a bye in the first round of the European Cup, then faced CSKA Sofia in round two. The Bulgarians were swatted aside and Ajax progressed with a 6-1 win over the two legs. Bayern Munich and Real Madrid were then both dispatched as the de Godenzonen were in no mood to loosen their grip on the trophy they had worked so hard to win over the previous two seasons.

For the second year running, Ajax faced an Italian team in the showpiece, this time in the shape of Juventus, but again the Italians were no match for the Total Football that was served up by the Dutch. An early Jonny Rep strike after five minutes was enough to seal a hat-trick of European Cups.

David Winner, writer of *Brilliant Orange: The Neurotic Genius of Dutch Football*, wrote:

> Johan Cruyff's miracles in Amsterdam were many. He and his coach Rinus Michels (a sort of John the Baptist figure) raised Ajax from obscurity. More important, they invented a new way of playing. Cruyff became the greatest exponent and teacher of 'totaalvoetbal' [Total Football]. His vision of perfect

movement and harmony on the field was rooted in
the same sublime ordering of space that one sees in
the pictures of Vermeer or church painter Pieter Jansz
Saenredam. It was the music of the spheres on grass.

The year of 1973 for Cruyff was one of change. Not only did
Ajax win the Intercontinental Trophy for the first time, but
Cruyff was also crowned the Ballon d'Or winner again. During
the madness, a transfer approach from his old coach Michels
at Barcelona was accepted by Ajax and, once the Catalans had
parted with six million guilders (approximately £1.5m), a world
record fee at the time, Cruyff found himself heading off for a
new life in Spain. Now I know what you're thinking – wow,
Barcelona, the mega club we all know today – but it wasn't like
that back then. They hadn't won La Liga for nearly 15 years,
despite winning the odd Copa del Rey. They had never won
the European Cup but had sat back and watched arch-rivals
Madrid lift it instead.

Cruyff was signed to bridge the gap and, for the first season
at least, it looked as if Barcelona had found their man. They
won the title by ten points as they swept through the Spanish
top tier, leaving Madrid in their wake. The title was clinched
on 7 April 1974 with a 4-2 victory at Sporting Gijón, striker
Marcial scoring a hat-trick in a dozen minutes. Cruyff called it
an 'unforgettable' experience, while his long-time friend Carlos
Rexach said, 'We won the league because we were so far ahead
so quickly that they had no time to react.' Football historian
Jimmy Burns stated, 'With Cruyff, the team felt they couldn't
lose. He gave them speed, flexibility and a sense of themselves.'

While Cruyff took the Catalans to his heart, his team could
never quite reach the dizzying heights that Michels and Cruyff
had climbed to within Ajax. By the time Cruyff had decided
to hang up his boots in 1978, all he and Barça had to show for

their efforts after that La Liga title were a runners-up medal and three European semi-final berths. He was a star in Spain but even his magic was powerless to propel this Barcelona team to the upper echelons of Spanish football, well not as a player anyway.

Retirement never came easy for Cruyff and, with itchy feet in 1980, he signed a deal to re-join his beloved Ajax. They were struggling down in 8th place in the league when he signed in the November, but both player and team-mates soon got into their stride. By the time the season finished in May, they had claimed a runners-up spot. Much of the squad from the previous decade had left, but the make-up and football were exactly the same, the Ajax way.

With a level playing field at the start of the 1981/82 campaign, Cruyff set out to drag this team one step further than the second place achieved the previous season. With 32 goals coming from Wim Kieft and the orchestrating of the team behind him by Cruyff, they claimed the Eredivisie, five points clear of PSV Eindhoven. Ajax were undefeated at home again, which meant that Cruyff hadn't lost a match in Amsterdam for nearly a decade, excluding his sabbatical of course.

The following season, Ajax went one better, this time adding the KNVB Cup to the trophy cabinet. A closely fought title race was eventually decided when old foe Feyenoord began to fall away at the business end of the footballing calendar. With the KNVB deciding to give the cup competition a little more of a European feel to it, 1982 saw a final of two legs. For Ajax and Cruyff, this was just an excuse to enjoy themselves even more, with the talisman scoring with an excellently taken right-footed shot as Ajax won both legs 3-1, in a 6-2 aggregate victory.

What unfolded during that season was something quite extraordinary. It had been done before but not for the best part of a quarter of a century. In a match against Helmond Sport,

Ajax were awarded a penalty. Placing the ball on the spot, Cruyff nonchalantly passed the ball sideways to the left, where an advancing Jesper Olsen was waiting. The Danish winger strode on with the ball, enticing the goalkeeper off his line before sliding the ball back across goal to Cruyff, who stood all alone on the edge of the six-yard box to tap in. It was this kind of quick thinking that set Cruyff apart from the others. If you want to see an example of 'Beauty and the Beast', go on YouTube and first watch Cruyff's, then watch the effort of Thierry Henry and Robert Pires. You're welcome.

The Arsenal duo were lambasted for their effort to try to 'take the piss' against Manchester City, but Cruyff, years later, didn't agree with that, telling Sky Sports News:

> I think when I was over two or three weeks ago people were complaining the game was a little more boring. I thought it was a very good idea to try the attempt. People were surprised in the first place and then they asked 'why did you do it?' But it is within the rules. It is disrespectful at 6-0 or 7-0 but to do it at 1-0, it is just another way to take a penalty. I don't understand why they say it is disrespectful. We were joking about it but then when the next game came up, we just did it. I would enjoy it [if attempted by one of his own players] – I like to watch players who try to take advantage of a situation. Normally it is virtually a 100 per cent score. It is a little surprising that they missed.

Cruyff's contract in Amsterdam was due to expire in the summer of 1983, and when the playmaker was called into the manager's office and told he wasn't to be handed a renewal, he took matters into his own hands and signed a one-year deal at the club's biggest rivals, Feyenoord. In an article written by Steven Scragg for *These Football Times*, he described the situation perfectly as Cruyff moved under a cloud from one city to another:

> Feyenoord probably needed Cruyff more than Cruyff needed Feyenoord. The club wasn't in a position of simply being subjugated by an all-encompassing Ajax; it was a little more complex than that. PSV Eindhoven had come on strongly during the second half of the 1970s, with three title wins in four seasons to add to a UEFA Cup success of their own in 1978. AZ Alkmaar also arose to prominence at the beginning of the 1980s to win their first title and contest the 1981 UEFA Cup final against Bobby Robson's Ipswich Town. By 1983, Feyenoord were being swamped by the new kids on the block as much as their old nemesis from Amsterdam.

Despite Cruyff's advancing years, he played every single match in a campaign that saw the team from Rotterdam not only win the Eredivisie for the first time since Cruyff had left for Barcelona, but also claim the KNVB Cup to boot. Cruyff was still pulling the strings in a team that had the very young but very talented Ruud Gullit, whose 25 goals helped seal a dramatic double.

Cruyff's team-mate Sjaak Troost told Sky Sports:

> Johan was Mister Ajax. He came to Feyenoord because Ajax did not listen to him. Some players had trouble with it in the beginning. In my opinion, the best Dutch national team in our history is still the national team in 1974. So, for me, it was not an issue

because I still think he is the best player there has
ever been. To be allowed to play football with him
was indescribable.

Cruyff only stayed for one season at the De Kuip Stadion. He
had proved to his former club that, even at the age of 36, he
knew how to get the job done. Feyenoord benefited from his
presence massively, so much so that Troost was said to be lost
without Cruyff on the opening day of the new campaign, seeing
that the playmaker was no longer lining up alongside him. 'I
already missed him after the first game of the new season,'
said Troost.

With his club career put to bed, it's only right that I try to
embody Cruyff's international career. The Netherlands weren't
anything like the footballing nation of the modern era. By
the time Cruyff made his debut in 1968, the Dutch had only
been a professional league for a little over a decade, so their
international quality was that of a footballing minnow, until,
of course, Cruyff entered the arena.

His opening two matches for the Oranje were quite hot
and cold, in fact they were polar opposites as the cheers from
scoring on his debut against Hungary were soon wiped away
in his second appearance, against Czechoslovakia. A red card
meant that an early bath was required for the teen, something
that didn't go down well at KNVB headquarters. They banned
him from the next few international matches to try to curb his
fiery ways but Cruyff was his own man.

In the 1970s, the KNVB had a deal with German
giants Adidas to produce all the kits for the national team.
Cruyff, however, was sponsored by Adidas rivals Puma, who
consequently produced a shirt for Cruyff to wear, which
sported two stripes on the arms and shoulders as opposed to
the Adidas global trademark of three stripes. On top of this,

Cruyff would wear the number 14 on his back, the first player to exceed the numbering system of 1 to 11. This, of course, set a trend.

Cruyff guided his Dutch team-mates to a World Cup Final in 1974, losing out to West Germany in the final despite the Oranje taking the lead in the opening minutes. The Netherlands had passed the ball around 15 times before Cruyff was eventually fouled in the penalty area. Johan Neeskens scored from the spot, but the Germans eventually turned the final around to win the World Cup at the expense of Total Football. The Dutch team of '74 were put in the class of the three best never to have won the tournament.

Rinus Michels was the coach of the national team and had instilled his footballing philosophy into all his players, with the Ajax lads having already tasted his ideology. The team played with skill, power and flair. They were by far the best team in 1974 but were undone by West Germany efficiency. Say what you want about the Germans, but they sure knew how to spoil a party or two. Despite the loss, the Netherlands drew accolades from all four corners of the planet. 'I am especially happy that I have been able to help make the Dutch way of playing famous all over the world,' said Michels later. 'If I had a tail, I would wag it.'

But had any player in world football had a piece of skill named after them before Johan? The second group match, against Sweden, although ending up as a 0-0 stalemate, will be remembered for including one of the most iconic moments in footballing history. In fact, the moment was so special that the movement is now coached and used the world over. The 'Cruyff turn' was born on this day in June 1974 as Johan Cruyff, facing his own goal on the left-hand touchline, rolled the ball with the inside of his foot between his own legs and turned the poor Swedish defender inside-out. It's rumoured to this day that they're still unscrewing Jan Olsson from the pitch in Dortmund.

Cruyff retired from the international scene in 1977, having helped the Netherlands secure their passage to the 1978 World Cup. Despite pleas to continue into the tournament finals, he turned down the offer. It was later rumoured that there was a kidnap plot against him and his wife in Barcelona if he went, although this was unconfirmed. His club record was 402 goals in just over 700 matches, while he also found the net 33 times in 48 appearances for his country. The Netherlands never lost a match in which Cruyff scored. 'Winning is an important thing, but to have your own style, to have people copy you, to admire you, that is the greatest gift,' said Cruyff.

Now not many players in this book will have a managerial focus but it feels only right to shine a quick light on the Dutchman's achievements. Having followed his idol Michels into coaching, Cruyff set about boring down on his philosophies, as his predecessor had done before him. He had many sayings and ideas on how the game should be played, but not just at elite level, in youth football too. The foundation would have to be correct for the player to learn and provide a base on which to showcase their talents. 'Every trainer talks about movement, about running a lot. I say don't run so much. Football is a game you play with your brain. You have to be in the right place at the right moment, not too early, not too late,' said Cruyff.

His managerial percentage is impressive, in fact its bordering on ridiculous. Managing first Ajax and then Barcelona, his win percentage after 500 matches in the hotseat reads just over 61 per cent. In his 551 matches he lost just 104, prompting one post-match interview to state: 'If you can't win, make sure you don't lose.' His ex-team-mate at Ajax, Barcelona and the Netherlands, Johan Neeskens said, 'If you look at the greatest players in history, most of them couldn't coach. If you look at the greatest coaches in history, most of them were not great players. Johan Cruyff did both – and in such an exhilarating style.'

With Ajax he won back-to-back KNVB Cups in 1986 and 1987, as well as leading them to European glory in the European Cup Winners' Cup in 1987, defeating Lokomotive Leipzig 1-0 in the final. In 1988, Cruyff returned to Catalonia to take up the head coach position at Barcelona. During his time in Spain, he managed not only to win four back-to-back La Liga titles from 1991 to 1994 but also to reach four European finals. He won the European Cup Winners' Cup in his first season, but he had to wait nearly four years for the big one.

Barcelona, unlike Real Madrid, had never won the European Cup. That was until that night in May 1992 when Cruyff took his 'Dream team' to Wembley Stadium to face Italian opponents Sampdoria. It took an extra-time strike from fellow Dutchman Ronald Koeman but Barcelona and Cruyff had both finally claimed a first. 'When we scored that goal, all I remember thinking was please, please Barça don't lose your mind,' said Cruyff. 'I knew that if my players hung on to their minds we would win.'

Cruyff had ended Barcelona's six-year wait to the league title, finishing above Real Madrid in 1991; however, the European Cup was the holy grail in Catalonia, with arch-rivals Real constantly rubbing their achievements in their faces. In five previous efforts, Barça had reached the semi-finals on three occasions, losing on penalties to underdogs Steaua Bucharest in their previous appearance in the final in 1986.

The Dutchman hadn't only brought a period of success in Catalonia but had also laid a foundation that is still being used today. Even the style of play is in the mould of the teams that Cruyff sent on to the Camp Nou turf. 'He [Cruyff] didn't have preparation methods and he trusted others to decide how to train, but he did have a playing method. He didn't move on to plan B, as he instead made plan A stronger,' said Pep Guardiola.

Cruyff had 14 rules that were his footballing blueprint.

Team player – To accomplish things, you have to do them together

Responsibility – Take care of things as if they were your own

Respect – Respect one another

Integration – Involve others in your activities

Initiative – Dare to try something new

Coaching – Always help each other within a team

Personality – Be yourself

Social involvement – Interaction is crucial, both in sport and in life

Technique – Know the basics

Tactics – Know what to do

Development – Sport strengthens body and soul

Learning – Try to learn something new every day

Play together – An essential part of any game

Creativity – Bring beauty to the sport

Gabriele Marcotti wrote for ESPN: 'You can separate Barça's history into BCE (Before Cruyff Era) and CE (Cruyff Era). And, yes, Barça are still, nearly 20 years after he coached his final game for the club, still very much in the Cruyff Era.'

Johan Cruyff was simply a football genius both on and off the pitch. Thanks for the past and the present, Johan. 'Choose the best player for every position, and you'll end up not with a strong XI, but with 11 strong 1's. In my teams, the goalie is the first attacker, and the striker the first defender.' – Cruyff.

6

Lionel Messi

*'Don't write about him, don't try to describe him, watch him.' – **Pep Guardiola***

IN THE modern-day football climate, never have two players at the same time divided so many people. Lionel Messi of Barcelona, Paris Saint-Germain (PSG) and Argentina, and Cristiano Ronaldo of Sporting Lisbon, Manchester United, Real Madrid, Juventus and Portugal have split football fans for over a decade on te question of who they believe is the greatest player on the planet. Fans across the globe hold a torch for one but normally tend to dislike the other. An Adidas campaign featuring Messi stated, 'When you've won four Ballon d'Or awards, #therewillbehaters.' More on Cristiano a little later.

Ironically, despite Pep Guardiola's advice above, I'm going to try to capture at least some of the talent that upped sticks from his native South America and headed east to the Catalonian province of Spain, swapping sun for sun and a footballing super country for a footballing super club. Prior to the move, Messi had spent his footballing youth in Rosario at Newell's Old Boys. It was here that he began a love affair with the ball glued to the end of his toes.

Newell's youth coach Adrian Coria shared his first impressions of the youngster: 'When you saw him you would think: this kid can't play ball. He's a dwarf, he's too fragile, too small. But immediately you'd realise that he was born different, that he was a phenomenon and that he was going to be something impressive.' A bold statement for sure, but it was something that resonated from the six years previous in which the 'The Machine of 87' was nearly unbeaten. Messi and his youth team-mates that had been born in that year were given the name after swatting aside nearly all before them, with the tiny forward notching nearly 500 goals during this period.

You may wonder how a teenage Messi wound up halfway across the globe in an age where youth players were normally kept on home soil.

Well, in 2000, Messi and his family took a trip to see relatives in Catalonia. It was while there that they had arranged a trial with Barcelona, chancing their arm with the multi-talented youngster who they could have packed in their hand luggage, such was the size of the lad at that time. Director Charly Rexach was wowed by the talents of the boy and looked to tie the deal up immediately. The other members of the board were unsure, as at the time it was nearly unheard of to transfer players from academies. However, in February 2001 a deal was done, albeit on a napkin, and Messi and his father moved to Spain.

The initial move was one of frustration for the youth, who was unable to register for the Barcelona infantiles due to the season being nearly two-thirds of the way through. Only friendlies and matches played in the Catalan league, which were few and far between, were available for Messi to begin his Spanish career. Messi had a dream, and that dream was to play for Barcelona. Speaking to Squawka.com, he said:

At the start … the truth is that it was tough, it was hard. The most beautiful thing is to play and not being able to play was really difficult. In the middle, I went through injuries too. When I was able to play here after two, three or four months, I got injured in my first game and I was out for another month and a half.

At the age of 13 I was still bowling around with my mates, hanging around till it got dark and my mum would call me in for my tea, never mind crossing the planet to unfamiliar territory to link up with kids you have never met, leaving behind all your friends and family.

I was alone, and they asked me what I wanted to do, if we stayed or left, that the decision was mine and that he [his father] would accompany me. I was always clear that I wanted to stay.

I think it's safe to say that the decision to knuckle down and earn his Barcelona stripes was very worthwhile, not just for the player himself, but for the whole footballing world.

With Messi having been at the famed La Masia academy for the best part of a year, his registration was finally accepted by the Royal Spanish Football Federation, meaning that the youngster was now eligible for all competitions and match types. This spelled big trouble for opposition teams; they just didn't know it yet. Having had to complete a course of growth hormone treatment due to his tiny frame, Messi was now beginning to mature in confidence in his new surroundings. He had befriended two of the La Masia students, Cesc Fàbregas and Gerard Piqué, who had taken a shine to the boy from Argentina, although he wasn't exempt from the traditions of initiations.

In an article written for *FourFourTwo*, the players explained how they managed to coax the quiet youngster out of his shell. 'We thought he was mute,' Fàbregas later recalled. 'Until he picked up the ball, and then any doubts were gone,' interjected Piqué. Messi still calls the central defender *'elamo'*, 'the boss', because it was often he who acted as the Flea's on-field minder. Increasingly, Messi came out of his shell, most notably during the prestigious 2002 Maestrelli tournament in Italy – his first with Barcelona. The team's four captains – Fàbregas, Piqué, Marc Valiente and Victor Vazquez – would always play a prank on the newest member of the squad, as a sort of welcome to the fold.

Vazquez, the team's centre-forward and most creative player after the Argentine, recalls:

> When we arrived at the hotel, Messi had brought his PlayStation with him and went to his room with Cesc, who he was sharing with. Piqué decided to go and take everything out of his room, as if it had been robbed. We went down for dinner and Gerard arrived late, as they had ransacked it. They took out the bed, his PlayStation, kitbag – literally everything. After we had eaten, everyone went back up to their rooms and Cesc and a couple of other players recorded Messi going into his room. He stood stock-still. His face was a picture! He didn't know what to say, because he was quite a shy lad, and so he just put his hands on his head. Then we told him it was something that we did to every new player. He really opened up after that.

That season in 2002/03 the Barcelona U15s swept everything before them, with Messi notching an impressive 36 times in 30 matches. The team were dubbed the 'Baby Dream Team', such was their dominance in this period, a reference to the great teams under Cruyff in the '90s. The group won the league as well as both the Spanish and Catalan cups. Tito Vilanova, who was nurturing the talents on display, told author Marti Perarnau in *The Champions' Way: From La Masia to Camp Nou*: 'I remember a game in which we were winning 3-0 after only three minutes. It's almost impossible, mathematically. I turned to my assistant and said, "And now what do we tell them? What can you say at the break when they're winning 8-0?"'

It was here that the Copa Catalunya was renamed by locals as *partido de la máscara*, the final of the mask. In the lead up to the showpiece, Messi had broken his cheekbone in the final league match of the season. Determined to play, he vowed to wear a protective face mask to appease the concerned team doctors. Feeling a little hampered by the aid and not playing particularly well, Messi removed it and scored twice in the space of ten minutes, before being substituted in a 4-1 victory over city rivals Espanyol.

At the tail end of this remarkable season, Messi's resolve was tested again as both if his best mates decided to move to England, with Cesc Fàbregas and Gerard Piqué moving to Arsenal and Manchester United respectively. Messi, however, had his eyes on the prize. He was determined to stay amid interest from Arsène Wenger and Arsenal. He had worked far too hard to throw away a chance of regularly making the Barcelona first team, seeing as in 2003/04 he had managed to debut for five different teams, including the men's.

With the Barcelona first team down to its bare bones due to injuries and international call-ups, it was a chance for the youngster to show what he could do. Even at the tender age of 16, he still managed to ruffle a few feathers in his first few training sessions. Frank Rijkaard's assistant, Henk ten Cate, said, 'It seemed as if he had been playing with us all his life,' while French winger Ludovic Giuly commented, 'He destroyed us all ... They were kicking him all over the place to avoid being ridiculed by this kid, he just got up and kept on playing. He would dribble past four players and score a goal. Even the team's starting centre-backs were nervous. He was an alien.'

In November 2003, Messi was finally presented with his opportunity. In a friendly against Jose Mourinho's FC Porto, the pocket-sized Argentine was given his head and instantly impressed the coaches with an exciting cameo. On 4 February 2004, Messi signed his first professional contract with the club, although he was still predominantly in the youth teams. Despite making his debut months earlier in a friendly, he would have to wait nearly a year before Rijkaard was brave enough to eventually let him have a crack in La Liga. On 16 October 2004, Messi was introduced to the footballing world with a ten-minute appearance against Espanyol.

Miguel Angel Lotina was the Espanyol manager when Messi made his debut in the match against Barça's Catalan rivals:

> When I first took over at Espanyol in 2004, assistant manager Tintin Marquez spoke to me about Messi. That was the first time I'd really heard of him. He told me he was a really, really skilful player and that he was brilliant in one-on-one situations. On top of that, he also scored lots of goals. We wanted to bring him to Espanyol on loan that summer. At the time, he didn't have a Spanish passport and Barça's three non-EU places in the first-team squad were all occupied. Then, around the time we were pushing for a deal, he played the second half of the Joan Gamper Trophy against Juventus. He played so well that Barça accelerated the issue with the passport so that they could have him with the first team that season.

With Ronaldinho already occupying the left-hand side of the attacking line, Rijkaard asked Messi to begin his career on the right. This was alien to the player but, wanting to make the team, he agreed to the foreign concept in a bid to get brownie points from the gaffer. His seven appearances as a substitute featured around 80 minutes of football, but even within that limited game time, it was a chance to get his foot in the door and show his boss that he was ready for the challenge. Barcelona would be crowned champions of La Liga in 2004/05, and even though Messi is credited with this in his honours, he contributed very little.

His first goal in professional football came at the tail end of the campaign in a routine win at home over Albacete. Ronaldinho, picking up the ball midway through the opposition's half, waited for the two centre-backs to commit themselves before scooping the ball over their heads into the path of Messi, who, as cool as you like, chipped the bouncing ball over the onrushing goalkeeper. Unfortunately for the Argentine, he had scored moments earlier with a similar move but the goal was flagged for offside. This time, however, it did count and Lionel Messi, sporting the No. 30 shirt, was off and running. His celebration was one of shock, jubilation, mixed emotions really. Ronaldinho joined him and hoisted him on his back, saluting the Camp Nou, the new prince, and king of Barcelona.

On Messi's 18th birthday, he signed a new contract to celebrate his now first-team status. On 24 June 2005, he put pen to paper on a lucrative five-year deal with the most significant part being his £150m buyout clause. Just weeks later, after a dazzling performance in the Joan Gamper Trophy, interest from Juventus and Inter Milan backed Barcelona into a corner. The yearly pre-season tournament held at the Camp Nou is in honour of the former founding member, player and later president. Inter weren't messing around and immediately activated the player's release clause, offering to triple his salary. Messi turned down the chance to move to Italy and, as a sign of goodwill, Barcelona again upped his contract.

Messi was beginning to establish himself in the first team, now sporting the No. 19 shirt and occupying the right-wing berth. He was also starting to form a good understanding with his team-mates Ronaldinho and Cameroon striker Samuel Eto'o. It was a bedding-in period for the young Argentine, who was thrown into some big matches during this period but also seemed to be left out at the drop of a hat. He appeared in the first of his El Clásico's and also starred in the tubthumping tie against Chelsea in the last 16 of the Champions League. Barcelona were victorious, but at a cost as Messi suffered a cruel injury that would curtail his campaign. Having scored eight times in 25 appearances, Messi was devastated to miss both the title run-in and the march to Paris in the Champions League. He battled back bravely against his torn hamstring, but with his place in the squad touch and go for the final, never made selection and would face his first real bout of disappointment. Barcelona claimed the La Liga and then turned a 1-0 deficit on its head to beat Arsenal 2-1 in the big one.

Messi was pleased for his team-mates, but his own pride got in the way of enjoying the occasion, something he later regretted. Speaking to *AS*, he said:

> I'm sorry I didn't [go out]. I didn't realise what was happening. At least I would have liked to be on the bench that night. Until my injury [against Chelsea in the round of 16], I participated in every Champions League game in my career. I was disappointed. I deeply regret that episode. We won that Champions

League and I was not sure that would happen again
because it is a difficult competition to win.

During the 2006/07 campaign, Messi was blighted with injuries,
although this didn't stop him from scoring an impressive 17
times, including a hat-trick against rivals Real Madrid in the
El Clásico in a pulsating 3-3 draw. There was also arguably
the greatest goal ever scored by the player, although there have
been so many that it's a viewer's prerogative to decide on that
narrative. However, his effort against Getafe at just 19 years
old was something else, although we had seen it somewhere
before. His goal in that match was an identical finish to that
of fellow countryman Diego Maradona against England in the
World Cup of 1986.

Messi, picking up the ball on the halfway line, beat two
players instantly before driving towards the penalty area.
With still plenty of work to do, he danced between another
two defenders, before coaxing the goalkeeper off his line
then rounding him to the right-hand side and slotting into
an empty net. It was as near as you could get to a carbon
copy of Maradona's goal just over 20 years before. If you had
placed tracing paper over the Maradona goal, Messi would
barely have gone over the lines. It was a moment of pure
genius from a player who was slowly becoming the focal
point of the team.

Despite Barcelona being so dominant in the previous
season, this time around they would have to settle for plenty
of silver medal positions. The form continued in 2007/08, as it
seemed the players were now beginning to lack focus, having
claimed a double just 18 months earlier. Even though they
had won the Champions League for only the second time in
their history, it wasn't enough for the president Joan Laporta
to consider Frank Rijkaard for another season in the dugout.

Ronaldinho had lost his form, which led to rumours of his partying ways but, either way, it wasn't good for Barcelona.

This decision by Laporta coincided with possibly the most glittering period in the Catalan club's history, arguably even surpassing Johan Cruyff's 'Dream Team' era of the early 1990s. With Rijkaard now heading out of the Camp Nou door in the summer of 2008, Laporta installed the Barcelona B coach, Josep Guardiola. Pep was an ex-captain of Barça and a keen student of the game. While in charge of teams below first-team level, he would study hours upon hours of footage of the opposition. The level of detail to win was unheard of at that time. Laporta knew this could be a gamble but also, if he got this right, it could unlock a period of domination for the team from Catalonia.

Ronaldinho was shown the door during that summer and Messi was handed the no. 10 shirt. Thierry Henry was signed from Arsenal to replace the departing Brazilian on the left flank. The new dawn for the club didn't exactly go to plan, though, as an opening day 1-0 defeat away to Numancia, followed by a 1-1 draw at home to Racing Santander, had the locals wondering whether replacing the manager was really the issue at all. Then suddenly it all fell into place. Barcelona won their first match at the third time of asking in a demolition job away to Sporting Gijón, 6-1, Messi bagging a brace to kick-start his campaign. They scored six again weeks later in a drubbing of Atlético Madrid and also against Real Valladolid and Málaga. Five were put past Almeria and Deportivo La Coruña. Barcelona had finally found their feet and were playing some absolutely scintillating stuff.

I truly believe that the Barcelona team of this period (2008–12) were the greatest club team to ever have taken to a football pitch. You just simply couldn't stop them. Messi was absolutely ripping it up and had contributed his best return in a campaign so far, with 38 goals in 51 matches. Eto'o and Henry made up the other 62 between them as the trio fired in 100 goals on the way to a historic first season for Guardiola. They first found glory in the Copa del Rey. At last, Messi was able to play in a final after missing out in 2006 due to injury. Barcelona destroyed Athletic Bilbao 4-1, with Messi scoring once and contributing an assist.

Under Pep, Messi's role had changed quite significantly, being used as both a false 9 and an inside-forward, who was able to cut inside on to his favoured left foot. The Argentine was used as a No. 9 in the El Clásico in Madrid as Barcelona ran out 6-2 winners. He was simply devastating on the day and left the field with a brace of goals and a standing ovation.

With the Copa del Rey firmly in Messi and Barça's pocket, the La Liga title followed just a few days later. It was the club's fifth domestic double, but now all eyes were on Rome and a Champions League Final with Manchester United. Barcelona had dispatched Sporting Lisbon, Basel, Shakhtar Donetsk, Lyon, Bayern Munich and Chelsea on their way to the Italian capital to meet the holders from the north-west of England. Manchester United were a team that, like Barcelona, were currently playing some fantastic football in both Europe and domestically. Cristiano Ronaldo had starred for the Red Devils, having pipped Messi to both the Ballon d'Or and FIFA World Player of the Year awards in 2008.

In the final, Sammy Eto'o provided the perfect start for Messi and co after just ten minutes, squeezing the ball in off the inside of Edwin Van der Sar's near post. Into the second half and, with United searching for an equaliser and beginning to leave holes at the back, a break by Barcelona ended with the ball at Xavi's feet in the right-hand corner of the Manchester United penalty area. He placed a fantastic cross to the back post, where Messi, definitely not known for his heading ability, leapt like a seasoned target man to loop his header back across goal to make it 2-0. It was like a classic Air Jordan moment, with the player seemingly hanging in the air for an age. Barcelona held on, despite the late pressure, and claimed a historic treble.

Sir Alex Ferguson acknowledged that his team had been well beaten on the night. 'You have to give credit to a very good Barcelona team – the better team won,' he said when quizzed after the trophy presentation. Barça club president Laporta tried to play down the media clamour to make out his 2008/09 team as the best that there had ever been. 'We're not the best team in Barça history but we've had the best season.' RTE commentator George Hamilton summed up the performance perfectly: 'It's not poetry in motion, it's geometry in motion.' Meanwhile, football writer and Barcelona expert Darryl Geraghty told *The Football Faithful*: 'It was like a statement to the world to say: the game has changed now, this is the new wave.'

Barcelona were now in the hands of Messi and, in the summer of 2009, they made him the highest-paid player in their history with a staggering £12m salary and a release clause of over £250m. By the end of 2009 Messi had claimed both the Ballon d'Or and FIFA World Player of the Year awards, cementing his status as the world's best player. Barcelona went on to break more records, with the Supercopa de España and UEFA Super Cup added in August. They also won the FIFA Club World Cup 2-1 against Estudiantes de La Plata on 19 December, with Messi scoring the winning goal via his chest (they all count) to secure an unprecedented sextuple of trophies in a calendar year.

While 2009 was a carnival year for the Catalans, the early part of 2010 wasn't as jubilant as the team bowed out of both the Champions League and Copa del Rey. Messi, however, had again improved on his goalscoring numbers and notched an impressive 47 goals in all competitions, including scoring all four of the goals in his team's Champions League victory over Arsenal. Arsène Wenger, who had tried to bring Messi to north London with Cesc Fàbregas, claimed, 'Messi is the best player in the world by some distance. He's like a PlayStation. He can take advantage of every mistake we make.'

Messi had fluctuated between playing as a false 9 and in the inside-right position but was starting to excel in a more central role. Summer signing Zlatan Ibrahimović was occupying the striking role but had seemingly fallen foul of his manager despite scoring a goal every other match. In his autobiography, *I am Zlatan*, the Swede wrote, 'Pep preferred to make Messi happy – he didn't value me.' The feud didn't end there, as when Barcelona crashed out to Inter Milan in the Champions League semi-final, Zlatan barked at his coach, 'You have no balls! You are shit scared of Mourinho.' The outburst signalled the end of Zlatan's short stay in Catalonia, but it meant that Messi would now get his wish of playing as the focal point in the team.

Despite Ibrahimović signing his own P45 with the club, there were rumours circulating that a text message to Pep Guardiola from Messi had in fact prompted the boss to have a rethink on his priorities. Spanish football writer Ben Hayward wrote, 'The exact wording of Messi's message is disputed, but the sentiment straightforward. "I can see that I am no longer important to the team, so …"'

Messi, still that shy boy from Rosario, was still a man of very few words, despite his accolades and importance on the football pitch. Zlatan was a big guy and also had a big character. He demands respect and a lot from his team-mates and is certainly no shrinking violet; in fact, the complete opposite in persona to the little Argentine. Guardiola had a decision to make, probably the toughest during his time in charge. Lose one of the greatest players he's ever seen at the expense of the flamboyant Swede or cut his losses on the £70m that he had lavishly splashed out just months earlier. Zlatan, however, grew increasingly frustrated by the show of faith in Messi and moved to pastures new in the summer of 2010.

With Guardiola seemingly low on attacking numbers, David Villa was signed to bolster the squad, signing for around £40m from Valencia. Thierry Henry had decided that his career would now unwind in the US and headed off to the MLS prior to the start of the 2010/11 season. Jose Mourinho had left European champions Inter Milan to head to La Liga rivals Real Madrid, who had started the campaign in emphatic fashion. Barcelona, meanwhile, had won one and lost one in their opening exchanges before a 5-0 demolition of Sevilla showcased that this was going to be a tighter affair this time around on the domestic front.

In November 2010, Madrid headed to the Camp Nou, unbeaten and ready to turn the tables on their bitter rivals. What unfolded was the birth of 'Tika-Taka' football, combined with the philosophies and principles of Cruyff's 'Total Football'. Barcelona blew away the team from the capital with a devastating display of football that bewitched Mourinho and his charges. The Madrid players were wearing all white, ironic that a white flag of submission be of the same colour. In a match in which Messi was more conductor than brass band, the Argentine was instrumental in the 5-0 mauling, despite not finding the net himself.

Sid Lowe, reporting for *The Guardian*, wrote:

> Jose Mourinho always said that his side would lose one day but he did not expect to lose like this – not after enjoying the greatest start of any coach in Real Madrid's history. His team, so impermeable before, were punctured. Five times. They were sunk. A 5-0 victory for Barcelona was described by the Madrid

coach as a 'historically bad result' for his club – it was the worst defeat he has suffered in his career. Barcelona did things that would be risky for any other side, playing out of the tightest corners. Soon, Camp Nou was roaring '*olés*' as their team swept the ball about.

The 5-0 win over their rivals had followed an 8-0 annihilation of Almeria. With form and football on a different stratosphere to the others, a hat-trick of La Liga titles followed, narrowly pipping Mourinho and Madrid. Jose and his troops would get their revenge in the Copa del Rey final as a 1-0 defeat for Barça ended hopes of another treble. Although this was seen as one-upmanship from Jose, the cruel blow he and his side had suffered on two fronts over the course of the 2010/11 season was enough to get the blood of the Portuguese coach pumping.

Barcelona had marched towards another Champions League Final and, on the way, had thwarted Rubin Kazan, Panathinaikos, FC Copenhagen, Arsenal, Shakhtar Donetsk and then Real Madrid. A feisty semi-final first leg saw both Barcelona and Madrid down to ten men, with the scores still level at 0-0. Mourinho may have protested way too much after Pepe had been given his marching orders, and he was sent to the stands for his protestations. It was from this viewpoint that the Real Madrid coach would see Messi in all his greatness as the Argentine scored two goals in the final 15 minutes to virtually secure a berth in the final.

One of the goals was a fine solo run from just inside the Madrid half. Messi, collecting the ball, played a neat one-two with Sergio Busquets. The little forward then glided towards the Real defence, slowly beginning to sway one way and then the other, like a cobra mesmerising its pray, before slaloming his way between the left-back and centre-back, then coolly finishing past the helpless Iker Casillas. If there was one player in world football who could take a match by the scruff of the neck and make something out of completely nothing, then it would have to be Lionel Messi. It would take just a few seconds of the opposition defence switching off and bang ... pick that one out.

And so on to Wembley and another final against Manchester United. Barcelona were a much stronger team than in Rome two seasons previously, whereas the Red Devils were winding down on Sir Alex Ferguson's reign. Ronaldo had moved to Madrid and the United backline were starting to move into their twilight years, and it showed. Barça were once again in superior form and, after Pedro had opened the scoring, it was always going to be one-way traffic. Wayne Rooney levelled for United, but early in the second half, Messi scored from 25 yards to ensure that, yet again 'ol' big ears was heading back to Spain. It was a rasping shot that whizzed past Edwin Van der Sar before the keeper even had a chance to see it. The match ended in a 3-1 win for the Catalans, who had sent Manchester United into a spin with their whirlwind football for the second time in three years. 'Nobody's given us a hiding like that. In my time as manager, it's the best team I've faced,' said Ferguson during the post-match interviews.

The performance was described as 'football perfection' by Jamie Carragher; however, he added that Barça:

> ... faced an opponent who enabled them to showcase their brilliance. Ferguson's common sense surrendered to romanticism. He was two years from retirement and knew this was one of his last chances to win the Champions League. The game was held at the venue where Sir Matt Busby won United's first European Cup in 1968 and if it was going to

signal the beginning of Ferguson's grand farewell on the continental stage, being part of a thrilling, end-to-end attacking final which he might lose served legacy more than constructing a turgid, dull match in which his team could compete by stifling flair and representing the antithesis of everything he stood for.

While there was talk from outside the Manchester United camp regarding the turgid display, Wayne Rooney was also not impressed by the two finals against the Catalans. 'We almost needed Jose Mourinho to manage us just for those two games in 2009 and 2011,' Rooney quipped. Natives from Barcelona, however, saw things in a completely different light, with midfield maestro Xavi commenting, 'The Wembley final was one of the best matches of that generation of players, without doubt. It was one of the best games in the history of Barça.' Boss Guardiola singled out the performance of Messi and mentioned that he was the best player he had ever seen. Quite some statement.

His outburst post final was backed up by Messi managing to find the net over 50 times during that campaign ... 53 to be precise. It was form he carried on into the 2011/12 campaign. He surely couldn't do it again, could he? I mean, rise to such lunar-type levels of goalscoring. You bet he could, except this time he exceeded even his own expectations and received a goal bonus on 73 occasions. Over 70 goals in a season that saw Barcelona as more bridesmaid than bride. Unable to catch the Real Madrid juggernaut, the Catalans had to make do with the crumbs left from the table. Mind you, the Copa del Rey, FIFA World Club Cup, Super Cup and Supercopa de España weren't a bad addition to the trophy cabinet.

On a personal level, Lionel Messi was beginning to break records at a rate of knots. Having claimed his hat-trick of

Ballons d'Or at the tail of 2011, he embarked on a mission to become the greatest-ever goalscorer. On 7 March 2012, Messi scored five times against Bayer Leverkusen in the Champions League knockout stages, the only player to have achieved this feat in the history of the competition. Just two weeks later, he scored a hat-trick against Granada to become Barcelona's all-time leading goalscorer. He was still only 24. As Messi boarded the coach afterwards with the match ball, Guardiola said, 'I feel sorry for those who want to compete for Messi's throne – it's impossible, this kid is unique.'

It was a parting compliment from the boss who had signalled his intentions to leave Barça at the end of the season. The man who had overseen the 'Tika-Taka' revolution was moving on to pastures new and leaving behind a legacy, as well as the greatest player on the planet. His replacement was already in place in the shape of his assistant Tito Vilanova. This was music to the ears of Messi, who had worked with the coach from the age of 14, so knew exactly what he was all about. Like Liverpool in the 1960s, '70s and '80s, from Shankly to Paisley to Fagan and then Dalglish, it was about continuity. Promoting from within and continuing the work from your predecessor. I mean, yeah, I'm sure they put their own stamp on things but if it isn't broke …

This Barcelona team were definitely not broken. In fact, they embarked on a barnstorming run of picking up 53 points out of 55, only dropping two in the El Clásico during the October, before finally succumbing to defeat on 19 January 2013. Messi had put the Catalans in front and, with Pedro doubling the lead, they looked set to secure another three points on the road. That was until a remarkable comeback and an injury-time winner from Real Sociedad ruined what had been, so far, the perfect campaign. Even with defeat in the Bernabéu in mid-March, Tito and Messi cruised to the La Liga title. Messi had been poor by his standards, I mean only managing 60 goals across all competitions, hardly worth getting out of bed for.

Joking aside, scoring that many goals at elite level competition is just insane. At the same time, Cristiano Ronaldo was running parallel with Messi and the pair were basically having their own golden boot shoot-out each season. But it wasn't all accolades and champagne. Midway through the title-winning season of 2012/13, Vilanova had contracted an illness that sidelined him for parts of the trophy run-in. Despite seeming well enough to lead the team to eventual glory, Vilanova had to step down after one season at the helm. Unfortunately, due to his illness, he passed away on 25 April 2014. Heaven has another head coach to add to its hall of fame. 'Tito was the first person who had faith in me because, at the time, I was a substitute or didn't play, and he was the one who made me a starter in the Under-16 category,' said Messi after hearing the news.

What followed after the La Liga title in 2013 was a low point for Messi in particular. First he had lost the coach who had been with him for over ten tears and then he was booed by sections of the Camp Nou. The Argentine had suffered niggling injuries during the 2013/14 campaign, but, despite this, still managed over 40 goals in a season in which Barcelona were moments away from retaining their crown, only to lose on the final day to eventual winners Atlético Madrid. 'In Leo we are talking about the best player in the world and when things are not going well you have to use him. Even if he is half lame, his presence on the pitch is enough to lift us and our play in general,' said Piqué.

Rumours of unrest between Messi and new coach Gerardo Martino were splashed across every tabloid, but the forward kept his counsel and insisted all was well. The president didn't seem to like the speculation and, in fear of Messi leaving, decided that a new boss would be the easier option. In came ex-captain Luis Enrique, a move very much in the mould of appointing Pep Guardiola a few years earlier. Someone who had the DNA of the club ingrained in their brain. It was a shrewd move and one that again ignited the fire inside Messi's belly. This was also coupled with the signing of Luis Suárez to bolster the frontline of Messi and Neymar.

The newly formed MSN were absolute dynamite. Remember the 100 goals scored in the first season under Guardiola? Well, this was eclipsed with an impressive 122 goals scored by the trio. Messi had been the main protagonist, contributing nearly half the goals, with 58 coming in 57 matches. It was after a poor first half of the campaign, which had led many to question whether this Barça team had the minerals for another title shot. They turned on the afterburners after Christmas and began to swat away their La Liga rivals, eventually pipping holders Atlético to the championship.

Messi was in arguably the form of his life. His 11-minute hat-trick, the 32nd of his career, on 8 March against Rayo Vallecano, reignited his love affair with the locals. Some had been questioning his form over the last eight to 12 months, with his future being heavily speculated on. With the title was in the bag, Messi scored possibly his best goal for the club in the Copa del Rey final against Athletic Bilbao in a 3-1 victory. For me, it's still Maradona's doppelganger against Getafe, but this has to be up there as a possible second place.

Standing on the right touchline and facing an opposition midfielder, Messi eased past the opponent and made his way down the flank. With two defenders now coming over to double up on him, Messi dropped his shoulder and squeezed his way past the traffic, evading the challenge from a third party. Moving into the penalty area, Messi feigned to head to the line before dropping his shoulder again to move the ball back on to his right foot, then arrowing a strike low into the bottom corner. It's moments like this when you just sit back and admire, because this really is the beautiful game.

Another Champions League Final followed, with Barcelona seeing off PSG, APOEL, Ajax, Manchester City, PSG (this time in the knockout stages) and Bayern Munich. It was the victory over the Germans that really caught the headlines as a deft chip over keeper Manuel Neuer had finished a superb run, during which Messi had bewitched Jerome Boateng on his way towards goal. It would become the year's most tweeted sporting moment, with the move going viral. Not only was Messi breaking records on the pitch for his goalscoring ability – but he was now also breaking the internet.

Barcelona faced Juventus in the 2015 final held in Berlin and, despite Messi not scoring in the showpiece, he contributed to a 3-1 victory over the Old Lady. Speaking after the final, team-mate Javier Mascherano said, 'Messi is indispensable, but the rest of us are dispensable. No, the club is bigger than any manager, than any player … except Leo. That's the reality, and you have to accept it.' It was a way of his fellow Argentine telling the footballing hierarchy at Barcelona that, whatever it cost, you had to keep this player at this football club.

With a second treble achieved in just under a decade, it was looking as if the Barcelona express train was at full speed. Enrique was getting a wonderful tune out of his charges and the MSN had been mesmerising to watch, but it didn't quite go to plan during the following campaign as Barça would have to settle for a runners-up spot in La Liga in a tightly fought race that went to the wire. Defeats to Deportivo La Coruña and Málaga in March and April respectively, handed the initiative to rivals Madrid, who didn't drop the baton in the final stretch.

There were still memorable moments in 2016, as first Messi and co battled back against PSG with a 4-0 deficit from the first leg in Paris to perform a footballing miracle in the Camp Nou. Luis Suárez opened the scoring after three minutes and, with Barça smelling blood, went to town to eventually run out 6-1 winners. Messi's second-half penalty was the pivotal moment in the match, with the momentum well and truly with the Catalans. Unfortunately for Messi, all his team's hard work would be undone with a convincing defeat in the semi-final to the previous season's finalists Juventus.

Another highlight of the campaign was a penalty scored by Suárez in a 6-1 home win over Celta Vigo. At the time, it was well documented that Barcelona legend Johan Cruyff was very unwell. Messi, placing the ball down on the spot, took a few strides back and, on completing his run-up, calmy side-footed the ball to the right, into the path of the onrushing Suárez to fire home. Cruyff had scored a penalty like this decades earlier and some say this was a special tribute to the Dutchman.

While it certainly isn't against the rules, it's thought of as not being very gentlemanly. Just ask Danny Mills of Leeds United when Robert Pires and Thierry Henry tried to pull the same stunt off … and failed. Speaking himself the incident, the old master couldn't help but crack a smile. He knew that to attempt such an effort takes balls:

> How is it possibly a lack of respect? Back then [when Cruyff performed the two-man penalty] nobody thought anything of the sort. It just doesn't make sense at all. It's football, it's entertaining, something different, and football is just that, entertainment, it's a game. And that's what Messi is about, having fun and entertaining people. And how can it be a lack of respect when Celta played so well? … What Messi did thrilled me. If anyone can get away with that, it's him.

The 2017/18 campaign saw more change at the club, with first Luis Enrique stepping down as coach to be replaced by Ernesto Valverde, and then a vital segment of the MSN was sold to PSG, Neymar making his way to the French capital for a reported £200m, a new world record. However, this didn't stop Messi and his counterparts from taking apart La Liga, having lost out the season before. Another 50-goal haul followed for the Argentine, who helped to guide Barcelona to a domestic double of Spanish championship and the Copa del Rey.

Valverde's team lost only one match on Spanish soil in the 2017/18 season, a dramatic 5-4 defeat in the penultimate fixture of an otherwise near-perfect campaign. Messi had again claimed the golden boot, his fifth, to add to his ever-growing personal collection. On 15 January 2018, he broke the record of league goals scored by a player for one club, which was held by Germany's Gerd Muller. His 365th La Liga goal was scored in a 4-2 win away at Real Sociedad. Just a few weeks later, Messi was having a personal battle with Cristiano Ronaldo, the Argentine scoring his 99th and 100th Champions League goals to nudge back in front of his rival.

Ronaldo would again retake the crown, but it really was a fascinating battle that the pair had during their time in Spain. In the nine seasons that CR7 was at Real Madrid, the Portuguese forward scored 450 goals in 430 matches. In the same period, Lionel Messi found the net on 472 occasions in 476 appearances. Quite staggering numbers from the pair, often billed as the best players on the planet. In the summer of 2018, Ronaldo headed to Turin to try his hand in Serie A and the whole dynamic seemed to change. Now, I'm not for one moment saying the departure of Messi's rival had anything to do with it but it certainly began a chain of events.

With Ronaldo now out of the picture, Messi again hit a bullseye of goals as his team managed to retain the La Liga title in 2018/19, but all wasn't as rosy in the garden this time around. Messi was named as club captain after the departure of Andres Iniesta and immediately took the mantle of leader in the dressing room. While he was quiet in comparison to his predecessors, Messi would show his professionalism and talent on the pitch. On 23 February, he scored the 50th hat-trick of his career and also provided an assist for Suárez, as he helped Barcelona come from behind to achieve a 4–2 away victory over Sevilla in La Liga. It was also his 650th career goal for club and country, and all this on the way to securing his tenth La Liga title for the club he grew up with.

The will he, won't he with Cristiano Ronaldo wasn't only held at golden boots in La Liga. The pair were basically on a ten-year domination of the Ballon d'Or awards too. If one didn't win it, then the other walked away with the prize. Between them, they won the award from 2008 to 2018, with Brazilian Kaká and Croatian Luka Modrić making the sandwich either side. By the year 2021, Messi had claimed the award seven times to Ronaldo's five, with the Argentine victorious in 2009, 2010, 2011, 2012, 2015, 2019 and 2021. The pair respected each other massively and were friendly towards each other both on and off the pitch, yet the media claimed it was some great rivalry … it wasn't.

So now it seemed as if there wasn't a focal point anymore. In the 2019/20 campaign, Valverde was sacked at the midway point and even Messi couldn't conjure his usual magic as he could only muster 31 goals. Imagine a forward only scoring 31 times in a season of top-flight football and it being disappointing. Wow. It just goes to show how high the bar was set by a player who hadn't scored as few as that in 12 seasons. Ironically, it was the same season that Barcelona last finished trophyless, until this one of course. Valverde was ousted and Quique Setien was installed in his place.

The new coach couldn't salvage anything from the remainder of the campaign by the time the ink was dry on his new contract and was shown the door in the summer of 2020. Dutchman Ronald Koeman, scorer of Barcelona's winning goal in their first-ever European Cup win, was given the reins. Luis Suárez was the next out of the exit door, sold to rivals Atlético Madrid. Messi was far from impressed that his mate was unloaded and the upheaval inside the club was being made public. Coaches were now coming and going and the club was undergoing a period of transition, with the Guardiola era well and truly finished.

On 25 August 2020, the first bombshell was dropped in Catalonia. Messi sent the Barcelona president a letter stating his desire to leave the club, he was so unhappy with the management of the club that he wished to play elsewhere, with Barcelona rumoured to be hundreds of millions of euros in debt. With Messi having such a large release clause in his contract, the only way he could leave the club was if he was going to force through a deal in the courts and there was no way that he was about to drag the club he loved through that. On 4 September, much to the delight of the Barça fans, he reversed his decision and decided to stay.

'I wasn't happy and I wanted to leave. I have not been allowed this in any way and I will stay at the club so as not to get into a legal dispute. The management of the club led by Bartomeu is a disaster. My love for Barça will never change,' said Messi in an interview with *Goal*. The player had one year left on his contract but there was no way that he would actually leave at the end of it … would he? In fact, he would. Barcelona's final season with Messi sporting their famous No. 10 shirt heralded only a third-place finish in La Liga.

In a will he, won't he saga, Messi looked as if he was about to leave the club, only to then offer to stay and play for a 50 per cent salary cut. Even the gesture towards the board wasn't enough to warrant the Argentine extending his stay at the Camp Nou, with the club in financial hot water. So, just like that, Messi would be clearing out his locker.

Sky Sports reported on the events that were unfolding in Catalonia:

> A spokesman for Barcelona reacted to the news and released a quickfire statement:
>
> Despite FC Barcelona and Lionel Messi having reached an agreement and the clear intention of both parties to sign a new contract today, this cannot happen because of financial and structural obstacles (Spanish Liga regulations). As a result of this situation, Messi shall not be staying on at FC Barcelona. Both parties deeply regret that the wishes of the player and the club will ultimately not be fulfilled. FC Barcelona wholeheartedly expresses its gratitude to the player for his contribution to the aggrandisement of the club and wishes him all the very best for the future in his personal and professional life.

It was a quite extraordinary scene for the player, who at his departing press conference just stood there and burst into tears, before announcing:

> I've been here my entire life, I'm not ready for this. And last year with all the nonsense, I was convinced of what I wanted to say, but this year it is not the same. This year my family and I were convinced we were going to stay here, that is what we all wanted more than anything. But today, I

have to say goodbye to all of this. I have so much respect for the club and so many beautiful things have happened. Also some bad things, but all this helped me to grow and improve and make me the person I am today.

Pausing to hold back more tears, the little magician drew breath before continuing: 'I hope I can come back and be part of this club again in any way and help it become the best in the world.' Pressed on how Barcelona would cope without him, he described the club as one of the best teams in the world. 'People will get used to it, at first it will be weird but like everything, people will get used to it. They have great players, a great squad and in the end, it will be easy for them.'

And, just like that, one of the greatest players ever to have kicked a football was in footballing limbo. Messi was a free agent, although speculation was rife that he would be joining either his old mentor Pep at Manchester City or his friend Neymar at PSG. It would be the latter and, on 10 August 2021, Messi put pen to paper on a two-year deal in Paris. Speaking to PSG.FR, Messi said:

> I am excited to begin a new chapter of my career at Paris Saint-Germain. Everything about the club matches my football ambitions. I know how talented the squad and the coaching staff are here. I am determined to help build something special for the club and the fans, and I am looking forward to stepping out on to the pitch at the Parc des Princes.

At the time of writing, Messi's stint in France has been anything but spectacular. In fact, he'll be lucky to break double figures for goals, despite his team looking like claiming the 2021/22

Ligue 1 crown. Messi scored his maiden goal for PSG in a 2-0 win over Guardiola's City, but that was about as good as it got for the forward, who looks like a Shetland pony standing on the start line at the Grand National. Injuries have arguably played a huge part in the downturn of form, or maybe his heart has been broken beyond repair and his love for Barcelona is so deep that he can't bear to score goals for another team. I highly doubt it's the latter … but coincidence? Maybe.

Messi's goalscoring record at club level currently sits at an outrageous 691 goals in 837 matches … and counting. I hope he manages to rediscover his goalscoring touch as I don't believe this is the end just yet. These are absolutely insane numbers from a player who in his first three seasons in professional football could only muster 36 goals. In his prime, he was as cold as ice in front of goal and not just in the 18-yard box. Even with half a pitch still to conquer, defences weren't safe from Messi's direct running, with his acute low centre of gravity. His prowess wasn't just saved for his club though. There was also the small matter of his homeland, Argentina.

On 17 August 2005, Jose Pekerman gave Messi his bow aged just 18 in a friendly away to Hungary. The little forward was on the pitch for just two minutes before being shown a red card and heading for an early bath in the 64th minute. 'He came through me and had hold of me and I wanted to break free, but the referee interpreted it as though I had tried to shove him away,' Messi explained. 'I went on with a lot of time left in the game, but then what happened happened. It was not like I had dreamed it would be.' It was not an ideal start to an international career and it caused quite a bit of controversy in both his homeland and around the world.

Messi scored his first international goal against Croatia in March 2006 but couldn't make an impact at the World Cup just months later. Mainly used as a substitute, he would have to wait another 18 months before his talents were recognised, winning gold in the 2008 Olympics, defeating Nigeria in the final and singled out by FIFA as the standout player of the tournament. From claiming the top of the podium, the story of the national team was one of decline, as between 2008 and 2012, Argentina were a team in major transition. Legend Diego Maradona had been installed as head coach but couldn't change the fortunes of the national team; however, he could see the talent that lay before him. Speaking to the press, he said, 'I have seen the player who will inherit my place in Argentinian football and his name is Messi.'

In fact, the national team hadn't hit the heights of the 1970s and '80s, nowhere near. Since Messi's debut, they had finished runners-up in the Copa America in 2007, 2015 and 2016. The World Cup had been a washout as well, apart from the extra-time defeat to Germany in the 2014 final, but even that team weren't heralded as a true Argentina. Messi had started to score at a similar rate to his Barcelona numbers, but even this wasn't enough for the nation to claim any major silverware, something that was often mentioned in the media. Oh well, he can't do it for Argentina was the refrain. He did, but try plugging a leaking dam with Swiss cheese.

Further disappointment came when Messi announced his retirement from international football in 2016 after a penalty shoot-out defeat to Chile in the Copa America. He told ESPN: 'I tried my hardest. It's been four finals, and I was not able to win. I tried everything possible. It hurts me more than anyone, but it is evident that this is not for me. I want more than anyone to win a title with the national team, but unfortunately, it did not happen.'

Messi had walked away from the national team. As you can imagine, this didn't go down well with the natives, who began a campaign to reinstate the player back in to the squad. Banners were held on every street corner, saying things like, 'Please don't go, Leo', and Argentina's President Mauricio Macri urged him not to quit, saying, 'We are lucky, it is one of life's pleasures, it is a gift from God to have the best player in the world in a footballing country like ours ... Lionel Messi is the greatest thing we have in Argentina and we must take care of him.' With the clamour to stay on board gaining momentum, Messi took a few weeks to digest the love for him and eventually completed his U-turn in August 2016. 'A lot of things went through my mind on the night of the final and I gave serious thought to quitting, but my love for my country and this shirt is too great,' he said.

Coincidentally, his 'rival' Cristiano Ronaldo had just helped Portugal become European Champions. This fuelled the fire further for the press, who could now boast that Messi had achieved nothing at international level, unlike Ronaldo, who now boasted a major honour. The 2018 World Cup was another bout of frustration for the player, who again shone for his country but was surrounded by what some would call inferior talent. Luka Modrić of Croatia said, after his country's 3-0 victory over Argentina, 'Messi is an incredible player, but he can't do everything alone.' A 4-3 loss to hosts to France in the last 16 signalled the end of another disappointing tournament, but there were better days ahead for Messi.

The forward was now also his country's leading goalscorer, overtaking the flamboyant Gabriel Batistuta. 'Did it annoy me that Messi took the record? A little, yes. You go around the world and people say, "He's the top scorer for the Argentina national team." But the advantage I have is that I'm second to an extra-terrestrial.' Messi was scoring goals just at the right time as Argentina headed into the 2021 Copa America, including in the opening match against Chile in a 1-1 draw. Argentina then took apart both Uruguay and Paraguay without conceding a goal.

In the quarter-finals, Messi again added to his goal tally with an injury-time goal in a 3-0 victory over Ecuador. The semi-finals were a different animal as Argentina faced a very stubborn Colombia team, with an in-form Luis Díaz. It was Díaz who levelled the match, ensuring an extra 30 minutes of football. With neither team shifting, a penalty shoot-out followed. Argentina were victorious, with Messi's former Barcelona team-mate Yerry Mina missing a crucial spot kick to hand the advantage to the team in sky-blue and white stripes. Another final and a chance to exorcise a few ghosts from previous campaigns, except the task in front of them was Brazil in the Maracanã.

Angel Di Maria's strike on 22 minutes was enough for Argentina to win their first major honour since their last Copa America win in 1993, nearly 30 years before. What made it even sweeter was the fact that it was on Brazilian soil, at the home of their bitter rivals. Messi told ESPN:

I have peace of mind of having achieved the dream that has been denied to me so many times. It was like a dream, a spectacular moment. I couldn't believe it had happened. I enjoy watching the images now more than at the time as I was in a daze. I didn't quite understand what was happening. A part of the media treated us as failures, saying that we didn't feel the responsibility of wearing the jersey, that we shouldn't be in the national team. We tried to be champions before, we were the first ones to want to. It's very difficult to win a World Cup or a Copa America. At the time they didn't value what we did, they only put emphasis on the fact that we didn't achieve the aim. The important thing is to feel satisfied that you have given your all ... luckily, the last time was different.

Messi can now hang his boots up with a smile on his face, knowing that he eventually helped his motherland to a major honour. His international tally currently sits at 97 goals in 183 matches and counting. Now, I doubt for one minute I even came close to describing the sheer brilliance of arguably the greatest footballer to have ever laced on a pair of boots. But like Pep Guardiola said, 'Don't write about him, don't try to describe him, watch him.'

7

Cristiano Ronaldo

'He gets 50 goals a season time and again.
Having Lionel Messi around at the same time
means he's been pushed to even greater heights.
Muhammad Ali needed Joe Frazier, Federer
needed Nadal, Larry Bird needed Magic
Johnson. You never spoke about one without
mentioning the other.' – **Rio Ferdinand**

CRISTIANO RONALDO stood in baggy jeans, with blond highlights in his wavy hair, as he flanked his new manager and the Brazilian signing, Kleberson. Ronaldo, who had impressed in a friendly between Sporting Lisbon and Manchester United weeks earlier, was signed for a fee of around £12.5m. This was a record at the time for the acquisition of a teenager in England, which highlighted the belief that Sir Alex Ferguson had in the player who had torn his team apart in front of his very eyes. Sporting had invited United over to play a friendly for the opening of their new stadium. The Portuguese team won the match 3-1, with the youngster causing the established United players a few problems.

Nicky Butt said:

> We'd got on to the pitch and this young kid was
> just electrifying. We were all just looking at him and
> thinking 'wow'. We were all making excuses after the
> game; we were tired, it was a rubbish game, and we
> ended up sat on the team coach for about three hours.
> Everyone is getting annoyed because we just want
> to go, but it turns out the manager and David Gill
> were in the stadium pretty much signing Cristiano
> Ronaldo there and then. He came to our training
> ground, a young, tall but skinny young lad; a really
> nice lad, he had bags of pace, bags of skill and he was
> very determined. You'd kick him in training and he'd
> get up, get the ball and run at you again and again.

Ronaldo himself remembered the whirlwind surrounding the
transfer, speaking at the launch of his range of Nike CR7 Boot:

> The first game I played against Manchester United
> was an unbelievable game, the perfect night. When I
> listened after the game some of my team-mates said,
> 'Listen, you are going to go to Manchester, trust me.
> Sir Alex Ferguson is there and wants to speak with
> you.' So, I went to the dressing room and he introduced
> me to the players, which for me was a little bit fun
> because I was a little shy. Alex Ferguson then said to
> me, 'I want you now.' Everything came so fast and
> two days later I spoke to the coach and they took me
> to England. Then I was in Manchester and I signed.

Prior to the signing, Ronaldo had spent his previous months
learning his trade on the job. Promoted from the Lisbon youth

team at 16, the young winger had impressed the first-team manager. By the time Ronaldo had made his debut, he had already represented the Under-16, 17, 19 and the B teams in the same season. Then on 29 September 2002, his break in the Primeira Liga came against Braga. A little over a week later, on 7 October, he scored two goals against Moreirense in a 3–0 win.

Already the interest in the boy was ramping up across Europe as his representatives were flirting with the likes of Liverpool and Barcelona. It was clear from an early stage that, although his roots were in Portugal, his future lay in pastures new. Those new surroundings were, in fact, nearly in London as David Conn reported for *The Guardian*:

> Ronaldo visited Arsenal's London Colney training ground to meet Wenger and the coaching staff on 24 November 2002. His representatives met Wenger again in January 2003, followed by David Dein, then Arsenal's vice-chairman, in February, and continued to discuss a move through the subsequent months, including at a meeting in June 2003 at the Hotel Concorde La Fayette in Paris. As late as 1 August 2003, the claim states that Tony Henry was meeting Jorge Mendes in Porto to discuss Ronaldo's prospective move to Arsenal, which Henry, who later worked as the chief scout at Everton, says was indeed priced at €6million. Just five days later United arrived in Lisbon to play the now-legendary friendly with Sporting to open their Jose Alvalade Stadium, in which the 18-year-old Ronaldo bewitched United's defence with the full palette of his skills.

Manchester United fans were still licking their wounds from losing their poster boy David Beckham just weeks earlier. The midfielder had reportedly fallen foul of the manager and had identified a change of scenery in Madrid, with the England captain moving to the Spanish capital for a fee of around £24m. Ronaldo, although hoping to take on Beckham's old shirt number, which he also wore at Sporting, was actually expecting to be given the No. 28. However, he was surprised to learn that he was going to be handed the exciting Beckham's No. 7, following in the footsteps of Eric Cantona, Bryan Robson, Steve Coppell and George Best.

The 2003/04 season saw United face Bolton Wanderers on the opening day at Old Trafford. The Stretford End, still reeling from losing one of their own, had a new, exciting talent to adore on the sidelines, not that they knew that at the time.

Ronaldo made his debut in the red shirt, coming off the bench with United already a goal up. His direct running and cheeky stepovers had the crowd off their seats, as this carefree youngster carried all before him. The match finished 4-0 and United fans had been mesmerised by the teenager, just like his manager and team-mates had in United's friendly with Sporting.

Ferguson wrote in his 2013 autobiography:

> The Bolton defenders ended up in knots. The right-back rattled him straight away in the centre of the park, took the ball off him, but Cristiano got straight back up and demanded another pass right away. 'He's got the balls, anyway,' I thought. The crowd on that side of the ground responded as if a messiah had materialised right before their eyes. The Old Trafford crowd build up heroes quickly. They see someone who gets their rears off seats and take to him right away.

Ferguson took it even further when he announced that 'Ronaldo had the biggest impact on Manchester United fans of any player since Eric Cantona'.

The adulation continued, with George Best lauding on the youngster after seeing his cameo on matchday one. Best was arguably one of the greatest players ever to have graced a football pitch, so to receive praise from the former Red Devil would have landed well with the young Portuguese forward, who said, 'There have been a few players described as "the new George Best" over the years, but this is the first time it's been a compliment to me.'

United still fielded a team of world-class players, despite one of their own megastars having moved on over the course of the summer. United's fans had felt the disappointment of the Beckham departure and the fact that the club had reportedly been close to signing Ronaldinho from PSG, only for the player to decide at the last minute that his future lay in Barcelona. Juan Sebastián Verón had also hot-footed it out of Old Trafford and joined Chelsea under their new regime, after being bought by billionaire Roman Abramovich. Players such as Roy Keane, Paul Scholes, Rio Ferdinand, Ryan Giggs and Ruud Van Nistelrooy still featured heavily in the team, albeit United were beginning to go through Sir Alex's next transitional cycle at the club. There were some good squad additions, but a lot of pressure was going to be inadvertently placed on the shoulders of the young Portuguese winger. His debut was fantastic, a real show, but moving on from that was always going to be a challenge in a tough league, as British football is famed for its hard work and tough tackling.

Ronaldo would soon learn that having dazzling, dancing feet, may not be enough for you to get by given the rigours of the Premier League. While that debut wasn't necessarily a false dawn, it did take him a while before he blossomed into a magnificent footballing machine at United. He was a slow burner as he worked his way into life in Manchester. His first goal in a United shirt came in a match against Portsmouth. A free kick on the left flank bounced and bobbled, but somehow made its way into the far corner. It was scruffy, but did he care? He scored five more times in his first season as United finished in third place in the Premier League behind big-spending Chelsea and the Arsenal Invincibles.

There was, however, a first trip to a final in the shape of the FA Cup. United made the showpiece in Cardiff's Millennium Stadium, where they faced Championship surprise package, Millwall. Cristiano opened the scoring with a fine header from a Gary Neville cross before a double from Ruud Van Nistelrooy ensured that United and Ronaldo headed back up the motorway with the trophy.

The BBC led a Ronaldo-style love-in, with first *Match of the Day* pundit Alan Hansen declaring he was the 'star of the final', as well as the BBC Sport website which praised the player to the skies in its report:

> Ronaldo, often pilloried by critics for over-playing this season, was the game's outstanding footballer. His trickery and incisive runs hurt Millwall time and again, with full-back Robbie Ryan bearing the brunt of the youngster's repertoire of skills. Millwall settled quickly, enjoying plenty of early touches as United struggled to get the ball. But Sir Alex Ferguson's team quickly unveiled their attacking threat. Ronaldo, wearing gold boots, crossed from the right after four minutes and Van Nistelrooy got across the Millwall defence only for his diving header to drift narrowly wide of Marshall's goal. More inventive work from Ronaldo again exposed Millwall shortly afterwards.

The 19-year-old turned Ryan inside and out and crossed, but after the ball broke to Paul Scholes the England midfielder failed to make contact from six yards.

Describing Ronaldo's Cup Final goal, the article read:

> Three minutes from the break Marshall only half saved a shot from Ronaldo and Darren Ward showed great positioning to hack the ball off the line. But Ronaldo's superb first-half display was eventually rewarded with a goal. United manoeuvred the ball crisply from left to right and Ronaldo attacked the far post to head Gary Neville's tempting cross past Marshall.

So not a bad first campaign for the player who had just missed out on the Community Shield champagne days before the season got under way. United bolstered their attacking ranks even further in the summer of 2004s with Wayne Rooney being prised away from his boyhood Everton after a dazzling display for England in Euro 2004. Unfortunately for England and Rooney, a damaged foot meant that his tournament was cut short and his United debut would have to wait a little while.

The 2004/05 season would see both United and Ronaldo falter, as neither could really find any momentum in a campaign that yielded little fruit. Jose Mourinho had just arrived at Chelsea and had already transformed them into a top footballing unit, with a little help from a blank cheque book, of course. Ronaldo upped his goal tally to nine in all competitions, but United could only manage another third-place spot and were mightily unlucky not to retain the FA Cup, losing on penalties to Arsenal in one of the most one-sided matches ever seen.

Unfortunately, in football, no player or team is guaranteed success. United had claimed eight Premier League titles in 11 seasons prior to Ronaldo making his debut. Ferguson and Ronaldo were looking to change that in 2005/06, but despite finishing runners-up, were miles off Jose Mourinho's all-conquering Chelsea. Two third places and a second was progression but not at the rate that either player or manager would have liked.

Despite United claiming the League Cup with a 4-0 win over Wigan Athletic in Cardiff, the Red Devils' campaign had seemingly stuttered to a halt. Rooney and Ronaldo both notched in that final, but with time and matches running out to catch Chelsea, a must-win at Stamford Bridge was eventually lost. To make matters worse, Rooney left the pitch on a stretcher, with a broken metatarsal for his troubles. United's season had come to an end, but with the World Cup in Germany on the horizon, the young England forward was desperate to be fit for action.

Ronaldo had already cemented himself in Portugal's national team. Having represented the Under 15s, 17s, 20s, 21s and 23s, he was always likely to filter seamlessly into the full squad. At just 18, he made his debut in a 1-0 victory over Kazakhstan, coming off the bench to replace Luís Figo. August 2003 was something of a watershed moment for the player, having just completed a move to Old Trafford and then representing his home nation in a full international. But things were going to start moving a whole lot faster for the Portuguese forward.

Euro 2004 was hosted in Portugal and Ronaldo was about to showcase his talents to a wider audience. The host nation made a dash for the final, only to be defeated by the tournament dark horses, Greece. Ronaldo had scored a couple of vital goals along the way, including a penalty in the shoot-out win over England in the quarter-final. Despite falling just short, Ronaldo was voted in the team of the tournament, an accolade highly deserved for a player who had shown no fear in his first big competition.

The World Cup in 2006 was the biggest stage of all. Wayne Rooney and the whole of England were praying that the young English forward would make the competition, following his injury at Chelsea just weeks before. It was a mirror image of the injury that had plagued David Beckham before the previous World Cup in Japan, when again the whole country held its breath for the wide man and captain to make the starting line-up.

Rooney had previous. The explosive forward had broken his foot in the defeat to Ronaldo's Portugal in the Euro 2004 thriller. Luckily for England, in the World Cup he only missed the opener against Paraguay. His return in the second half of the victory over Trinidad and Tobago was a much-needed boost for the England squad. In a cruel twist of fate, Sir Alex Ferguson's young guns were again pitted against each other in another quarter-final knockout. England and Portugal faced each other for the second time in two years at the same stage of a knockout competition.

England were desperate for revenge this time around. Unfortunately, for the second time, Rooney was unable to complete the match. This time, however, he was shown a straight red card after stamping on Chelsea's Ricardo Carvalho. The referee seemed to take an age to make a decision, but who was leading the charge in his efforts for the England man to be sent off? Cristiano Ronaldo. His protests were fierce and he clearly had no remorse for his Manchester United team-mate. Rooney shoved his 'friend' away, but once the red card had eventually been flashed, Ronaldo walked away from the incident and winked at his bench, while Rooney headed down the tunnel for an early shower. England eventually lost the match as their gallant effort with just ten men fell short. To rub salt into the wounds, who should step up to dispatch the winning penalty? Cristiano Ronaldo. I can tell you're getting good at this guessing game now.

The English press had a field day, but instead of turning on the Three Lions, which is the norm after a tournament exit, they brought their criticism to the door of Ronaldo. His winking action had been seen by the cameras, with most of the media labelling him a 'Winker'. The witch hunt had well and truly begun. Ian Wright, working as a BBC pundit that day, was shocked by Ronaldo's actions: 'Look at that ... has he just winked there?' Fellow pundit Alan Shearer summed up what the majority of English fans were thinking that day: 'I think there is every chance that Wayne Rooney could go back to the United training ground and stick one on Ronaldo.'

Rooney, though, speaking to the *Manchester Evening News*, had a different view on things:

> I had my phone in my hand and I was getting all these messages about Ronaldo. Of course, when he ran over to ask Elizondo to send me off I pushed him away. In that moment I couldn't believe what he was doing. But sitting in that dressing room gave me time to calm down and think. I put myself in Ronaldo's shoes. Would I do the same? Probably. Would I be in the ref's face to make sure he got sent off? If he deserved the red, if it would help us win – yes, no question. I'd do it tomorrow. I thought: 'Actually, I tried to get him booked in the first half for diving.' And the wink thing, I didn't see anything in that at all. It was nothing.

Despite Rooney's reputation for being a hot-head in his younger days, he displayed a maturity beyond his years post-match:

So, I calmed down. I went over to him afterwards in the tunnel. I felt it was important to speak to him while it was still fresh and to do it face to face. He gave me a look as if to say sorry but by then I had my United head on. I said I've no issues with you. Enjoy your tournament and good luck. I'll see you in a few weeks – and let's go try and win the league.

On the pair's return to pre-season training, Sir Alex Ferguson wasted no time in getting the two into his office in a bid to ensure that there was no animosity between the players. Gary Neville was also brought in to make sure that there would be no hangover from the World Cup fallout, as United looked to end a Premier League trophy drought, which was now stretching to four years. With Chelsea seemingly getting stronger under Jose Mourinho and Arsenal looking to find their invincible form once again, it was key for the boss to steady his ship prior to setting sail on the 2006/07 Premier League campaign.

Speaking to Sky Sports, Gary Neville said of the meeting:

First day back in training, I was called into the office with Wayne and Cristiano by the manager, he wanted to see if there were any problems, any hangovers. They were actually really good friends, they used to socialise – Patrice Evra, Rio Ferdinand, Cristiano and Wayne were very close to each other. Because the whole of the country was against him [Ronaldo], it did feel like a David Beckham-type moment in our dressing room. There was this thing about England and Manchester United, with England fans having a go at the United players, there was no love lost anyway.

Neville had already lived through this kind of media attention before, back in the summer of 1998, after his best friend and team-mate Beckham was sent off for the Three Lions during the World Cup in France:

> When Beckham came back in 1998 everyone at United rallied around him, and it was the same with Cristiano in 2006, and it helped him go and prove everybody wrong. It was the first morning of pre-season, they shook hands, there was no problem whatsoever. To be fair, Wayne is knowledgeable enough to know that on a football pitch, anything goes – we had the same mentality at United. Cristiano was trying to win for his country, Wayne would not expect anything different and neither would I.

What was noticeable with United and Ferguson on that occasion was that the 'them and us' attitude was ingrained into the squad prior to the season kicking off, something that ultimately blossomed as the Red Devils ended the 1998/99 campaign with a historic treble of Champions League, FA Cup and Premier League. Any concerns that the pair wouldn't see eye to eye in the same team were soon put to bed as an opening-day victory over Fulham confirmed that both forwards were ready for business. United were 4-0 up after 20 scintillating minutes at Old Trafford, eventually running out 5-1 winners. Rooney and Ronaldo scored three goals between them, with Rooney bagging a brace in an emphatic start on the inaugural day of the new footballing calendar.

They didn't stop there. By the turn of the year, the pair had scored 20 goals between them, with many of them being assisted by the other. Ronaldo was dovetailing beautifully with the attacking options of Rooney, Louis Saha and Ole Gunnar

Solskjaer. His goalscoring exploits weren't just saved for the Premier League, though, as there were further strikes to add to his impressive tally during the bombardment of teams in both the FA Cup and the Champions League. United were purring on three fronts and reached both the FA Cup Final as well as the Champions League semi-final, although they would crash out against a very well organised AC Milan team, who had a revenge mission against Liverpool in the final firmly on their minds.

Ronaldo and Rooney had both scored in a 3-2 home win in the semi-final, but were soon sent crashing back to earth with a heavy 3-0 defeat in the San Siro just two weeks later. Just after that, Ronaldo's pain was turned to sheer pleasure as a 34th-minute penalty against City in the derby ensured that United had ended a mini break from the top of the English football summit. Ferguson's United had dethroned Jose Mourinho and his impressive Chelsea team, who had finished six points behind the team from Manchester.

Mourinho and his charges didn't have to wait too long to extract their revenge, mind you. With both teams having reached the first FA Cup Final under the new Wembley arch in 2007, many were predicting a real humdinger of a showpiece. In reality, calling it a spectacle was quite frankly taking the piss. It was a shocking match. With both teams failing to break the deadlock, it moved into extra time, where a Didier Drogba toe-poke meant that the trophy was to make a short trip from Wembley across London to Stamford Bridge.

Despite the final upset, Ronaldo was chuffed to have won his first league title as a professional. Speaking to Sky Sports at the trophy presentation, while wrapped in a Portugal flag, the player said, 'I feel great, you know when you win a title, everyone is happy, the team is happy. It's unbelievable. Unbelievable atmosphere for supporters and everyone. It's an amazing day for me and for Manchester United.'

In all competitions, Ronaldo scored an impressive 23 goals in 49 appearances, a fantastic stats for a player who at this time was still regarded as a winger. As well as picking up a Premier League medal with his team-mates, Ronaldo also bagged himself the Professional Footballers' Association Player's Player, Fans' Player and Young Player of the Year awards, as well as the Football Writers' Association Footballer of the Year award, becoming the first player to win all four main PFA and FWA honours. He was also named runner-up to Brazil and AC Milan magician Kaká in the 2007 Ballon d'Or awards.

The set-up in the Manchester United team suited Ronaldo, with some even suggesting the system was shaped around the Portuguese winger. United strengthened further in the build-up to the 2007/08 campaign, bringing in some midfield flair and a loan move that turned into a master stroke from the boss. Luis Nani and Anderson were signed from Sporting Lisbon and FC Porto respectively, but the real ace in the deck was the two-year loan signing of Carlos Tevez from West Ham United. The Argentine forward seemed a strange transfer from the off, with the likes of Saha, Rooney and Ronaldo all being so prolific in front of goal, but what it did do for the squad was to make the attacking options interchangeable, like the way Ferguson had rotated his four strikers during the treble-winning year.

United's defence of their title in 2008/09 wasn't exactly swashbuckling, with both the team and Ronaldo struggling to hit their stride. With two draws and a defeat after the opening three matches, United found themselves in the relegation zone until a 1-0 win over Spurs kick-started their campaign. Ronaldo had also seen red in a moment of madness in the draw with Portsmouth. Once back from his ban, though, he began a devastating partnership with both Rooney and Tevez. It didn't matter who played where and, if all three were playing, it led to the opposition team having absolutely no idea who was supposed to be playing in which position, such was the rotation and movement of the trio.

Ronaldo and United were rampant. Another Premier League trophy was added to the collection and in Europe this time United made the Champions League final, to face Premier League opponents Chelsea. Jose Mourinho had been axed from Stamford Bridge, but the Blue machine just kept rolling on. United had pipped Chelsea to the title, so a clash in Russia was always going to prove a mouth-watering occasion. Speaking to the *Daily Mail* prior to the final, Ronaldo said:

> I have been totally surprised by how many goals I have scored as I am not even a centre-forward. But to be the best in the world I have to win titles like the Champions League and the Premier League. I am a winner and I have a dream that we will win the Double this season. It would be madness if we did but why is it not possible now? It is not easy to win anything, especially not the Champions League. I think if you win that then you go down in history and that is what I want.

Ronaldo opened the scoring for United with a fine header past Petr Čech before a Frank Lampard strike levelled things up for Chelsea just before half-time. With the match still tied after extra time, a penalty shoot-out followed, as local clocks struck midnight. In the pouring rain, Ronaldo was the first player to not convert his spot kick. Chelsea just kept on scoring, until captain John Terry strode up from the halfway line with the ball in hand, just one kick away from sealing Chelsea's first-ever European Cup/Champions League win. The skipper placed the ball on the spot and sent United keeper Edwin Van Der Saar the wrong way. Unfortunately for Terry, he had slipped during his run-up and his shot had been scooped on to the outside of the post. United then pounced and, by the time Nicolas Anelka missed his penalty, both Chelsea players and Ronaldo were spread across the turf in floods of tears.

Ronaldo had scored 41 times in a campaign that saw United claim a league and European double. While this was great for both club and player, what was bubbling on the horizon wouldn't be music to the ears of everyone at Old Trafford. Real Madrid had sat up and taken notice of the prolific forward, who had made no attempt to hide his support of the team from the Spanish capital. Meanwhile, Ronaldo left Manchester and headed off to join up with his Portugal team-mates ahead of the 2008 European Championships. He told *Terra* magazine: 'I want to play for Real Madrid, but only if it is true they are eager to pay me and Manchester United what they have been saying they will.'

Sir Alex Ferguson had a job on his hands to keep his star man. Having already lost David Beckham to Real Madrid a few years before, the United manager was in no mood to let history repeat itself. In his autobiography, he explained how he persuaded Ronaldo to stay for one more season, as he recalled:

> Real Madrid paid £80m in cash for him [in 2009] and do you know why? It was a way for Florentino Pérez, their president, to say to the world: 'We are Real Madrid, we are the biggest of the lot.' Ramon Calderon, Pérez's predecessor, had claimed the previous year that Cristiano would one day be a Real Madrid player. I went to Carlos Queiroz's house in Portugal to find the boy expressing an urge to go to Real Madrid and told him: 'You can't go this year, not after the way Calderon has approached this issue.'

The United boss was adamant that the deal would only be done on his terms. Ferguson said:

> 'I know you want to go to Real Madrid but I'd rather shoot you than sell you to that guy now. If you perform, don't mess us about, and someone comes and offers a world record fee, then we will let you go.' I did well to calm him down. I told him the reason I was refusing to sell him that year was because of Calderon. 'If I do that, my honour's gone, everything's gone for me, and I don't care if you have to sit in the stands. I know it won't come to that, but I just have to tell you I will not let you leave this year.'

Ronaldo agreed to stay for one more year and again he was an integral part of a team that not only retained their Premier League crown but also reached the Champions League final for the second successive season. A stunning strike against FC Porto in the knockout stages of the tournament earned him the inaugural FIFA Puskás award. This brand-new honour was to be awarded to the male or female judged to have scored the most aesthetically significant, or 'most beautiful', goal during that calendar year. 'It is important to preserve the memory of those footballing greats who have left their mark on our history. Ferenc Puskás was not only a player with immense talent who won many honours, but also a remarkable man. FIFA is therefore delighted to pay tribute to him by dedicating this award to his memory,' said President Sepp Blatter at the inauguration of the award in Budapest.

United had also secured the Club World Cup in Japan, with Ronaldo claiming the Silver Ball, but his first major honour of that season was the FIFA Ballon d'Or. Winning this prestigious award meant that Ronaldo was the first player at Manchester United to win the individual award since George Best, 40 years earlier in 1968. Even with all the accolades that were now beginning to land at the feet of Cristiano Ronaldo, he still wanted more. In this case, a new challenge.

Luis Nani admitted that Ronaldo had openly stated that he was leaving to his team-mates. He said via the *Daily Mirror*:

> We would stay at the end of training to do competitions and they [Anderson and Ronaldo] were my team-mates; everyone has best friends or some they feel more comfortable with and they were my support. Some days he was telling us openly, 'I'm here six or seven years now, I think it's enough for me.' He said that a couple of times. But it was always, 'I will see, I will see, I will see,' but we never thought it would happen so fast.

Ronaldo's 26 goals in 53 appearances cemented his move to the Spanish capital and ended his time in Manchester. Ahead of the 2009/10 campaign, world transfer record holder Ronaldo was unveiled at the Santiago Bernabéu in front of over 80,000 enthusiastic Madridistas. The bumper crowd had surpassed the quarter of a decade-old record that was set by another transfer record breaker, Diego Maradona. Madrid had splashed out a cool £80m on the Portuguese forward. Los Blancos already boasted an impressive frontline of club icon Raúl and Argentine Gonzalo Higuaín. This was as well as the signing of French forward Karim Benzema from Lyon, although this deal was a more low-key affair, despite the £30m price tag.

Within just 34 minutes of his home debut, Ronaldo casually dispatched a penalty into the bottom right-hand corner past the Deportivo goalkeeper to open his account in a 3-2 opening-day victory. Real Madrid's No. 9 was off and running with his new club. The No. 7 shirt that Ronaldo had requested was still being worn by another goalscorer on the day, Raúl. Ronaldo would settle for his new number, which was presented to him by a former user of the digit in Madrid's record goalscorer, Alfredo Di Stéfano.

The goals kept on coming. After the first four matches of the season, Ronaldo had racked up an impressive five goals. He took to life in Spain like a duck to water. His goals kept Madrid pushing for the title against Pep Guardiola's all-conquering Barcelona. Despite scoring on 32 occasions in all competitions, it wasn't to be enough for Cristiano and co as Madrid would end the campaign empty-handed. It was a feat not often achieved in the capital and was to be the one and only season in which Ronaldo wouldn't be hoisting aloft some silverware.

Madrid finished on 96 points, just a win behind Barça, who had played some absolutely scintillating football. Lyon had also put Los Blancos out of the Champions League in the round of 16, going through 2-1 on aggregate. But a hat-trick on 5 May 2010 away at Mallorca signalled to the Madridistas that even though the team were potless, they had arguably the greatest player on the planet in their ranks, bar Lionel Messi, of course, although I doubt he would ever come into any Madrid fan's thinking. Speaking to *The Guardian*, Ronaldo said of his first campaign: 'I really enjoyed the season that I've done, but what's missing is winning a title. I'm very happy here in Madrid and my team-mates have helped me a lot, but the team has not won anything. We have to keep fighting and I am confident we will win many titles in the future.'

Club symbol Raúl vacated the No. 7 shirt in the summer of 2010 as he headed to Germany to finish his career, so Ronaldo jumped at the chance to wear his old number and was once again reunited with his much-favoured father figure. Jose Mourinho had just been named as the head coach at Madrid and was about to embark on a roller coaster ride at the helm. Barcelona were playing champagne football, something that maybe Mourinho had been accused of not performing. Some of his critics had accused the coach of becoming much more pragmatic after his time in Italy, where he was very successful during his stay in Milan with Inter.

Ronaldo was red hot again. For the first time in his career, he scored four goals in a match during the 6-1 demolition job of Racing Santander on matchday eight. The Portuguese forward had already notched five times in the opening seven matches, showing glimpses of his 2008 Ballon d'Or-winning form, in a season that saw him take the match ball home on a further four occasions, having scored trebles against Athletic Bilbao, Levante, Villareal and Málaga. Mourinho's Madrid were certainly not goal shy. In fact, they scored over 100 goals in La Liga alone, but this was still not enough to topple the swashbuckling Catalans from Barcelona. Real Madrid finished on 92 points, four adrift of Guardiola's men.

More heartbreak was to follow as Pep hoodwinked his old club-mate Jose in the Champions League semi-final, in which the El Clásico overspilled into the European scene. Barça were 3-1 victors, but despite Jose being left holding the baby on this particular occasion, the revenge mission was complete in the Copa del Rey final. For the fourth time that campaign, the two had clashed, except this time the trophy was heading back to the Bernabéu. With the final tied in extra time, Madrid played a neat one-two down the left flank before a beautiful cross was headed back into the far corner of the net by Cristiano Ronaldo in the 103rd minute. He had leapt like a salmon to produce a moment of magic, ensuring that he would get his hand on his first trophy on Spanish soil. He would also claim some individual awards, as his goal tally of 53 meant that he would walk away with both the Pichichi Trophy and the European

Golden Shoe. Real Madrid were close, so close, to winning the La Liga title, but it just turned out that arguably the greatest club team in the history of the game were strutting their stuff at the same time.

Some people would crumble at the challenge of trying to overcome that Catalonian machine but not Jose Mourinho and Cristiano Ronaldo. They had the bit between their teeth. In the closing minutes of the Copa del Rey final, a skirmish broke out between the two sets of players as well as coaching staff. Jose Mourinho was accused of attempting to gouge Tito Vilanova in the eye from behind. Vilanova turned and pushed Mourinho in the back, sparking his bodyguard to jump in to halt proceedings. In the press conference post-match, Jose was asked about the incident with Vilanova. He said he didn't know who 'Pito' was. The Madrid fans loved Mourinho for this as 'Pito' is Spanish slang for prick. Some quarters of the Madridistas had doubts about the appointment of Mourinho for having links to Barcelona. This dissipated any of their concerns; he was one of them. So much so that in the final pre-season match before the start of the domestic season, Real Madrid entertained Galatasaray at home. Directly in front of the director's box, there was a huge banner that celebrated the roguery of Mourinho. It read, 'Mou, your finger shows us the way.'

For two seasons now, Ronaldo had played second fiddle to Messi and his mates over at the Camp Nou, but this time it seemed it was personal. Jose had only been in Madrid for 12 months, but that was long enough to get the feel of the place and, having tasted defeat at the hands of Guardiola when it really mattered, he was in no mood to let the experience happen again. Raphaël Varane was signed to bolster the defence, although with the number of goals that were being scored at the other end, Madrid would normally always outshoot the opposition in a gun fight.

171

Madrid fans, do you remember the 2011/12 season? Well, you really should. I mean, how could anyone forget?! The media named it 'La Liga de los Récords', Spanish for 'The League of the Records', for the number of records that were sent tumbling by Madrid during that campaign. Tomas Roncero, a journalist with *Diario AS*, wrote:

> Real Madrid that season were a very physical team – aggressive, but not violent. For it to function – and to beat Barça in particular, a team which was playing like a violin at the time under Guardiola – it needed 11 players who were united and committed. Maybe because of the importance of this structure, Cristiano was more liberated in attack, but the rest of them used to go at opposition teams like they were in the army.
>
> Rival teams took note. Real Madrid never lost a physical battle. When Real Madrid went to Pamplona in March, for example. In other times, it used to be a hostile stadium where Osasuna fans intimidated Real Madrid, but not this team. They ate them, scoring five goals. It was because Real Madrid were more superior in the physical battle. They were warriors. Men like Sami Khedira, Pepe, Ramos. They were very difficult to beat.

Ronaldo had yet again scored an astonishing number of goals that season. He found the net on 60 occasions in a campaign that concluded with him holding aloft the La Liga trophy, finally managing to edge Barcelona out of the title race, and that included Ronaldo scoring the winner in the Camp Nou to end the reign of the Catalans. Madrid scored 121 times, amassing 100 points to secure the championship. Again, on a personal level, Cristiano claimed the Pichichi Trophy as well as the European Golden Shoe, titles he would secure again in 2013/14 and 2014/15. Madrid had scored seven past Osasuna, six past Real Zaragoza, Rayo Vallecano and Sevilla. They also secured five-goal hauls on four occasions, and four goals in ten matches. Despite the all-conquering domestic accolades, yet again they fell just short in Europe. Real crashed out on penalties to Bayern Munich at the semi-final stage, losing there for the second year running.

Now that the first La Liga title was in the bag, it was time for the real business to begin. Ronaldo would claim a second La Liga title at the end of the 2016/17 season, but what happened in between that period was a sustained attack on the European scene. Having reached the brink of the finals for the previous two years, finally Real Madrid were about to embark on a fairy tale run to a final. But not just one final, oh no. In a five-year period from 2013 to 2018, they wouldn't just appear in four out of five finals, but win them all as well. Jose Mourinho had left to return to Chelsea, which meant that Carlo Ancelotti was given the chance to lead the team that had just finished runners-up in La Liga. The squad clearly had bigger fish to fry.

Ronaldo had tasted both success and defeat in previous Champions League finals with Manchester United, having defeated Chelsea in 2008 before losing to Barcelona a year later in 2009. The Portuguese forward had been in imperious form on the way to the final to be held in his native land, with the showpiece in the Estádio da Luz, Lisbon. Madrid faced neighbours Atlético in the first 'all city' final in the competition's history. Diego Godin scored midway through the first half for Diego Simeone's Atlético before a very late equaliser from Sergio Ramos forced extra time. With Atlético tiring, Gareth Bale, Marcelo and Ronaldo all scored to put the game to bed and claim a 4-1 win. It was the tenth occasion that Madrid had lifted the famous trophy, with the celebrations being labelled 'La Decima'.

Phil McNulty, writing for BBC Sport, reported on the match:

> The emphatic score line after extra time does no justice to the drama that unfolded at Estádio da Luz as Atlético stood moments from winning the trophy for the first time only to end exhausted and well beaten.
>
> Diego Godin capitalised on an error from Real's veteran goalkeeper Iker Casillas to give Diego Simeone's newly crowned La Liga champions a first-half lead, one they protected with fierce intensity until 90 seconds from the end of five minutes of stoppage time when Sergio Ramos headed in Luka Modrić's corner.
>
> Atlético wilted visibly after that, and Real ruthlessly completed the job of becoming the first club to claim the trophy 10 times, an achievement known as 'La Decima' [the 10th]. Bale, who had wasted earlier chances, headed in from an acute angle after goalkeeper Thibaut Courtois blocked Angel Di Maria's shot with 11 minutes left. This was effectively the match-winning moment.
>
> The Welshman kept going despite not being at his best and this was the sort of contribution that he and Real had in mind when he made his £86m move from Tottenham last summer. Substitute Marcelo added a third with a shot Courtois should have saved before Cristiano Ronaldo salvaged something from a disappointing personal performance, scoring his 17th

goal of this Champions League campaign from the
penalty spot after he was fouled by Gabi.

The Champions League trophy was heading to the Bernabéu,
as well as the Copa del Rey, which had been secured a few
months earlier. Ronaldo had again scored a shed load of goals,
with his new partnership with record signing Gareth Bale
beginning to blossom. A few knocks and niggles had bumped
the forward out of his stride, but he still managed over 50 goals
in an otherwise impressive campaign.

He went one better the next season, as yet again Ronaldo
strived for footballing perfection. Despite his 61 goals, Real
Madrid were easily dethroned in the Champions League,
crashing out in the last 16 stage. Barcelona had wrestled the
title away from Atlético, meaning that Madrid would settle for
a UEFA Super Cup and World Club Cup double. Not exactly
empty-handed at the end of the 2014/15 campaign but hardly
what the paying punters wanted either. In fact, it wasn't nearly
enough to keep Carlo Ancelotti in his job as Florentino Pérez
pulled the trigger and ended his short but decorative reign.
Even winning the biggest prize of all doesn't guarantee you
time in the Madrid hotseat.

Rafael Benítez was the next manager to be thrown to the
lions at the Bernabéu. A dismal start to the 2015/16 season
was rounded off in January 2016 as Benítez was shown the
door, with Madrid floundering in La Liga. Assistant Zinedine
Zidane was promoted to head coach and again Madrid were
back on full attack. They made great headway on the domestic
scene, with only one defeat coming in their last 22 matches,
but were unable to close the gap, meaning another runners-up
berth for Los Blancos.

On the European scene, Madrid were back to their inspiring
best. They marched through to the Champions League final

in Milan, where they yet again faced Diego Simeone's Atlético Madrid. Simeone must have been sick of the sight of this city rivals by this time. Yet again the city rivals headed to extra time after drawing 1-1 in the regulation 90 minutes. The match then went to a penalty shoot-out, in which Real Madrid scored all five of their kicks before Juanfran missed to ensure that Real had again beaten their neighbours when it really counted.

However, the final was shrouded in controversy after some wretched refereeing by Englishman, Mark Clattenburg. Madrid's opener, scored by Ramos, was clearly offside, yet the goal was allowed to stand. So, to try to even things up, Clattenburg took it upon himself to gift Atlético Madrid a penalty, which they missed, before eventually levelling through Carasco. Clattenburg said to the Brazilian Shirt Name podcast:

> When the ball gets delivered, I knew there was a touch by Gareth Bale in the middle. That then went to [Sergio] Ramos who scored. I said to my assistant, but it was very difficult with the noise: 'Did you know there was a touch in the middle? You know there's a touch?' But he just froze. I could see him looking at the big screen. He completely froze, so about a minute later I restarted the game because I had to.

It was reported that the earpiece to communicate between the officials had somehow been disconnected and there had been a total loss of sound at the most vital time. Not ideal for Mr Simeone and co that's for sure. Clattenburg then said:

> I was very fortunate that two or three minutes after half-time, I'm presented with a 50-50 penalty. Fernando Torres was really clever getting in front of Pepe to draw a foul. It's one you wouldn't want to

settle a game on. I gave it to give back the balance. It was one of those perfect scenarios in refereeing and I gave the penalty.

Ronaldo and new gaffer Zidane couldn't care less. Yet again Madrid were champions of Europe, an honour that they would hold for the next three seasons. The record meant that it would take the best part of four years before they tasted defeat in the competition, when they were humbled in the last 16 of the 2018/19 campaign by Dutch giants Ajax. In between this, Zidane and Ronaldo had struck gold with the football that was being served up in the Bernabéu as Madrid won the full shebang in 2016/17. Los Blancos won the La Liga title, Champions League, FIFA World Club Cup and the UEFA Super Cup.

By this time, Cristiano Ronaldo had also overtaken Raúl as the club's leading marksman. With every Champions League title, the Ballon d'Or followed. The individual title was won in 2008, 2013, 2014, 2016 and 2017. If Lionel Messi hadn't been on the same level as Ronaldo domestically, then there would have been a hoard of records smashed in Spain as well. With every season, it seemed there was a new record to be beaten, a new aim to guide Ronaldo to the zenith. By the time he had claimed another Champions League victory in the 2017/18 final against Liverpool, it was his fifth in the competition with two different clubs. After that final, Ronaldo spoke to the press, referring to Madrid in the past tense, which sparked immense speculation on the forward's future. He was Madrid's all-time leading goalscorer, but despite all the team and personal accolades accumulated in the Spanish capital, he was clearly searching for a new challenge as he began to move towards his twilight years. On 18 July 2018, Juventus paid around £100m to lure the Portuguese hotshot to Italy.

Ronaldo wrote a heartfelt letter to the fans of Madrid:

> Real Madrid has conquered my heart, and that of my family, and that is why more than ever I want to say thank you: thanks to the club, the President, the directors, my colleagues, all the technical staff, doctors, physios and incredible workers that make everything work, that tirelessly pursue every minute detail.
>
> Thank you infinitely once more to our fans and thanks also to Spanish Football. During these nine exciting years I have played against great players. My respect and my recognition for all of them.
>
> I have reflected a lot and I know that the time has come for a new cycle. I'm leaving but this shirt, this badge, and the Santiago Bernabéu will continue to always feel part of me wherever I am. Thanks to all and, of course, as I said that first time in our stadium nine years ago: Go Madrid!

And so, to the Old Lady of Turin. Different country, different stadiums, same outcome. His first goal came in a 4-1 victory over Sassuolo on 16 September 2018. In the first two seasons at Juventus, Ronaldo scored 65 times in just under 90 appearances, with the first campaign yielding a Serie A and Coppa Italia double for Juventus. The second wasn't as successful, but, yet again, the league title was claimed to ensure that, despite his advancing years, Ronaldo was still the cream of the crop. His goal against Sampdoria had all but secured the Scudetto and the club had won it for the ninth season in a row.

With the Juventus squad being a dominant force domestically, they were unable to match Ronaldo's ambitions abroad, with only a Champions League quarter-final to show for their efforts.

Even in Ronaldo's final season in 2020/21, despite his 23 goals in all competitions, Juve were unable to hit the dizzy heights the forward had found in Spain. In fact, Juventus could only muster a fourth-place finish in a dismal campaign that had seen Ronaldo beginning to fall out of love with his time in Italy.

There were murmurings of board members allegedly being unhappy at paying a salary so high for a player of Ronaldo's age. Even so, his record of 101 goals in 133 matches meant that his time in Turin would be fondly remembered. While I may do his stint in Italy a disservice, it's to be noted that, while it was still imperious, it paled into insignificance compared with the way that for nearly a decade he absolutely obliterated Spanish defences on a weekly basis. Well, any defence across the whole of the world actually, as his goals record and trophy haul can most certainly attest to.

From the moment Cristiano left Manchester United, there was an air of accountability from the club. He had been nurtured in Manchester and ultimately became one of the greatest players ever to have played the game. So much so that, in nearly every transfer window following 2009, Ronaldo would in some way be linked with a return to Old Trafford. He had returned to pre-season training in 2021, but it was clear that his future lay elsewhere than in Turin. Rumours were that he had cleared his locker and was on a plane headed to Manchester to sign terms with striker-less Manchester City. The story from here on in is that Sir Alex Ferguson made a call to the player and asked him to change his mind. The media were already releasing the press statements of Ronaldo in a City shirt on some social media platforms. As the plane touched down at Manchester airport, it was to be revealed that, yet again, the

Portuguese forward would ply his trade in red and the fairy tale return had finally rung true.

Ronaldo said:

> Manchester United is a club that has always had a special place in my heart, and I have been overwhelmed by all the messages I have received since the announcement on Friday. I cannot wait to play at Old Trafford in front of a full stadium and see all the fans again. I'm looking forward to joining up with the team after the international games, and I hope we have a very successful season ahead.

He scored a brace on his second United debut on 11 September 2021, as United beat Newcastle 4-1. More important goals were to follow as he single-handedly helped the Red Devils qualify for the knockout phases of the Champions League, with last-minute goals against Villareal and Atalanta. Another brace in a 3-2 victory on 4 December ensured that Ronaldo had scored his 800th top-level career goal, absolutely insane numbers.

Finally, we must not forget his contribution to his homeland. He made his debut at just 18 years of age, replacing Luís Figo as a substitute, when Portugal defeated Kazakhstan 1-0 on 20 August 2003. Ronaldo scored the first of his international goals in the 2-1 defeat by Greece in Euro 2004, a competition in which he was later named in the team of the tournament. In 2007, at the age of just 22, he was made captain of his country as his goalscoring exploits continued to impress. With Portugal struggling to qualify for the 2014 World Cup, Ronaldo banged in a hat-trick in the second leg of the play-offs to ensure it was they and not Sweden who marched through to the tournament. In taking home the match ball, he also equalled Pauleta's record of 47 goals for his country. On 14 March 2014, Ronaldo bagged a brace in a 5-1 victory over Cameroon to take his place as the country's leading scorer. He was leading the team from the front; mind you, they had some pretty decent players behind him with the likes of Deco, Pepe, Thiago and Bruno Alves.

The pinnacle at international level came at the European Championship in 2016. Ronaldo and co were uninspiring during the group stages with three draws, but managed to progress. They roared into the semi-finals, where they faced a very stubborn Wales team that, like Portugal, were being dragged along by their talisman, in this case Gareth Bale. Ronaldo scored the opener in a 2 0 win, equalling Michel Platini as the competition's all-time top scorer with nine goals. Portugal faced hosts France in the final and, like a decade or so previously, inflicted defeat on the team staging the tournament, as Greece had done to Portugal in 2004. Ronaldo was carried off after a tackle from Dimitri Payet ended his final after just 25 minutes. Urging his team on from the sidelines, Ronaldo cajoled and barked instructions to his mates, as if he was the head coach, never mind what actual manager Fernando Santos was saying. The match went into extra time with both sides unable to break the deadlock until the 109th minute when Eder found the net and secured Portugal their first-ever title.

After the heroics in France, Ronaldo addressed his team-mates, backroom staff and waiting press:

> I would like to thank this man right here [Fernando Santos], first of all without him none of this would be possible. Second, to all the players, all the staff, everyone involved in this conquest. No one believed in Portugal, but the truth is we made it. All of us, we did it. I am very happy; this is one of the happiest days of my life. Forget the individual trophies, Champions League – this is one of the happiest moments of my

life. I have cried three of four times already and my
brother had to tell me to calm down.

Holding back the tears, Ronaldo tried to carry on:

It's true, from the bottom of my heart, I swear on
my son's life, I am so very, very, very happy. I could
repeat this 100 times. I am so happy. This is the
trophy that was missing. Thanks to all of you players,
all the staff and you again coach. All the faith you
had, honestly, it touched me. From the bottom of
my heart, I am truly happy. We deserved this. We
are now in the history of Portugal. We are the first
team to achieve this.

On 1 September 2021, Ronaldo scored two headers in a 2-1
win against the Republic of Ireland to overtake Ali Daei's
international record of 109 goals. Even at the age of 36, he's
showing no signs of letting up and has already found the net
11 times for Manchester United so far. How much longer can
he go on for? He and Lionel Messi are just simply on another
planet to the rest of the footballing world. 'If Cristiano
Ronaldo was not a football player, I would have already won
three Champions League titles with Atlético Madrid.' – Diego
Simeone.

   Viva Ronaldo …

At the time of writing, Cristiano Ronaldo's record for both club
and country are as follows: 115 goals in 184 appearances for
Portugal, while his club record currently stands at 801 goals in
1,097 matches. Incredible numbers.

8

Ronaldo – Il Fenomeno

*'I was in Spain when he was playing for
Barcelona, and I can tell everybody that he was
one of the best. He was impossible to mark, he had
an acceleration that made him difficult to stop,
he was scoring goals for fun, he was doing things
that the rest couldn't do. He was the special player
during my time in Spain.'* – **Gus Poyet**

BRAZIL HAS been the birthplace of some of the most talented players to have ever played football, particularly those who have been lucky enough to have ever pulled on the famous yellow jersey. One of the most gifted of all time is without doubt Pelé. His goalscoring record speaks for itself as well as his golden appearance in the film, *Escape to Victory*. Zico, Romário, Carlos Alberto, Garrincha, Socrates, Jairzinho, Ronaldinho and as recently as Neymar have all lit up the Maracanã and further afield. This stage, though, is set for Ronaldo Luís Nazário de Lima or, as we know him, Ronaldo.

Il Fenomeno (The Phenomenon) was sprinkled with something a little more than stardust. From his early days of playing on the streets of Rio de Janeiro, people knew that it was only a matter of time before this young star shone the brightest and became a household name. Ronaldo's family never had much, but when the youngster was only 11, his parents split up. It was at this point that Ronaldo decided that he no longer wanted to waste his time on his academic studies at school and decided to drop out. His love for football was such that he decided to withdraw himself from learning to dedicate as much time as possible to learning his craft. 'I always found him on the street playing ball with friends when he should have been in school. I know, I lost my battle,' explained his mother.

At the age of just 12, he joined a local futsal team. Futsal played a huge part in developing his skills, which would later prove vital on his journey to superstardom. In the futsal league that he joined, Ronaldo led the scoring charts in the first season with 166 goals. His silky skills caught the attention of retired Brazilian footballer, Jairzinho, who was the coach of São Cristóvão youth team. Wasting no time at all, he recruited Ronaldo into the fold, where he excelled in both the Under-17 and Under-20 teams while still only 15 years old. With Ronaldo constantly performing for São Cristóvão, Jairzinho then recommended him to Cruzeiro.

Prior to his move to Cruzeiro, Ronaldo had his heart set on joining boyhood club Flamengo, but upon being offered a trial, couldn't afford the fare to get to his first training session. His opportunity was dead in the water, but he was not to know that opportunity would come knocking on another door fairly soon. At just 13 years of age, he was approached by two agents, Reinaldo Pitta and Alexandre Martins, who swooped to take the youngster on their books. When asked years later about their thinking in taking a punt on an unknown teen, they quipped, 'We saw right away that he could be something different than most other players.'

With his new-found representation, offers were now starting to roll in for the boy. São Paulo and Botafogo were both turned down before a £50,000 offer from Cruzeiro was finally accepted. Ronaldo wasted no time in impressing his new club by bagging four goals on his youth-team debut. This caught the attention of the coach, Carlos Alberto Silva, and on 25 May 1993, Ronaldo earned his first-team debut in a match against Caldense in the Campeonato Mineiro.

His first senior goal came that summer in a friendly against Belenenses of Portugal. Again, the forward impressed those looking on, particularly against FC Porto, who submitted a bid for the player immediately after the match. Cruzeiro turned down their offer of £500,000. This player was going to be the jewel in their crown, and they knew it. Half-a-million quid was certainly not going to be enough to prize him away from them, even though it was a huge mark-up on the sum they had dished out themselves only six months previously.

The gamble from the board paid off as, by November, the whole nation now knew who their explosive teen forward was after an impressive five-goal haul against Bahia. Ronaldo scored a variety of goals, including two penalties and two what you would call more traditional strikes, but it was the fifth that showcased his footballing brain. The Bahia goalkeeper had made a save, playing up to the crowd, which had been giving him a torrid afternoon. He placed the ball in front of him as he lay on the ground, grimacing, playing the role of pantomime villain. Ronaldo, wasting no time at all, dispossessed the keeper to notch his fifth of the day. Sporting behaviour? No. Did he care? Absolutely not.

Brazil international defender Cafu had recognised the prowess first-hand. 'The first time I saw him play was at Cruzeiro. He was still a kid. It was in a game where he ended up scoring five goals. From that point on he showed he was truly a phenomenon.' Ronaldo had no fear despite his tender years. His skills learned on the street playing futsal and in the cages had geared him up for the physicality of professional football, where men were men and only the strong would survive. They had livings to make and cared less for fancy dan kids trying to make a name for themselves; everything had to be earned.

The 1993/94 season wasn't just a breakthrough campaign for the youngster but also a red-letter affair for his club as they not only won the title for the first time in seven seasons but also claimed a first-ever Copa do Brasil. Ronaldo's 44 goals in 47 matches assured the forward of his first taste of silverware at men's level and his performances had attracted the attention of the national coach, Carlos Alberto Parreira. He called upon the youngster to join his squad for the friendly against rivals Argentina, in Recife, where he made his debut on 23 March 1994.

Ronaldo's first international goal came just weeks later when he notched in a 3-0 win over Iceland, during a warm-up match for the upcoming World Cup in the US. His maiden strike for the Seleçáo was a sweet half-volley from the edge of the penalty box to announce himself on the world stage. His performances over this period were good enough to warrant a place in the squad for the 1994 World Cup, but the youngster was to be an onlooker as his team-mates reached the final and eventually won, beating Italy in a penalty shoot-out. The experience was both rich and educational for Ronaldo, as when quizzed by a reporter on his return, he remarked that he was 'overjoyed' by the whole thing.

Despite being born and raised in Brazil, as with most of the talent from South America, Ronaldo's footballing future would lie further east. PSV Eindhoven were interested in the player and, with his national team-mate Romário having already played for the Dutch giants, urged the youngster to spread his wings and move to pastures new. 'Romário told me that PSV is one of the most professional and best organised clubs in Europe. He said it would be best to acclimatise in Europe and learn about European football. I think he is right,' Ronaldo said.

On 28 August 1994, Ronaldo made his debut for PSV and his search for a goal in his new homeland would last a mere ten minutes. Receiving a long pass, the Brazilian brought the ball under control with his first touch, before firing home right-footed into the far corner of the net. Like his compatriot before him, Ronaldo found scoring in the Netherlands a task no more complicated than back in his motherland. The pitches were still grass and the concept was still the same, despite the language barrier. In fact, the only language Ronaldo really knew was scoring goals, and that was multinational. His first campaign in the Netherlands yielded 36 goals in as many matches, which included seven braces and two hat-tricks.

PSV ended the campaign trophyless despite the truck load of goals scored by Ronaldo and co. They managed 85 in the Eredivisie, but ultimately fell well short of champions Ajax, who had absolutely blitzed the opposition. A third-placed finish and early exit from two cup competitions weren't the best as a collective, but introducing himself to a new league and culture, Ronaldo seemed to take to his new surroundings like a duck to water.

In the first round of the UEFA Cup, PSV faced German team Bayern Leverkusen. Ronaldo bagged himself a hat-trick and walked off with the match ball. Unfortunately for him, for all his scoring abilities at the top end of the pitch, the defenders behind him weren't of the same quality. PSV lost the first leg 5-4, which led to an exit from the competition, as the Dutch team failed to overturn the result and crashed out 5-4 on aggregate after a goalless draw in Eindhoven. Leverkusen striker and Germany World Cup winner Rudi Völler stated in a post-match press conference, 'Never in my life have I seen an 18-year-old play in this way.'

Ronaldo was also attracting praise from the written press. Reporting for *The Guardian*, Nick Miller described the impact that the teenager had in his debut season:

> What's striking about Ronaldo in that first year at PSV is how complete he looks, even as a skinny teenager. Everything that would come to define him – the lightning pace, the blurry stepovers, the implausible impression that he was faster with the ball than without it, even the exceptional upper-body strength – was all there.

The phrase 'those blurry stepovers' was a reference to the move that Ronaldo perfected and continued throughout his career. In today's footballing hipster dictionary, it's often described as a 'Flip Flap'. To all of those lucky to witness it at the Philips Stadion, who watched in awe as the Brazilian bewitched his opponents, the footwork will always be known as Ronaldo's '*Elastico*'.

Gary Thacker, writing for *All Blue Daze*, described the move beautifully:

> Faced with an opponent Ronaldo would pause for a moment over the ball, swaying slightly like a cobra hypnotising its prey. Then, with the defender's concentration awaiting the first move, he would slightly nudge the ball in one direction, hypnotically inducing the defender to shift his balance and counter the anticipated move, and in that moment

Ronaldo had his opponent beaten. A quick snap of the ankle would then flick the ball in the opposite direction allowing the mercurial striker to scamper past the beaten defender, leaving him floundering like some dupe, a victim of a conjurer's sleight of hand.

The Guardian's Rob Smyth concurred with the magician metaphor: 'In many ways Ronaldo was the first PlayStation footballer. His stepover was a form of hypnosis, and his signature trick, the *elastico*, could certainly have come from a computer screen.'

The superlatives for the teenager were coming from all quarters. At a time when the new Champions League format was really starting to take shape and even more European football was beginning to be beamed live to our homes, players who had gone under the footballing radar were now about to be thrust into the spotlight.

Ronaldo returned to pre-season to prepare for the 1995/96 campaign but had some discomfort in his knee. A case of Osgood-Schlatter Disease was diagnosed. It's characterised by a painful bump just below the knee that's made worse with activity and improves with rest. Episodes of pain typically last a few weeks to months. For Ronaldo, it would impact on his second season in Dutch football as his appearances would be somewhat limited compared to his first jaunt. No surgery was required, only rest, but Ronaldo began to grow impatient at missing out on large portions of the campaign. Again, PSV failed to make an impression on the Eredivisie, but they did walk away with the Dutch cup. Even with a dent in his own development, Ronaldo finished his second year in the Netherlands by taking his total to 54 goals in 58 matches, a quite astonishing return from a player who was just ending his teen years.

Interest in the player was beginning to grow. European powerhouses Barcelona and Inter Milan were at the head of the queue for the player, despite rumours circulating that he now had dodgy knees. Bobby Robson, ex-England manager, was the boss in the dugout of the Camp Nou and was certainly keen on bringing the youngster through to the Catalan capital. Robson had been seen as a stop-gap choice for Barça as the club jolted from the Johan Cruyff era towards another Dutch leader in Luis Van Gaal. The problem with Van Gaal was that he was unavailable for another season, so, as an interim measure, decided to plug the gap with the senior Robson.

Barcelona had endured a torrid past 24 months, finishing fourth and second in the league. The locals were starting to become restless after the break-up of Cruyff's dream team, which featured Ronaldo's old pal Romário. Robson had a remit from the board to win but entertain at the same time. He recalled: 'The president said to me, "We need bums on seats, we need a top-class striker, do you know where there is one?" I said, "Yes, I know there's a young kid at PSV that I like very much. I think he's terrific, but he's a risk."' The board took the risk and a world record fee of around £12.5m changed hands with PSV, so Ronaldo found himself heading south to Spain.

The 1996/97 season started a little slow for the striker, who took 210 minutes to score the first of his 47 goals that year. He then notched three braces in his next four matches as Barcelona began to pick up speed in La Liga. Sandwiched in that run was another brace as Barcelona defeated Atlético Madrid in the Supercopa de España. A 5-2 victory at the Camp Nou meant that within a month of arriving in Catalonia, Ronaldo had one hand on his first trophy. They went over the line in the second leg a week later, claiming a 6-5 aggregate win.

That was cup number one in a season littered with a hat-trick of trophy wins in cup competition. Barcelona lost out on the title, agonisingly, by just two points. The shock defeat away to Hércules with just three matches remaining broke the momentum of the team, resulting in them finishing second in La Liga on 90 points, just behind Real Madrid on 92. So near but yet so far for Robson and Ronaldo.

The Brazilian's six goals in four appearances helped Barça to reach the final of the Copa del Rey. Having beaten both Madrid teams en route to the final, Barcelona were left to face the very unfancied Real Betis in the Bernabéu. Ronaldo was missing for the final due to injury, with a long season beginning to take its toll on the player. This seemed to give the underdogs of Betis a lift, which culminated in the dark horses taking the lead after 11 minutes. Barça fought back and eventually won in extra time. That was trophy number two, but the best was yet to come. And who else was to deliver it to the man who had trusted Ronaldo to bring success?

Barcelona's European Cup Winners' Cup adventure had pitted them against AEK Larnaca, FK Crvena Zvezda, AIK Solna, Fiorentina and finally PSG. Ronaldo scored seven goals on his way to the final, where he would face the French in familiar surroundings in Rotterdam. PSG weren't the team or club that you find today. They were the poor relatives of Ligue 1, with the French powerhouses such as Marseille, Monaco and Saint-Étienne leading the way. However, they had top players such as Bernard Lama, Bruno N'Gotty, Leonardo and Patrice Loko. The stage was set. In the 38th minute, Barcelona were awarded a penalty and up stepped Ronaldo to calmly stroke the ball into the Parisians' net. Barça held on and the third cup was added to the campaign's haul.

Ronaldo had scored an impressive 47 times that year, which led him to claim the La Liga Golden Boot and the European Golden Shoe. Robson's gamble on the youngster had definitely paid off. Quinton Fortune remembers playing against the forward in La Liga at the time: 'He was physical perfection, and he seemed like a mythical figure. I love Lionel Messi, I played many times with Cristiano Ronaldo and I adore him, Neymar is outstanding, Ronaldinho was exceptional – but if you put all of them together, you might get what Ronaldo was that season.' Sid Lowe of *Sports Illustrated* stated, 'That season Ronaldo was unstoppable. He was slim and powerful, skilful, fast, and deadly. He was ridiculously good.' At the end of 1996, aged just 20, Ronaldo became the youngest player to win the FIFA World Player of the Year award.

Unfortunately for both Robson and Ronaldo, despite the hat-trick of trophies, the boss was still replaced by Van Gaal. It was a move that upset some of the players, who were beginning to warm to the man management style of the Englishman. Ronaldo particularly relished working under the coach, who had brought him into the club from PSV, ironically the club where Robson would find his next role.

Speaking after the passing of Sir Bobby Robson, Ronaldo said:

> I'm proud to have worked with him. He was an awesome coach and an awesome person. He was like a father to me. I have had a lot of managers in football but the difference between all of them and Sir Bobby was his humanity and the relationships he had with the players. He was always like a father to everyone. At Barcelona he spoke to me in Portuguese because, at the time, my English wasn't good. He was very patient. I remember there were a lot of players for Barcelona from different countries at that time and Sir Bobby managed us all and brought us together. It didn't matter what language you spoke or what colour you were. He was great.

The unrest at the club didn't just fall at the manager's door. Ronaldo had signed a deal on his arrival in Barcelona that would hardly have left him on the breadline each week, but he wasn't the highest paid at the club either. With the goals and the trophies seemingly flowing hand in hand, Ronaldo and his representatives demanded that they sit down with the board to renegotiate something a little more fitting for the new World Player of the Year. Barcelona president Josep Lluís Núñez declared, 'He's ours for life,' when questioned about the saga, only to commit a dramatic U-turn 24 hours later to the media and announce the deal was dead.

Speaking to ESPN, Ronaldo stated, 'I had reached an agreement to renew my contract just a month before that season finished, but a week later the lawyer and the president of Barcelona agreed that that contract was absurd.' This resulted in a stalemate in proceedings and again alerted clubs to the fact that the forward could be available. This time around, however, Inter Milan weren't to be beaten to the punch and immediately activated Ronaldo's buyout clause, which stood at a then whopping £27m. His move to Inter signalled another world record fee paid, becoming the second player in history to twice break the transfer record, following in the footsteps of Diego Maradona.

News of the saga had spread worldwide, with the *Washington Post* reporting on the goings-on between Inter Milan, Barcelona and the player. The headline read 'Inter Milan Signs Brazilian Ronaldo', and reported:

> World player of the year Ronaldo signed a five-year contract with Inter Milan on Friday. The announcement was made by Ronaldo's representative, Alexandre Martins, and the representative of Inter, Luis Suárez, who arrived in this city Thursday evening

to finalise the agreement. Suárez confirmed that his team paid $32 million to the Spanish federation RFEF to transfer Ronaldo from FC Barcelona to Inter. Ronaldo, a 20-year-old forward, is playing with the Brazilian national team at the Copa America in Bolivia. Details of the agreement will not be revealed until July 1 in Milan. Italian media reports have said Inter is prepared to pay Ronaldo $3 million a year after taxes. He would also get a $14 million signing bonus. 'We have solved all the legal problems that stood in the way of Ronaldo joining,' said Suárez. 'In the name of Inter, I'm very happy to have such a magnificent player.'

Martins said Ronaldo had 'a great desire to leave Barcelona. In Inter he will find a great warmth. It was the first European club he became interested in when he entered into conflict with Barcelona.' The much-anticipated signing took place soon after one of Ronaldo's legal team handed over a $27.5m cheque to the Spanish federation to free him from his contract with Barcelona.

Ronaldo was walking into the San Siro to join a team already littered with stars. Gianluca Pagliuca, Javier Zanetti, Youri Djorkaeff, Aron Winter, Diego Simeone, Paulo Sousa, Ivan Zamorano and Alvaro Recoba were just some of the dazzling talents that would be lining up alongside the Brazilian. The season's opening match against Brescia on 31 August 1997 was Ronaldo's debut for the Nerazzuri. Inter won 2-1, coming from behind to start the campaign with a win. Bologna away was their second match and, just after the half-time break, Ronaldo opened his account for his new club.

It was a trend that the striker continued as he managed to find the net on 34 occasions in all competitions that season.

Inter Milan hadn't mounted any form of title charge since 1989, but with the firepower of Ronaldo and Recoba, were now classed as serious contenders to the throne. They flirted with the top of the table until defeat to rivals Juventus in April 1998 derailed their push for the Scudetto. Unfortunately for the Nerazzuri, they faltered at the final fence, finishing runners-up to the Old Lady by four points.

Ronaldo's presence had got spectators into the stadium. For the Milan derby, over 80,000 fans crammed into the San Siro to watch a pulsating 2-2 draw, with Ronaldo giving Inter the lead midway through the second half before a late penalty for Milan evened the scores. The biggest crowd of the season had witnessed a match of true derby status. The Brazilian was proving that he wasn't just a flat track bully; he scored goals against everyone.

Having tasted European Cup Winners' Cup success months earlier with Barcelona, Ronaldo was now having his first sortie in the UEFA Cup. He scored against Neuchâtel Xamax, Strasbourg, Schalke 04, a brace in the semi-final against Spartak Moscow and the third goal in a 3-0 win against Lazio in an all-Italian affair in Paris. Ronaldo scored what would be his trademark goal. Running through the defence, he went one on one with Lazio goalkeeper Luca Marchegiani, feinted to go right, then left, without touching the ball, leaving Marchegiani on his backside, before going right and slotting the ball into the empty net. I think the kids call it 'going for a hotdog' nowadays.

For a second consecutive season, Ronaldo was tasting European champagne.

On a personal level, he also picked up the FIFA World Player of the Year award for the second consecutive year as well as the Ballon d'Or. Along with his 25 goals in Serie A, he was voted the Serie A Player of the Year. Not bad for your first year in Italy. His Inter team-mate Youri Djorkaeff stated, 'Ronaldo was phenomenal. He proved that he was a cut above the rest that season.'

Inter Milan failed to capitalise on their UEFA Cup win and started the 1998/99 campaign in terrible form. So much so that coach Luigi Simoni was given his P45 by November. By March, Inter were looking for their third manager of the season as Mircea Lucescu was also given his marching orders by Massimo Moratti. The chairman was struggling to find a solution to his problems and eventually gave the job to Roy Hodgson, who steadied the ship, albeit far too late to salvage their season. Inter finished in eighth position and crashed out of the Champions League at the quarter-final stage, losing to eventual winners Manchester United.

Ronaldo had also struggled. His troublesome knee was beginning to flare up and a momentary loss of form didn't help his cause. However, despite the lows, he still ended the campaign with 15 goals in all competitions. The upheaval of coaches during the season had clearly taken its toll on the forward, who was then asked to carry out roles that he wouldn't normally undertake. Tracking back and tucking in when not in possession certainly didn't suit the marksman's game, instead of playing high up the pitch, waiting for a counter.

The World Cup in France during the summer of 1998 was a welcome distraction for the striker. Brazil were red hot favourites heading into the competition as they weren't only the current holders but also boasted a star-studded squad, including the current Ballon d'Or holder. Jacob Steinberg of *The Guardian* wrote: 'In 1998, no one was as ferociously talented as Ronaldo, whose supernatural mixture of power, pace and skill had made him the player every child in the playground wanted to be at the age of 21, the hopes and dreams of a nation rested on his shoulders.'

Despite a poorer league campaign than normal, Ronaldo burst into life in France. He wasn't only scoring goals but also assisting his team-mates, as his all-round play was now starting to benefit his home nation. On the march to the final, he scored four and made three as the Seleçáo looked to claim a second successive World Cup title. Ronaldo scored and set up Bebeto in a 3-0 group match win over Morocco. He then scored a brace in the 4-1 victory over South American rivals, Chile. During the 3-2 win over Denmark in the quarter-finals, he turned provider, with two assists in a closely fought encounter with the Danes.

The semi-finals loomed, where a highly fancied Dutch team lined up to face Brazil in the Stade Velodrome in Marseille. Ronaldo opened the scoring just after the restart and those in yellow looked to be heading into the final until Patrick Kluivert equalised in the 87th minute to bring extra time into the equation. There was to be no break in the deadlock and the match went to a penalty shoot-out. Ronaldo stepped up first and stroked the ball home. Brazil didn't miss a kick and, once both Philip Cocu and Ronald de Boer failed to notch, Ronaldo and co were heading to another final.

France, who were the hosting nation, had also made it through to the showpiece in Saint-Denis. As you can imagine, there was a huge public interest in the final as well as a worldwide audience looking forward to settling down and watching two great teams battle it out for the title of world champions, the greatest team on the planet. What unfolded prior to kick-off was something that no one could quite put their finger on. Something sinister? A plot to shake up the tournament, Skulduggery?

The party line is that hours before the team sheets were due to be handed in, Ronaldo suffered a convulsive fit. At first, he was removed from the starting line-up just 72 minutes before the match, and the team sheet (with Edmundo as his replacement) was submitted to the FIFA delegate. The Brazil line-up without Ronaldo was released to a stunned world media. The BBC's John Motson stated, 'The scenes in the commentary box have been absolute mayhem and chaos.' Ronaldo was gunning for the tournament's golden boot. Surely he would be fit to play.

Just an hour before kick-off, Ronaldo pleaded with coach, Mario Zagallo. He stated that he was now feeling fine and that he wanted to play. Eventually, after much persuasion, Zagallo changed his mind and the forward was brought back into the team. However, Ronaldo didn't seem to click in a match that got away from the Seleçáo, as the hosts stunned Brazil with a 3-0 win to lift the trophy in front of a partisan home support.

But something still wasn't sitting right about the Ronaldo saga. Jacob Steinberg from *The Guardian* stated that Ronaldo 'sleepwalked' through the final, which also saw him injured in a collision with French goalkeeper Fabien Barthez. Zagallo later admitted the fears over Ronaldo had affected his team psychologically and stated, 'For the whole of the first half I was wondering whether to take him off.' But the coach was wary that there would be a public outcry in Brazil had he done so.

The main conspiracy theory is that sponsors Nike forced Ronaldo's inclusion. There had long been a feeling that the sportswear company's £105m sponsorship deal had earned them too much control over the team's management. Some even claimed that there was a clause in the contract and that Brazil were obligated to play Ronaldo, one of Nike's biggest stars, as long as he was ruled fit. Rumours also circulated that it was Ronaldo's job to mark Zinedine Zidane at corners (both of Zizou's goals in the final came from corners), which he later admitted, and that his situation was part of a bigger fix involving FIFA and an £18m bribe. Others say Ronaldo reacted badly to an injection in his troublesome knee.

Ronaldo eventually had his say on the matter when speaking to *FourFourTwo* magazine:

> I decided to get some rest after lunch and the last thing I remember was going to bed. After that, I had a convulsion. I was surrounded by players and the late Dr Lidio Toledo was there. They didn't want to tell me what was going on. I asked if they could leave and go talk somewhere else because I wanted to sleep. Then Leonardo asked me to go for a walk in the garden in the hotel where we were staying and explained the whole situation. I was told that I wouldn't play in the World Cup final but all the essential medical exams didn't show anything was abnormal – it was like nothing had happened.
>
> After that we went to the stadium with a message from Zagallo saying that I wouldn't play. I had test results in my hand – with Dr Toledo giving the green light. I approached [Mario] Zagallo at the stadium and said: 'I'm fine. I'm not feeling anything. Here are the test results, they're fine. I want to play.'
>
> I didn't give him an alternative. He had no choice and accepted my decision. Then I played and maybe I affected the whole team because that convulsion was certainly something very scary. It's not something you see every day. In any case, I had a duty to my country and I didn't want to miss it. I had my honour and felt that I could play. Obviously it wasn't one of the best matches in my career, but I was there to fulfil my role.

Edmundo, who was the makeweight during the whole saga, added fuel to the fire when probed about the incident. Taken back out of the starting XI, 'The Animal' later suggested that Nike influenced Ronaldo's return to the team. 'Nike's people were there 24 hours a day, as if they were members of the technical staff. It's a huge power. That's all I can say.'

No one will ever really uncover the mystery of the pre-match goings on in the Brazil camp, but something never quite sat right for anyone associated with Ronaldo. The parliamentary inquiry was unable to find any wider conspiracy, although the Brazilian public remained unconvinced. Reporting for CNN's news channel, Don Riddell wrote, 'It's one of the great mysteries of our time: not the Loch Ness Monster, Stonehenge or the Lost City of Atlantis; it's the case of the missing striker – not so much a whodunit, more a kind of a what the heck happened?'

Despite the controversy, Il Fenomeno claimed the Golden Ball award, which is given to the player of the tournament. This was due to his performances en route to the final, which included not only goals but scintillating play and assists. The World Cup appeared to see him at the peak of his powers. Amy Lawrence from *The Guardian* described the rise of the striker beautifully:

> The way he combined powerhouse athleticism with a poetic touch made for an awesome sight. In the 1990s, in his physical pomp, in his free-flowing prime, there was nothing remotely like him. By the time the 1998 World Cup came along his reputation had extended to the point of fully formed marvel. A happening.

A return to Milan and new hope for a new season. Ronaldo re-joined his team-mates back in Italy and, having endured plenty of upheaval in the previous campaign, hoped for a more consistent season ahead. Marcello Lippi had taken the hotseat in the San Siro dugout and had made his intentions quite clear by busting the world transfer record in signing Christian Vieri for £32m from Lazio. The striker was bolstering an attack that included both Ronaldo and Roberto Baggio.

The new partnership seemed to click instantly. Vieri wasted absolutely no time in introducing himself to his new team-mates and, by the hour mark on his home debut, had notched goal number three to send the home fans into ecstasy. By match six, the front two had scored eight goals between them and were dovetailing beautifully on the pitch. The Nerazzuri sat pretty at the top of Serie A and all was rosy in the garden until a 6-0 home win against Lecce in November 1999 signalled a turning point in both Inter's season and Ronaldo's career. Soon after scoring a penalty in the 49th minute, Ronaldo limped off the pitch with discomfort plain for all to see. His knee had seemingly buckled from underneath him and, once in the medical room, he was told he would require surgery on a ruptured tendon.

Inter Milan's luck didn't improve as, with Ronaldo already sidelined for an extended period, they also lost Vieri for large parts of the campaign. Their flying start caught up with them and the black-and-blues finished in fourth spot. To make matters worse, Ronaldo was nowhere near ready to return. With Inter struggling to retain a title push, they might have rushed him back a little too hastily from his injury. Although he had made good progress in rehabilitation, it was probably a little too premature to expect him to play any part at the tail end of the 1999/2000 season.

Ronaldo did return for the Coppa Italia Final against Vieri's old club, Lazio. Just six minutes of his comeback were on the clock when disaster struck. Ronaldo was prone on the pitch, holding his knee. The Inter physio, Nilton Petrone, described it as the worst injury he had seen in football. Speaking to *FourFourTwo* magazine, he said:

> At the beginning of 1999, Inter had already called Dr Saillant to monitor Ronaldo's tendons, both in the right and the left kneecap. It was known that the degeneration was relatively big but no one thought about surgery before his injury. The injury happened on November 23, 1999. After 20 minutes, Ronaldo was about to spin and then suddenly stopped. I was on the bench and at that moment we noticed that something wasn't right. He asked to be replaced and walked normally but when I arrived in the locker room and bent his knee I saw that the centre of the tendon was ripped. This was Ronaldo's first injury. I did the monitoring and then he went to Paris to have an operation with Dr Saillant. We then did all the rehabilitation monitoring and at the beginning of every month we would go to Paris.

Even the professionals can sometimes make the wrong call, as Petrone was about to find out:

> Around the beginning of April, we started to think that he was training normally. He was playing and had already been released by the doctor who performed the surgery and told he could possibly make his return to the pitch. But Inter are very meticulous with rehabilitation, so at the beginning of that month we travelled, with Dr. Franco Combi, who was Inter's doctor at the time, to talk to Dr. Saillant about the possibility of Ronaldo playing

in the final of the Italian Cup against Lazio or the match against Juventus which was two weeks later.

We took Ronaldo to Paris to see the doctor and he said that it was okay for him to play in the match against Lazio. We asked him how much time he would be able to play for and he said 15 to 20 minutes. When he returned for that match, he ripped the kneecap tendon completely. His kneecap actually exploded and it ended up in the middle of his thigh.

To make matters worse, Inter lost 2-1 on aggregate to Lazio to end another season potless. Ronaldo was broken both mentally and physically. His knees were in tatters and he endured a lengthy period on the sidelines, missing the entire 2000/01 campaign. His road to recovery was a long one, but even the horrific injuries that had occurred couldn't keep Ronaldo from focusing on becoming the player he once was. Battling back from knee injuries is one of the toughest acts as an injured footballer. Slowly but surely Ronaldo worked his way towards full fitness. Physio rooms can be lonely places for players while team-mates are all out together working on the plan for the coming weekend. You can start to feel isolated and this can seriously affect your wellbeing. Ronaldo showed great character to come back from the same injury twice in 24 months.

During his spell on the sidelines, Brazil staggered and stumbled towards qualification for the 2002 World Cup, to be held in South Korea and Japan. Ronaldo hadn't played many minutes during his recovery process, but was training hard and was already being lined up to join the squad for the tournament. To be honest, there would have been a national state of emergency declared had Luiz Felipe Scolari not picked Ronaldo to join the squad in the Far East. Despite his lack of match time, Ronaldo's club-mates could see that he was now ready to roll. Inter Milan team-mate Youri Djorkaeff said, 'When we were training, we would practically stop to watch him. It was extraordinary.'

With the scars not yet healed from France '98, Ronaldo felt that he had a point to prove heading into the tournament. Not only had his Brazil team folded in the final against the hosts, France, but there was also the controversy that surrounded the player regarding his fitness prior to the final. Tim Vickery, the South American football expert, wrote: 'Without Ronaldo, Brazil were a shambles, fortunate even to get to the tournament. With him, it was a different story.'

Brazil embarked on another title tilt, with wins over Turkey, China and Costa Rica to top Group C. Ronaldo was in fine fettle, netting four goals in three matches. He scored again during the 2-0 last-16 win over Belgium, but drew his first blank in the quarter-final victory over England. There were question marks over Ronaldo's performance against the Three Lions as he looked jaded, with many starting to question whether his lack of matches during the regular season was now catching up with him after starting five matches in only a couple of weeks.

With so much talk of fitness issues, Ronaldo decided to take matters into his own hands and rocked up to training with the most bizarre haircut I think anyone has ever seen on a footballer. A completely shaved head was left with a wedge at the front. Like a fringe that just stopped at the top of the forehead. Was Ronaldo having a Britney Spears-style meltdown? Was it a cry for help? Ronaldo explained to ESPN:

> I had an injury in my leg and everybody was talking about that. I decided to cut my hair and leave the small thing there. I come to training and everybody saw me with bad hair. Everybody was talking about the hair and forgot about the injury. I could stay more

calm and relaxed and focused on my training. I'm not proud about the hair itself because it was pretty strange. But it was a good way to change the subject.

Ronaldo later apologised to all the mums in the world in an interview with *Sports Illustrated*, for all the kids who were now going to copy his new hairstyle.

The semi-final against Turkey saw Brazil clinch a tightly fought match, with Ronaldo scoring an elaborate toe-poke to secure a third final in three consecutive tournaments. This time around, Ronaldo wasn't going to let anything other than his football do the talking.

Germany were the opponents in Yokohama. The match was goalless and very even in the first half, with both teams hitting the woodwork, before Ronaldo opened the scoring in the 67th minute. A shot was spilled by Germany keeper Oliver Khan and fell kindly into the path of Ronaldo, who slotted the ball into the empty net. Just 11 minutes later, he struck again to put the match out of reach of the Germans. After a neat pass to the forward, who was standing on the edge of the penalty area, he took a touch and side-footed the ball into the bottom left-hand corner of the net. Brazil were world champions for the fifth time and the winners of two of the last three competitions.

Ronaldo was emotional at the end of the match and, speaking to the media while hugging the trophy, said, 'I've said before that my big victory was to play football again, to run again and to score goals again. This victory, for our fifth world title, has crowned my recovery and the work of the whole team.' Gérard Saillant, the French surgeon who operated on Ronaldo's knee, was in the crowd as his guest, and stated after the final, 'This gives hope to everyone who is injured, even those who aren't sportsmen, to see that by fighting you can make it. He's back to where he was; it's hugely satisfying and I am very moved.'

Over in Spain, stories were beginning to develop about a possible transfer to the Spanish capital for Ronaldo. Real Madrid were currently in full swing of their Galactico project, having already secured the signings on Roberto Carlos, Zinedine Zidane and Luís Figo. It was going to take an extraordinary amount of money to prise Ronaldo away from the San Siro and Massimo Moratti stood firm in his stance until eventually a fee of around £45m was agreed. After 59 goals in 99 matches for Inter, Ronaldo was heading to pastures new.

Ronaldo was injured when he signed his contract in the autumn of 2002 but still managed to pass his medical. This meant that the fans in the Bernabéu had to be patient to see their new star in all white, whose transfer to the Spanish capital had smashed all records for shirt sales on his first day. By October, he was ready to return to action and, on his first appearance, took just 61 seconds to open his account for his new employers after coming on as a second-half substitute. He scored again 12 minutes later to seal a 5-2 win over Alavés in front of his new supporters, who would see the hitman notch a further 28 times as his first campaign with Madrid produced 30 goals in 44 appearances.

Ronaldo's goals ensured that Real Madrid held off Real Sociedad to clinch the La Liga title by two points. He also scored the opener in a 2-0 win over Club Olimpia to secure the Intercontinental Trophy. This was added to the European Super Cup, which had already been claimed after a 3-1 win over Feyenoord at the beginning of the season. A body blow for the striker was that the club weren't able to capitalise on a good run in the Champions League, falling at the semi-final stage to Juventus. Despite the defeat at the hands of the Old Lady, it was a good first season for the striker, nonetheless. He had wowed the footballing world with a scintillating hat-trick at Old Trafford in the quarter-final, which led to a standing ovation from the Stretford End when he was eventually substituted.

When asked about his performance and the fact that both sets of fans applauded his contribution, Ronaldo said, 'It remains a very beautiful, very special moment.' Manchester United coach Mike Phelan witnessed the display from the technical area. 'He got the standing ovation he deserved from the crowd. That's the first time I really felt a special player was out on a football field. I don't think there was anybody in the stadium who didn't stand up, and I count myself in that as the opposition coach. You just understand when you see quality.'

Following on from their title-winning season, Real Madrid couldn't muster another championship challenge the next season, as this time the team from the capital could only manage a paltry fourth-place finish. Ronaldo had continued to find the net with consummate ease, taking his tally in Spain to nearly 50 goals in two seasons. The Brazilian also scored the second goal in a 3-0 victory over Mallorca in a 4-2 aggregate win to claim the Supercopa de España.

The Brazilian forward then topped the goalscoring charts again in both the 2004/05 and 2005/06 seasons, but despite his still golden touch, Real Madrid were unable to compete with his fellow Brazilian Ronaldinho over at Barcelona. Los Blancos failed to land any silverware over the course of 24 months, crashing out of the Champions League in the last 16 in both campaigns.

The 2006 World Cup in Germany was to be the last for Ronaldo. Persistent knee troubles and concerns about the player's weight were beginning to surface on as even more regular occurrence. Brazil's team were revered for their quartet of magical stars going into the tournament, with Ronaldo,

Ronaldinho, Kaká, and Adriano all set to feature for the then world champions. Unfortunately for the fans back home in Rio, it never quite materialised in that way as Brazil were knocked out in the quarter-finals by a fine Thierry Henry goal as the French advanced at the expense of the Seleçáo. Despite Brazil's failure to advance any further in the tournament, Ronaldo's team-mate Kaká, paid homage to his team-mate. 'Ronaldo is the best player I have ever played with. I have seen Il Fenomeno do things nobody else has ever done.'

Ronaldo was jeered by sections of support due to his 'size' and immobility. He seemed to struggle to get around the pitch, although he did score twice against Japan to equal the then record of 14 goals in a World Cup held by West Germany's Gerd Muller. Against Ghana in the round of 16, Ronaldo made the record his own by scoring goal number 15. It was a deed that was recorded in the *Guinness Book of World Records*. 'I am proud of my career and of the records I set. But I know that one day they will be broken,' Ronaldo said when quizzed about his achievement. The record was later beaten by another German. Miroslav Klose set a new record, which currently stands today, during the 2014 World Cup, netting five times to take his tally to 16 goals in 24 matches. Like Ronaldo had said, records are there to be broken.

Not only was Ronaldo's time in yellow coming to an end, his stint in Madrid was also reaching its conclusion. Madrid had signed Ruud Van Nistelrooy from Manchester United and, with injuries beginning to show, Ronaldo was starting to feel a little forced out. He could still find the net, there was no question about that, but maybe those terrible knee injuries that he had suffered at his absolute peak were now beginning to catch up on the body of the explosive forward. Van Nistelrooy hadn't been in Madrid very long, but he could already see the qualities that the Brazilian possessed. The Dutchman said, 'Ronaldo was the best natural talent I ever played with. His innate ability went beyond anything that I'd ever seen or played alongside.'

In January 2007, Madrid accepted an offer from Milan, although this time it was the red and black rather than the blue-and-black stripes. AC Milan tabled a bid of around £7m and Real Madrid snapped their hands off. Ronaldo had scored an impressive number of goals for Los Blancos, 104 in 177 matches to be precise, but despite this, his coach wasn't keen on the way he conducted himself. This prompted a heartfelt goodbye from the forward, who left a thinly veiled dig behind for his ex-gaffer: 'I would like to thank the fans who've supported me all the time and thank all the team-mates that I've had here and all the coaches I've had – except one.' Fabio Capello had been making noises for some time regarding the fitness issues surrounding the player, and once Van Nistelrooy had found his feet, it was time to pack the bags of the Brazilian. Capello, who wasn't going to be drawn into a media war of words, responded with, 'I wish him the best of luck in doing what he used to do which is being a great player.'

So, back to Milan, where on 26 January 2007 Ronaldo was unveiled as an AC Milan player, joining a long line of players who had crossed the divide over the years. He managed to score in his first Milan derby as a La Rossoneri, but in 2008, while jumping for a cross, he suffered another knee injury that ruled him out for the remainder of the campaign. His time in the fashion capital of Italy was a lot shorter the second time around, only scoring eight times in just over 20 appearances.

Like most South Americans, Ronaldo headed back to where it all began. He signed for Corinthians in Brazil and helped them to secure a league and cup double in 2009 before more controversy followed, relating to drink, gambling and even drug use. Let's not dampen the career of Il Fenomeno as he was arguably one of the greatest No. 9s of the modern era and possibly of all time. His statistics could have been scary had he not suffered such terrible injuries. In a club career that saw him score 352 goals in 512 appearances, coupled with 62 strikes for Brazil in 96 matches, it's clear that the player could score at will, whenever he found the need. His coolness in front of goal was what made him so ruthless. In fact, 88 of those goals were scored by sitting the goalkeeper down on his bum, dribbling around him and sliding the ball into an empty net. That's just an absurd number of times, considering some professional footballers won't have even scored 88 times throughout their whole career.

Sid Lowe of *Sports Illustrated* wrote, 'When he was one on one with the goalkeeper, you knew that he would score. He was so natural, so cool, so utterly in control. He would dip the shoulder, step over, and bang.'

Rob Smyth writing for *The Guardian* said, 'There were two Ronaldos: the one that returned after long-term injury in 2002 was a great goal scorer, but the 1990s version was a great everything. At his fearsome peak for PSV, Barcelona, and Inter Milan he was arguably the most dangerous striker the world has ever seen.'

Hard to argue with this fact as, on his day, no defender in the world could live with him. Injuries have robbed so many great players of their best years, with Ronaldo being a case in point. Marco Van Basten was another hotshot who was cruelly sidelined with a lot of good years still ahead of him.

Ronaldo's coach at both PSV Eindhoven and Barcelona echoed the sentiment of Smyth. Bobby Robson had seen the teenager turn into a man while under his tutelage. 'Ronaldo could start from the halfway line and the whole stadium would ignite. He was the fastest thing I've ever seen running with the ball. Had he managed to stay free of injury, he had every chance of becoming the best footballer ever.' Brazilian team-mate

Ronaldinho called him 'the most complete striker the world has ever seen', with even Argentine sensation Lionel Messi claiming that 'Ronaldo was the best striker I have ever seen'.

Some top accolades there from some of the best in their trade. Rory Smith wrote a cracking article for ESPN on how Ronaldo had changed the striker's role:

> Ronaldo, as so many of those who looked up to him acknowledge, changed what it is to be a centre-forward. Every time you see a striker who is expected to hold the ball up, beat players, win headers, shoot from range, drop deep, do everything a striker can possibly do – it might be worth remembering him. He shifted boundaries, challenged convention, just as much as Messi and Cristiano Ronaldo have altered our perceptions of what a winger might be. Ronaldo, the original Ronaldo, inspired a phalanx of imitators, players we see on our screens every weekend. But he also turned the game so that it will always look just a little bit like him. More than most, he made that No. 9 his own.

Ronaldo Luís Nazário de Lima, Il Fenemeno, The Original Ronaldo, or just Ronaldo. However you want to address him, I think it's fair to say we should put some respect on his name. Obrigada Ronaldo!

9

Thierry Henry

*'I've used this analogy before and I make no apology for using it again. When he hit top gear and ran past you, it was like trying to chase after someone on a motorbike. When Arsenal were "The Invincibles" in the period between 2003–2004, Henry rivalled Ronaldinho as the best in the world. A great goal-scorer, not to mention a scorer of great goals, he is the finest player I have seen in the Premier League. His game didn't have a weakness.' – **Jamie Carragher**

THEY SAY that there are three certainties in life: birth, death and taxes. You would have to add to that list the sight of Thierry Henry picking up the ball in the left-hand channel, cutting inside his man and arcing a ball into the far corner of the net. You know it's coming but just try to stop it. You can't. It was like gravity was pulling the Frenchman to that side of the pitch, like a magnet drawing him over into the danger zone. Danger for the opposition, anyway. Henry grew into one of the greatest forwards that the modern era had ever seen.

As an adolescent, Henry had an ability to blow teams away. This was demonstrated in a youth match in which he scored all six goals in a 6-0 win for his team. Scout Arnold Catalano had spotted the prospect, aged just 13, and immediately offered him a chance to join Monaco without even having to attend a trial. Henry signed schoolboy terms and was sent to join the famous Clairefontaine academy. This prestigious school is an elite facility in France where the best young footballing talent would go to hone both their skills on the pitch as well as their academic abilities. Players from the age of around 13 to 15 would attend there, as part of their development.

Once Henry had completed his spell at the academy, he was sent back to Monaco to join up with the first team and his new boss, a man who was about to have a massive impact on the career of Thierry Henry. Arsène Wenger was the coach for the principality club. He gave Henry his debut on 31 August 1994 in a 2-0 defeat to Nice. Little did Henry know then the huge influence that his manager was about to have on his career.

Wenger's first task was to move Thierry out to the wing. His thinking was that the gangly forward would have more success against full-backs than against big burly centre-backs at a time when there was still a lot of physicality in the game. Just weeks after Henry's debut, Monaco sacked Wenger and in came ex-France international, Jean Tigana, who found no need to switch Henry from out wide as he already had a goalscorer in David Trezeguet.

Henry's first two seasons in professional football yielded just six goals, but by the end of the 1996/97 season, he was beginning to find his feet and had helped his team claim the French title. His ten goals in all appearances were small in number but big in stature as teams were now beginning to appreciate the promising talent that Catalano had uncovered nearly a decade before.

Henry was voted the Young French Footballer of the Year in 1996 and, in the following campaign, having claimed a domestic title, was part of the Monaco team beaten 6-4 on aggregate by Juventus in the Champions League semi-final. The winger had found the net on seven occasions en route to the final four, but was unable to thwart the Old Lady of Turin, who at the time boasted one of the best squads in Europe.

Henry's form at club level was coming together at just the right time as France were about to host the 1998 World Cup. He made his international debut in a 2-1 win over South Africa on 11 October 1997. Aime Jacquet, the French head coach, had studied him in the Under-20s and had liked what he had seen, so had no hesitation in bringing the 20-year-old along for the ride. He made the full squad for the World Cup finals and not only did he impress, but he also finished as the team's top scorer with three goals.

Despite his touch in front of goal, Henry had to settle for a place on the bench in the World Cup final as a red card for Marcel Desailly meant that Jacquet had to make defensive changes to his team during the match. The irony here is that, at that time, the French were crying out for a striker. David Trezeguet was still a year or so away from breaking through and Stephane Guivarch was hardly pulling up any trees. He was later to be named by the *Daily Mail* as the worst player ever to have played in the Premier League. The striker's reply to such a statement was, 'It is truly a crap newspaper.'

France triumphed 3-0 over Brazil in the final, but even though Henry was an unused substitute, he had claimed the biggest prize of them all. He said, 'Jacquet told me at half-time I would come on and I immediately went to warm up. But then Marcel was sent off and the coach changed his plans. So, he didn't send me on. I was frustrated at first but then I realised I would lift the trophy and that felt good. I was only 20, it was not like it was the end of my career.'

Not only was Henry now a World Cup winner, but he was also made a Knight of the Legion of Honour. This accolade is the highest order of merit in France and was instituted by Napoleon.

With the noise beginning to grow around Henry, Juventus had been keeping tabs on the winger after their Champions League encounter in 1997. Thierry had showcased his talents in not only the biggest club competition in the world but also on the biggest stage internationally. This prompted Juve to eventually make their move for the man who had a strike rate of one goal in five at Monaco. His 20 goals in 105 appearances were a solid footing on which to base the rest of his career. His explosive pace scared the life out of defenders, so if he could begin to find the net on a regular basis, the world would really become the Frenchman's oyster.

In January 1999, Henry switched from the south of France to the north of Italy. Juventus had splashed the cool sum of around £10m on the player, who they thought would fit seamlessly into their black-and-white jigsaw. They were wrong. Henry struggled in Serie A, with tight Italian defences and sweeper systems that allowed little to no room whatsoever behind the full-backs, the area that Henry liked to attack. Reflecting on his time in Italy, Henry said, 'I wasn't enjoying myself at all. I felt like I'd lost the desire to play football.' Three goals in his first 18 matches were hardly record-breaking.

Having joined midway through the 1998/99 season, Henry returned to pre-season with mixed emotions. It was a chance to start afresh, but he was finding it tough on the pitch as he was being moved around from his position on the wing, even to the point that he found himself playing as a wing-back. Eager to impress, he just laced up his boots and got on with the task in hand. Little did anyone know at the time that Juventus had potentially one of the world's deadliest finishers on their books.

One man who did know was Henry's old boss, Arsène Wenger. The Frenchman was now the manager of Arsenal and, on a day of no match, he ventured to Italy to watch Juventus play against Udinese. Wenger had pushed Henry into a wider position during his time at Monaco due to the physicality of the game and to aid his development at a young age. He was shocked to see that not only were Juventus still using him in such a way, but he was also playing a lot deeper than how a winger would normally operate.

There was an opportunity to correct this when the pair later met on the same plane home after the match. Speaking to Arsenal.com Henry recalled:

> We were playing Udinese, they had a good team and he had come to see the game, I don't know who he came to see. I didn't know he was at the stadium in all fairness but [later] I was going back to Paris where I'm from, a suburb of Paris, and he was on the same plane that I was. We exchanged numbers and he told me, 'I don't know why you're playing on the wing,' which at the time I was not actually, I was playing as a wing-back! He said, 'You are wasting your time, I remember you as a nine. It would be great if we can meet again.' And the rest is history.

The decision for Henry to up sticks and move just seven months after arriving in Italy was an easy one. He had a huge admiration for the man who had given him his head at a very young age and showed great faith in him while coming through the Clairefontaine academy, issuing little snippets of advice along the way. Henry said:

If he was not there, I don't know if Patrick Vieira would have gone there, if Emmanuel Petit would have gone, if Nicolas Anelka would have gone there. Suddenly there was a massive following in France of Arsenal. Before, it was Leeds because Eric Cantona went there, and then Newcastle because David Ginola went there.

Nicolas Anelka had absolutely ripped it up since joining Arsenal in February 1997. The teenager from France was signed for £500,000 and made an immediate impact in the first team. He was like lightning. His finishing wasn't too bad either. In his first full season, Anelka spearheaded an attack with Dennis Bergkamp and Arsenal went on to lift a Premier League and FA Cup double, with Anelka firing in the second in a 2-0 win against Newcastle United in the Cup Final. The following season, despite Arsenal not claiming any silverware, Anelka was still named the PFA Young Player of the Year.

His stock was rising, but his performances towards the tail of the season, when Arsenal were gunning for both Premier League and FA Cup glory, dipped. Some sections of support had even started to boo the youngster amid speculation that his entourage were trying to engineer him a move away from the club. In the summer of 1999, Real Madrid came calling for the young forward, who was hot property at the time. Arsenal were unwilling at first, but when it seemed that the player could make things difficult, eventually accepted a fee of around £22m.

On 2 August 1999, Anelka packed his bags and was heading out of Highbury. Arsenal wasted no time in spending some of their new income. On that same day, Davor Suker was signed from Real Madrid for a fee of around £3.5m, although this had no relevance to the Anelka deal going the other way. Wenger had a hole in his armoury and didn't hesitate in remobilising his frontline. 'It was imperative that we strengthened the strike-force at Arsenal before the start of the season and Davor is a special talent who will help boost our campaign,' said Wenger. 'He is a quality striker with experience in the Champions League and will undoubtedly be a great asset for us.'

Still not convinced that there was enough in their arsenal to fire Arsenal to another title, Wenger sat down with the club vice-chairman and explained to David Dein that Thierry Henry must be signed at all costs. Trusting in his manager, Dein opened the chequebook for the second time in two days and paid Juventus around £11m for the Frenchman. Juve were laughing all the way to the bank as they had retrieved all the money originally paid out for the player just half a year earlier. They would be laughing on the other side of their faces a few years later.

North London now boasted a little corner of France, with Arsenal beginning to move the country's occupants across the English Channel one by one. Wenger urged the fans to get behind their new man, insisting that he was nothing like the departing Anelka:

> Thierry is much more of an extrovert than Nicolas was. He is a team player who will work hard for the whole team. He has a good spirit and a good mentality for a young player and he has gained a lot of experience already at international level. He gives you a lot of options. He can play wide or in the centre and makes anything possible when he has the ball. Thierry has pace, power, and great dribbling. I would like to move him into the centre either as the second striker or the main target man.

After all the high praise to the board and the supporters, the start of the 1999/2000 season didn't exactly get off to the dream start that both Wenger and Henry had anticipated. The manager was, however, a man of his word and moved Henry into a more advanced position, with the Dutchman, Dennis Bergkamp, asked to drop a little deeper to link up the play. After seven matches, Henry hadn't mustered a single goal. Things were beginning to lay heavy on the mind of the player, who was even thinking about asking the boss to be put back on the wing.

With confidence low, Henry began to wonder whether he was the man who could fill the boots left by his fellow countryman or whether it was another case of not being able to adapt to life in foreign country. He also had to learn to play with the magician alongside him. Bergkamp, like Henry, had faced a torrid time in Italy, in his case with Inter Milan. 'Although I arrived a world champion, I was nobody,' Henry admitted. 'And rightly so. I hadn't won anything at Arsenal, so who was I? I was just a follower at the beginning.' Fair play to him, though, as instead of throwing in the towel, he showed great character and got on with the job in hand.

Against Southampton at The Dell, Henry came off the bench for his ninth appearance and with ten minutes remaining received a slide-rule pass to his feet from Tony Adams, spun his marker and struck a fantastic curling shot into the far left corner to claim all three points for the Gunners. Prior to his match-winning strike, Henry had fluffed his lines when it seemed far easier to score than miss and, despite proving to be the match winner, *The Times* was still unconvinced and wrote: 'Henry was still snatching at chances that Anelka would have converted.' Henry had secured the win despite the tabloid comments. 'If we hadn't won the game I would have felt as if I'd let everyone down,' he said post-match. 'I looked at the clock and knew I had nine minutes to put it right.'

It was a bit of a false dawn for the striker, who instead of kicking on, struggled to find his feet again. It was really starting to get to the player, as he only managed one more goal to make it two in his first 17 matches. He spoke openly about his struggles, feeling that sharing his burden would take the weight off his shoulders rather than bottling it all up inside. 'I think the boss wants me to play in a more central role. That's fine, but it means having to learn about timing your runs in a completely different way. That takes time.' Rome wasn't built in a day, but it was well worth it once the job was completed. Thierry Henry, the striker, was certainly no exception. He was everything the Italian capital was and more.

On 28 November 1999, the worm finally turned for the forward. Derby took a shock lead at Highbury through Dean Sturridge but Henry equalised soon after. Moments after the second half had begun, he struck again to clinch a 2-1 victory. *The Times*, which hadn't been complimentary to Henry, was now beginning to understand what Wenger could see in his frontman. His goals that day were described as 'a thing of classic beauty, combining pace with sureness of touch and swiftness of eye [that] showed the Arsenal following he can finish'. They were indeed finishes of the highest order, those of an experienced centre-forward.

Henry claimed that he needed to 'rediscover the scoring instinct, that automatic reaction in front of goal'. After four difficult months in England, he conceded, 'I've literally had to go back to school and be re-taught everything about the art of striking.' After his early barren spell, David Dein admitted that it was an education for Henry, something that the player still recalls to this day. 'I remember Mr David Dein giving me a DVD of Ian Wright and he said, "Thierry, this is what you need to do." I said, "Wow! I'll try."' Wright was the club's all-time top goalscorer at the time with 185 goals in 288 matches.

Suddenly Henry's game just clicked and by the close of the season he had found the net on 26 occasions, extraordinary numbers considering his opening half of the campaign represented the form of a central defender in front of goal rather than that of a forward. He scored a cracking double in the London derby against Chelsea and a belter against Leeds United in a 2-0 victory. His boss was full of praise. 'He would not have scored that three months ago,' said Wenger. Arsenal had finished runners-up again to Manchester United and had been beaten in the UEFA Cup Final by Galatasaray, as even with the red hot form of Henry, Arsenal finished another season trophyless.

With his new position and new-found confidence, Henry headed off to Euro 2000 with the French squad, where he was yet again France's top scorer in the competition. He opened his account in the group stages with a goal in the first match against Denmark and followed it up by scoring in a 2-1 win over the Czech Republic. France progressed through the knockout phases where they beat Turkey and Portugal in the quarter-final and semi-final respectively. Henry's third goal in the tournament came in the 2-1 last-four win over the Portuguese.

On to another final. This time, it was Italy who were waiting in Rotterdam. Henry's old club-mate, David Trezeguet, scored the golden goal in extra time to ensure that France had claimed back-to-back tournament titles with a 2-1 win. Thierry was also named man of the match in an exhilarating showpiece, in which both teams showed their teeth in a gripping finale to the competition. It was already beginning to look like a good year as, by the turn of the century, Henry had completely transformed himself.

He arrived back at Arsenal's training ground in London Colney with a nice shiny European Championship medal around his neck. However, he was still waiting to taste victory champagne at his not-so-new club and would have to wait a little longer, as yet again Manchester United marched on to Premier League success in 2000/01, a third successive title. There was also another final defeat at club level, which was a bitter pill to swallow for both Henry and Arsenal as the Gunners had led Liverpool in the FA Cup Final, only for Michael Owen to strike twice in the last seven minutes to break Arsenal hearts.

On a personal level, it had been a decent campaign for Henry, who had yet again been the club's leading marksman with 22 goals. The pick of the bunch came at home against rivals United, where, with Denis Irwin seemingly too tight for Henry to do anything once he received the ball, the Frenchman, facing his own goal, just flicked up the ball, swivelled and volleyed past his fellow countryman Fabien Barthez. It was a truly outstanding finish, which was then celebrated in a style mimicking the then famous Budweiser advert where people would shout down the phone, 'Wassup!'

Henry scored on the opening day of the 2001/02 season as Arsenal put four past Middlesbrough in the north-east. He then continued to find the net with ease, including a brace against rivals Manchester United, to send Arsenal to the summit of the Premier League. By the time Gunners fans were tucking into their Christmas Day turkey, Henry had bagged an impressive 15 goals in the league. His form continued well into the new year, including a brace at Fulham. United were hot on Arsenal's heels, but were starting to slip away right at the business end when it really mattered.

Having lost the FA Cup Final in 2001 in dramatic fashion, Arsenal were keen to ensure that this time around there wouldn't be a repeat in Cardiff, this time running out 2-0 winners over Chelsea. Henry had finally won his first trophy as an Arsenal player and was looking to add to that just a few days later when they headed to Old Trafford, with United clinging on to their tails and the Gunners looking to win the title for the first time in four years. Henry was injured for the trip but was part of the travelling party, who really did party all the way back down the M1 after a Sylvain Wiltord goal put paid to the Red Devils' title challenge and brought Henry and co a league and cup double.

Sam Carney, writing for *These Football Times*, summed up the double-winning team beautifully:

> Perhaps it's understandable why the brilliance of this Arsenal crop has been superseded in the collective mind. But at the time, it seemed as if they'd never fail to win again. No matter what Manchester United, Liverpool, Newcastle, Leeds threw at them, they'd inevitably come up with an answer. And Arsenal were so good that if the league's top scorer Henry didn't get you, one of Pires, Wiltord, Ljungberg, Kanu or Bergkamp would.

That Arsenal team of 2001/02 hold the current record for having scored in every match they played that season. Henry chipped in with 32 goals across all competitions, a feat he would achieve again the following season as Arsenal lost their grip on the title but reclaimed the FA Cup with a win over Southampton. By now, the trademark style of Henry was beginning to seem familiar in the form of him starting his position out on the left flank before cutting inside and bending the ball perfectly into the far corner. His partnership down that side with fellow Frenchman Robert Pires was very special. You know it's coming, but just try to stop it. If one player went down the outside, the other would go inside. This made it so difficult for defenders, who often wouldn't know whether to stick or twist.

Henry opened his account again as ten-man Arsenal beat Everton during the curtain-raiser at Highbury in 2003/04. He then followed that up by scoring goals against Middlesbrough and Aston Villa before a 0-0 draw at Old Trafford halted Arsenal's near-perfect start to the campaign. The finale of the match in Manchester drew comparisons with the 'Battle of Old Trafford' in 1991. Both teams were deducted points for a brawl that occurred after a bad tackle saw both sets of players pile in for a tussle. A red card for Patrick Vieira and a missed penalty in injury time from Ruud Van Nistelrooy amplified the red hot atmosphere and animosity between the two sets of players. Arsenal players didn't know it yet, but that penalty miss was to prove vital in their season as they continued on their way towards another title push.

Henry continued his hot streak with a brace against Wolves and a penalty in the home match against Middlesbrough, but he saved his best goal of the campaign, and arguably one of the most important in his Arsenal career, for Liverpool. A week before this, he had scored a 25-yard fizzer past Barthez in a 1-1 draw with United, so he was in decent nick at the time. Arsenal weren't only looking strong at the top of the table, but coming into April, were still to taste defeat in the league.

Liverpool started brightly and opened the scoring after five minutes when Sami Hyypiä headed the visitors in front. Henry equalised soon after, but just before the interval, Michael Owen was the scourge of Arsenal once again. The Gunners regrouped and, within four minutes of the second half getting under way, found the net twice in a minute to turn the game on its head. Robert Pires struck to level proceedings before a wonder goal from Thierry lifted the roof off the North Bank.

He picked up the loose ball deep inside the Liverpool half and ran at Didi Hamann, who was powerless as he just glided past him. Then, with a wall of Liverpool white in front of him,

Lionel Messi facing three men. Nothing unusual for the Argentinian wizard.

Thierry Henry adding to his record-breaking haul for Arsenal.

Johan Cruyff gliding past an opponent in a European Cup match for Ajax.

Ronaldo executing his trademark finish by rounding the goalkeeper in a European Cup Winners' Cup match.

A cheeky selfie from Totti after his equaliser in the Rome derby.

Gazza in full flight was a beautiful sight.

Captain Marvel in action during the 1990 FA Cup Final against Crystal Palace. Robson would lift the trophy in the replay.

A divisive character but my word what a player. Maradona was pure box office. Napoli fans worship him after his title heroics.

Eric Cantona scoring his second goal in the 1994 FA Cup Final. Second penalty, same outcome.

You can kiss it now Stevie, you deserve it. Gerrard put in a heroic performance to help Liverpool secure the 2005 Champions League.

Cristiano Ronaldo scoring one of the most outrageous headers you will ever see, jumping around 2.4 metres high.

Pele will always be revered as one of the greatestgoal scorers to ever grace the field. He was dynamite for Santos.

Puskas (10) celebrates as his strike finds the net as Hungary dismantle the Three Lions at Wembley.

Zidane's glancing header helps France to secure the 1998 World Cup.

the Frenchman just coaxed Jamie Carragher half a yard towards him and, in that split second, played the ball from his right foot to his left, danced past the static backline and side-footed the ball past the keeper into the far left-hand corner. It was so elegant but yet executed at such pace. Henry then clinched the match ball with a hat-trick to finish off the 4-2 win.

Arsène Wenger, speaking to *The Independent*, said, 'It just looked as if he decided to score. He made it look simple when you know at this level how difficult it is to go past players and score.' Henry simply said, 'It was something I did on the spur of the moment.' The win was pivotal in Arsenal's quest for the title and it put them seven points clear at the top of the table. Both managers that day had high praise for the Gunners in their post-match interviews with BBC Sport, with Wenger commenting, 'I felt the way they responded was absolutely magnificent', and opposition boss Gérard Houllier saying, 'I thought Arsenal were stunning in the second half.'

Arsenal did go on to clinch the title that season and did it without losing a single league match. The 'Invincibles' of 2003/04 will take some beating, as history would suggest going a season unbeaten is virtually unheard of at elite level. Thierry Henry chipped in with another 39 goals as he rightly received the PFA Players' Player of the Year award and the Football Writers' Association award. His impressive talent in finding the net meant that he also scooped the European Golden Shoe.

However, what goes up must eventually come back down. Jose Mourinho had arrived in West London and was spraying his chairman's money around like a Formula 1 driver with the champagne on the winner's podium. Arsenal were unable to regain their crown in 2004/05, despite Henry again breaking the 30-goal barrier. Arsenal did manage to claim the 2005 FA Cup, but Henry was sidelined for the showpiece. On the final day of the 2005/06 season, Henry bagged a hat-trick against

Wigan Athletic in the last match to be staged at Highbury, with Arsenal about to move into their brand-new stadium in the summer.

Unlike Chelsea, Arsenal were now a team in transition. The Invincibles were an ageing squad that was now beginning to break up. Patrick Vieira was heading out the door, which meant that Henry was now given the captain's armband. It was a move that was frowned upon in some quarters, even by sections of the home support, with Arsenalnewsreview.co.uk saying:

> Thierry Henry is the Mahatma Gandhi of football, an apostle of peace, brotherhood and non-violence. With him, it's a love-in: I'm a nice guy, I won't kick you, so don't kick me. If I knock you down, I'll pick you up and give you a kiss. Yes, he is a huge star and legend and an astonishing goal scorer. But he is not a captain and never will be. I said that last season when he sulked after Vieira was sold and I'm saying it again now.

On 17 October 2005, Henry broke Ian Wright's goalscoring record with a brace in a Champions League match against Sparta Prague. It was at the beginning of the competition in which the Gunners would eventually reach the final, staged in Henry's homeland. He had gained revenge on his old club Juventus by dumping them out in the quarter-finals of the Champions League as well as beating Real Madrid and Villareal on their way to a showdown with Barcelona. Henry was in imperious form throughout the competition, but was unable to prevent the Catalans lifting the trophy in Paris after a 2-1 defeat. Jens Lehman, Arsenal's keeper, had seen red after 18 minutes and, even after taking the lead through Sol Campbell, Henry was severely hamstrung in the final, with

Arsenal having to play nearly 70 minutes a man down. He had, however, caught the eye of the opposition, who were quite keen on bringing the forward over to Spain.

Arsenal's move to their new stadium in 2006 wasn't the smoothest for Henry, as against a backdrop of contract talk, injuries curtailed his 2006/07 campaign. By the time the Frenchman had finally freed himself from the brand-new Emirates Stadium physio room, Barcelona had beaten down the door with a £22m pound offer. There was also unrest at that time between the board and David Dein, with speculation mounting around Wenger's future also. Henry knew this was the right time to leave the club, albeit with a heavy heart. 'I always said that if I ever left Arsenal it would be to play for Barcelona,' he said when quizzed about the move.

It was a sad day for Gunners fans. Tom Pheby, host of the 'It's an Arsenal Thing' podcast, reflected on Thierry's time in north London:

Thierry Henry was touted as a direct replacement for Nicholas Anelka when he arrived at Highbury in 1999, but his former manager, Arsène Wenger, had originally planned to establish the pair as a formidable strike partnership based on their athleticism and speed. Henry was seen as a winger at his previous club Juventus. The youngster had hardly set the world alight having registered 23 goals in 121 appearances in Italy and Monaco yet Wenger saw something special in a player that was destined to become an Arsenal legend and one of the finest players the Premier League has ever seen.

The Arsenal manager was handsomely repaid for his modest outlay of £11m as Henry delivered 26 goals in his debut season but Henry was more than just a goal machine. He was an artist, blessed with pace, vision, balance, football intelligence and fabulous technical ability. Henry was the final piece of the Arsenal puzzle which consisted of world-class players that had a wealth artistry and the necessary resilience to win. He was surrounded by the sublime talents of Dennis Bergkamp, Patrick Vieira, Robert Pires and Freddie Ljungberg and goals were easy for the Frenchman to come by.

From the polished but ordinary looking flick or tap in, to the spectacular looking volley or mesmerising solo goal, Henry had it all in his locker plus that '*Catonaesque*' arrogance that only world-class players are entitled to. It's hard to imagine seeing the likes of another Henry, he was unique and the ultimate striker for the modern game, a mobile, agile player that could happily go out wide or drift inside in the more traditional number 9 role.

In February 2020 *FourFourTwo* magazine stated:

No one assisted more in a season. No one has terrorised defenders with such a combination of bewitching grace and phenomenal power. He remains Arsenal's highest goalscorer with 228 goals in all competitions. He's number one in the club's official top 50 players and was inducted to the Premier League hall of fame in 2021.

So, Thierry Henry left Arsenal as a legend and their highest-ever scorer. Some honours after only eight seasons at the club. But now it was time for him to shine in Barcelona. Frank Rijkaard played Henry in a wider role than he was used to at

Arsenal, but it didn't take long for him to get off the mark, scoring his first goal for his new club on 19 September 2007 in a Champions League match against Lyon. Just ten days later, he was getting back on the bus with the match ball as he scored an impressive hat-trick in a 4-1 win over Levante. His debut season with the Catalans was bordering on average, though, as a goal return of just 19 meant that he hadn't hit the spectacular heights he had reached with Arsenal. It was a weird period with Barcelona as the coach was eventually relieved of his duties after a poor season in which they had failed to claim any silverware. Frank Rijkaard was relieved of his duties and reserve coach Pep Guardiola was handed the reins.

Guardiola had a shaky start to life in the hotseat, but soon turned things around. He married the front three of Henry, Eto'o and Messi together to form an unbelievable attack. The trio amassed over 100 goals in the 2008/09 season, with Henry chipping in with 26 plus ten assists in a campaign that not only brought domestic glory but also success on the European stage. Barcelona walked La Liga, claiming the title with an eight-point gap over their rivals in Madrid. They also battered Athletic Bilbao in the final of the Copa del Rey in an impressive 4-1 victory, but their crowning glory was the Champions League final win over Manchester United in 2009.

United had already claimed a Premier League and Champions League double the year before and were looking to do it again in Rome. Barcelona, though, were on another footballing planet that year. I still believe that the Barcelona team from 2008 to 2012 is the greatest club side that's ever played the game. Eto'o and Messi scored for the Catalans in a 2-0 win, but Henry was now part of a Champions League-winning team. He almost never played, though. His injuries were now becoming a little more frequent as he reached the conclusion of his career, but there was no way he was missing this one for anything.

Henry told *Mundo Deportivo* after the celebrations:

> I have lost count of the games I played injured, but that final was very special to me. People don't know, but it was my daughter's birthday and I had never won the Champions League as everyone knows. I had come to compete, we were going to win the six cups as the song says and I couldn't bend my knee and I couldn't run well, but I had to play, as simple as that. What if I was fine? I do not think so. What if I helped? I hope I did, but I was there. I played as much as I could and lied, because they asked me if I was okay and I said yes, of course I did. I'm never going to say I'm not okay, that's the way it is.

Unfortunately for Henry, his injuries did finally catch up with him as a staggered start to the 2009/10 season saw him in and out of the team. Also, the emergence of Pedro wasn't helping the ageing star, but he battled through lack of fitness and form to complete his third season in Spain and help land a sextuple of trophies in a calendar year. Not only had Barcelona won the treble in the previous campaign, but the following year they added the UEFA Super Cup, Supercopa de España, FIFA World Club Cup, and then finally reclaimed the La Liga title in May 2010.

Henry had managed just four goals in 32 matches and, with a crop of exciting youngsters coming through at the club, Guardiola decided to free the Frenchman from his wage bill. On returning from the 2010 World Cup, Henry would soon find himself heading to a completely different continent as his next destination was to be North America and the MLS. His time in Barcelona had been relatively short but most definitely sweet, finding the net on 49 occasions in 121 matches.

The US would be the home for Henry for nearly five years, but, try as he might, he just couldn't quite get the New York Red Bulls to the finals. He could still find the net, even if that explosive pace that had propelled him to the top of his game had started to evaporate. While he was unable to secure any silverware in the MLS, he did manage an impressive 52 goals in 132 appearances for the franchise.

Henry was back training with his beloved Arsenal during the MLS off-season and, in January 2012, signed a two-month deal with the club, meaning that Thierry could play in the FA Cup tie at home to Leeds United. This sparked fan frenzy, as once again the Emirates was going to host their star. With the tie poised at 0-0, Wenger rolled the dice and Henry entered the fray to score a trademark goal from the left flank, just like in his Highbury glory days, to seal a 1-0 win. As if that wasn't enough for the fans, who were beside themselves at their hero returning not only to play, but also to score, Henry would again score the winner in his final appearance before signing off, in a 2-1 stoppage-time win over Sunderland.

Former Arsenal striker Alan Smith commented on Henry: 'I have to say I haven't seen a player like him. He's an athlete with great technical ability and a tremendous desire to be the best.' Henry returned to the MLS briefly, but soon retired from playing in 2014. Arsenal's website, Arsenal.com, wrote some words on the player's departure the first time around, but they were echoed after his fleeting appearance in the winter of 2012:

> As someone who has written more words in tribute to Thierry Henry than probably anyone else, it is difficult to sum it all up for one final time. Arsenal. com has waxed lyrical perennially in our Player of

the Season award and, in October 2005, all prayed at the altar of Henry 186 when he broke the Club's goalscoring record. It goes without saying Thierry is one of the finest players to wear an Arsenal shirt. He arrived as perhaps an 'ugly duckling', out of favour for France and Juventus. But he became the most elegant swan under Wenger's protective wing.

Goalscorer, penalty taker, captain, talisman, assist maker, free kick taker, corner taker – those were his responsibilities. Speed, strength, accuracy, precision, technique, mental tenacity – those were his qualities. Charismatic, emotional, enigmatic, talkative, open – that was his character.

The 'ugly duckling's' record in club football reads 366 goals scored in 813 appearances. His international numbers are also up there alongside the very best. Despite his French team never really kicking on after the two opening tournament successes they achieved in 1998 and 2000, Henry found the net on 51 occasions in over 100 matches for the national team. He was also part of the squad that reached the World Cup final in 2006 but lost on penalties to Italy after Zinedine Zidane had been given his marching orders for a headbutt on Marco Materazzi.

Henry was a master at improvisation. As well as his trademark finish, he would also boast the no-look pass in his locker, something he liked to wheel out on many occasions. He would sometimes look uninterested in matches and then, bang, would pull a rabbit out of the hat and it would be over. Maybe it's a French thing. Cantona had it, David Ginola and Laurent Robert had it, as did many other players from France from an earlier era.

In a match against Charlton Athletic in the 2004/05 season, Jose Reyes played a short pass to Henry, who was facing away from goal on the corner of the six-yard box. With Charlton defender Jonathon Fortune pinned tight against his back, it looked a certainty that Henry would lay the ball back to either Reyes or the onward advancing Dennis Bergkamp. Feeling the defender pressed behind him, Henry slightly leaned forward, lifting the defender just enough from the floor to nonchalantly back-heel the ball past both player and goalkeeper. It was quite an extraordinary finish from a player who around that time could have won the Grand National, had he entered it. BBC Sport described it as a 'sizzling effort', which we can't deny, as Henry's form around this period of his career was as hot as the mid-day sun.

Paul Merson said, 'Thierry Henry would play for Arsenal like he was a 20-year-old playing in an Under-12 league, and I've never seen that before.' Henry was a record breaker and, in his pomp, one of the best finishers on the planet. He's now commemorated in statue form outside the Emirates Stadium. Immortalised in bronze where he made others look like mere mortals. Va Va Voom, Titi.

10

Francesco Totti

'The reason I've got so much respect for him is
because he's got all the pressure on his shoulders in
Rome. He's the king of Rome.' – **Steven Gerrard**

ROME. THE capital city of Italy. Home of the Colosseum, the Spanish Steps, the Vatican, the Trevi Fountain and crazy moped drivers who are clearly in more of a rush than you are. The Colosseum is arguably Rome's most famous landmark and used to be home to around 80,000 spectators, cramming into the concrete theatre to watch gladiators do battle. Nowadays it's the Stadio Olimpico that hosts the gladiator-like performances, most notably from Roma's favourite son, Francesco Totti, L'Ottavo Re di Roma (The Eighth King of Rome).

Both Lazio and Roma share the stadium and have done since the 1953/54 season. Totti, who spent his whole career at Roma, was born in the city and very nearly signed for rivals Lazio while plying his trade in youth football. 'I was eight years old, I played at AS Lodigiani. Milan and Lazio had supervised me and wanted me. Lazio even offered money. My mother and grandfather loved Lazio, my family hoped that I would go, except my father who was a big fan of Roma. An agreement was close,' said Totti, whose patience was finally rewarded with a call from Roma.

'Lodigiani,' remembers Gildo Giannini, who was then in charge of the Giallorosso youth system, 'had already promised Totti to Lazio, but his mum Fiorella came to me demanding that Roma took him. I didn't need much convincing – we already knew about him – and I got Lodigiani to sell him to us.'

As a youngster, Totti had no problems playing with the bigger boys in the street. 'I was also a bit of a crook,' recalled Totti. 'I used to steal footballs. In the summer we would play all afternoon until sunset. Often, before going home, I took the ball, played it cool, and took off. I had a real collection. I gave them all back in the end. I wasn't the best at school, but I always paid attention and was well behaved, because of Mama.'

Totti had spent three seasons in the youth team at Roma before opportunity knocked and he found himself on the bench as a tender 16-year-old lad. Roma's league campaign was nothing short of a disaster as they found themselves in mid-table. Totti was a substitute in a 2-0 away victory over Brescia on 28 March 1993. Coach Vujadin Boskov's decision to call upon the teen started a love affair with the locals that I don't think will ever be forgotten. Totti will certainly never forget either. 'When the gaffer told me to warm up, I thought he was talking to Roberto Muzzi sat next to me,' Totti later recalled of his debut. 'As it turned out, he had me in mind! I couldn't believe it, the emotions I felt were indescribable.' He added, 'I warmed up for about ten seconds. I only touched the ball a couple of times – I was too excited and happy!'

Roma failed to win any of their last nine league matches, with Totti only making a single appearance in that time. That summer, coach Boskov was replaced by Carlo Mazzone. The new man at the helm could see that he had a Rolls-Royce of a player on his hands and didn't hesitate in selecting him for the first team. Totti was deployed behind the centre-forward, playing a little bit deeper between midfield and attack. This allowed him plenty of time to get on the ball and grow in confidence with each match.

Totti would have to wait for his first goal, finally notching at the 13th time of asking in a 1-1 draw with Foggia on the opening day of the season, 14 September 1994. The ball was hoisted into the Foggia penalty area by Swedish midfielder Jonas Thern, Daniel Fonseca, holding off his marker, nodded the ball back towards the edge of the penalty area. Totti, who was wearing the No. 9 shirt, raced on to the loose ball and lashed his shot into the bottom corner with his left foot. This was just weeks before his 18th birthday. He had taken his chance in the season's curtain-raiser due to an illness to Abel Balbo. In those days, the shirt numbers were still issued from 1 to 11, based on who was starting in which position. Guiseppe Gianni and Daniel Fonseca were already custodians of 10 and 11 respectively, leaving Totti to claim an unusual No. 9. Unusual in a sense that he would be made famous by the double digits that were soon to adorn his back.

A crowd of 58,797 saw Totti's first strike for the Giallorosso, although one 'fan' wasn't entirely impressed with the team's performance. President Franco Sensi was scathing in his post-match comments after his new coach could only steer Roma to an opening-day stalemate. 'You can't draw this sort of game. I am not pleased at all,' quipped Sensi. It was a comment that was not lost on his coach, who responded by trying to deflect the attention away from both himself and his new employer. 'The president is a fan, and fans make observations like this. Above all, it's those who ask him the questions that are wrong,' said Mazzone.

With belief now beginning to show in Francesco's play, he added to his tally just three weeks later with a goal coming in a Coppa Italia tie against Fiorenzuola, Roma running out eventual winners, 2-1. The campaign was a huge improvement for both club and player as Roma would end their 1994/95 season in fifth spot, thus qualifying for a UEFA Cup berth. Totti had racked up seven goals in 24 appearances across all competitions.

European football was now on the horizon for the youngster, a chance to experience even more footballing variety with a host of foreign opponents now to contend with. Domestically, though, Roma were much of a muchness under Mazzone with another fifth-place finish, but again achieving a UEFA Cup place.

Meanwhile, the back of the net was proving harder to find for Totti, who wouldn't pick up his first goal bonus of the season until the end of November, when he finally broke his duck in a 2-1 home win against Bari. He would only add one more goal to his Serie A tally that season, equalising in the return fixture at Bari to help Roma on their way to a 2-1 win. The I Galletti must have been sick of the sight of Totti that year.

A little flirt with European competition had whetted Totti's appetite. His first goal came in the second-round demolition of Belgium's Eendracht Aalst. Roma made light work of their Flemish counterparts and led 4-0 after the first leg. A 0-0 draw in the return was enough to send them to round three, where they would face Danish opposition in the shape of Brøndby. Roma were caught short in the first leg and were trailing 2-1 at the halfway stage in the tie, but second-leg goals from Totti, Balbo and Carboni ensured that they went through to the final eight of the competition.

Slavia Prague from the Czech Republic lay in wait. A tricky tie in Prague meant that Roma had it all to do again back in the Stadio Olimpico, needing to come back from a 2-0 deficit after the first leg. However, the Romans couldn't quite muster a comeback of biblical proportions and crashed out on away goals after a mammoth effort to win 3-1. Carlo Mazzone paid the price for ending the campaign in an uninspiring fashion and was replaced in the summer of 1996 by Argentine coach, Carlos Bianchi.

Unfortunately for Totti and Roma, the following campaign didn't provide much in any way, shape or form. After an early exit from both the Coppa Italia and the UEFA Cup, and languishing in the bottom half of the league table, Sensi wasted no time in pushing the button after a 2-1 defeat away at Cagliari on 6 April 1997. Bianchi was gone. His tenure at the club had been short but also strained, as was his relationship with the club president as well as Totti, who was at breaking point.

Totti had been in and out of the team during the season and was struggling to find any kind of form due to a stop-start campaign. 'The 1996/97 season was really a very difficult time for me,' he admitted. 'I was very close to Sampdoria, but a week before the deal took place, it had changed a lot. I am on the list of Roma youth teams participating in the international friendlies including many other tough clubs like Ajax, Mönchengladbach and playing well.'

Totti was referring to mini tournament that had been arranged by one of Roma's sponsors in February 1997, which included teams from the Netherlands and Germany. Totti was still eligible to compete in this youth set-up and was sent for experience and minutes by his coach. The format consisted of three matches, each lasting 45 minutes. They were scheduled as follows: Ajax v Borussia at 19:30; Roma v Borussia at 20:30; Roma v Ajax at 21:30. Before that, however, the event kicked off at 18:15 with an exhibition involving Roma youth teams, which saw a 13-year-old

Daniele De Rossi make his debut on the Olimpico pitch, playing two 20-minute halves.

Roma won both their matches, beating Ajax 2-1 and Mönchengladbach 3-0, with Totti scoring in both matches. This meant that Roma had topped the mini table and lifted the invitational Torneo Città di Roma trophy. It wasn't all champagne and smiles for Francesco, though. The rumours of his supposed departure had been circulating prior to kick-off and some of the fans inside the stadium voiced their discontent at the young player. How dare he want to break away from their beloved Rome?

Reporting for *La Gazzetta dello Sport*, Ruggiero Palombo wrote:

> Totti, who had previously been jeered in the same way as [Francesco] Statuto (the Romans in Rome aren't so well-loved these days), first sparked the move for Roma's second goal (lovely play involving Totti, Moriero and Delvecchio) with a pass that was the stuff of champions. He finished off the humiliating 3-0 win with a solo effort culminating in a Maradona-esque lob.

Palombo also commented that Totti was jeered before the tournament kicked off. This was most likely due to the Giallorossis' poor run of form and the rumours that the young talent was close to joining Paolo Mantovani's Sampdoria. However, jeers soon turned to cheers after Totti's carnival football. The move away was never going to materialise as, behind the scenes, Sensi had already blocked the move and told Bianchi in no uncertain terms that he must nurture the precocious talent at his disposal and find a way for him to blossom. Ultimately, Bianchi couldn't find a way and he was sent packing by the powers that be. Sensi didn't have to look too far for his new man. In fact, he was right under his nose, at neighbours Lazio.

Zdenek Zeman had spent all his years coaching in Italy despite hailing from the Czech Republic, which was then part of Czechoslovakia. Totti had looked on with great interest as Zeman brought through a raft of youngsters into the Lazio first team, most notably Alessandro Nesta. One of the first actions of Zeman was to move Totti out to a left-wing/inside-forward position. His reasoning was that he could exploit more space to attack and therefore create more one-on-one situations. Another advantage of Totti playing from the left was that he could cut inside on to his favoured right foot to get shots away.

Another result of Zeman's arrival was Totti being handed the No. 10 shirt. All of a sudden, the player was going from a coach who didn't really fancy him to one who showed that he totally believed in him. Roma then switched from their rigid style of 4-4-2 and played a more slick, dynamic 4-3-3. It was during this time of change that Totti enjoyed his most prosperous campaign to date, netting on 14 occasions during the 1997/98 season. His brace against Bari in a 3-1 away win was a particular highlight. The first goal was a rocket of a free kick that flew past the goalkeeper into his bottom right-hand corner. The second, and the pick of the two, was from a cross from the right-hand side, which he volleyed into the top corner. Despite his efforts in front of goal, Roma were still miles away from their rivals in Serie A.

Totti trumped his own goal tally by scoring 16 the following season, as well as being handed the captain's armband at the tender age of 22. Life was beginning to change quickly for the home-grown talent, who was now leading his boyhood team out on to the pitch at the Stadio Olimpico.

In November 1998, Totti scored his first goal in a Rome derby, which really ignited the love affair with the natives. Trailing Lazio 3-1 with just 12 minutes remaining, Totti set up Eusebio Di Francesco to make it 3-2 before etching himself into the hearts of all Roma fans by scoring the equaliser with less than ten minutes to go. By the time the Lazio goalkeeper was picking the ball out of his net, Totti was already behind the advertising hoardings with his shirt in hand, bowing to the throngs of people celebrating in the Curva Sud.

Even with the heroics of the boy wonder, Roma could only manage consecutive sixth-place finishes in 1998/99 and 1999/2000. Zeman was therefore relieved of his duties and former AC Milan supremo, Fabio Capello, was installed as the new head coach. Capello could sense that something was bubbling in Rome, with the club looking to build around the talent of their talisman. Again, Totti's position on the field was switched, this time into a more central role behind the front two. He was now charged with supplying the bullets as well as finding the net himself.

Totti opened his account on matchday one of the new campaign, helping himself to a goal against Bologna. His link-up play with Vincenzo Montella and Gabriel Batistuta was beginning to prosper as, by Christmas, Roma were top of the pile. It was a position they would hold for the entire campaign, eventually lifting their third-ever Serie A title, Totti's first. The team from the capital managed to hold off the juggernaut from Turin, claiming the championship by just a two-point margin over Juventus. Personal accolades followed as the playmaker was awarded the Italian Footballer of the Year award. He was also nominated for the Ballon d'Or for the first time in his career. Totti said, 'To claim even one Scudetto for your childhood team, in the city where you were born, is special.' Totti had said before that winning a Scudetto in Rome is worth ten in any other city.

Despite Roma lifting the Supercoppa Italiana the following campaign, they didn't managed to retain the league title, agonisingly missing out by a single point as Juve were back to their formidable best. Totti was now beginning to score consistently, but the fragilities of the team around him were to hold back the player who was seemingly desperate for more silverware in his own city. He was going to have to get used to a silver medal spot on the podium as Roma weren't only runners-up in the league in 2001/02 but also again in 2003/04, 2005/06, 2006/07 and 2007/08. As if this wasn't bad enough for Totti and the supporters, Roma also fell short in the Coppa Italia Final in 2002/03, 2004/05 and 2005/06, before winning it back to back in 2006/07 and 2007/08.

Fabio Capello was now long gone and Luciano Spalletti was giving out the orders. Another new coach meant that there was another new position for Totti, who was now being asked to operate alone in a central striking role. It was during this switch that he scored his 107th league goal for the club, making him the highest scorer in Roma's history. He was now beginning to revel in the role and scored one of his most iconic goals with a superb chip past Julio Cesar in the 2005/06 campaign. It was to be a trademark goal as more of this ilk followed.

In 2006, Totti was part of the Italian squad that lifted the World Cup in Germany, beating France in a penalty shoot-out. He had chipped in with goals along the way, having arrived at the tournament after having had a metal plate inserted in his foot, which nearly ruled him out completely. He ended the competition with the joint-highest number of assists as well as scoring the winning goal in injury time in the last 16 via the penalty spot. His contributions were recognised when he was named in the 23-man All Star team. He soon retired from the international scene, though, with his real love Roma taking up all his attention.

Totti's 80 goals in that four-year period between 2004–08 were pivotal in a team competing at the top of the table and in the cup competitions. In 2007/08, he helped Roma to within a whisker of a historic treble, winning both domestic cups but missing out on the Serie A title by just three points. It was another oh so close moment that was becoming a theme for the striker, domestically anyway. The cup successes were sweet, but it was the title that was the utopia that Totti was reaching for.

In January 2008, on the way to the Coppa Italia final, Totti notched his 200th goal for the club in a 4-0 win over Torino. The following month, he broke Roma's record for league appearances, reaching 386 in the colours of his beloved team. In March, on his 500th overall appearance, Totti scored a penalty in a 2-0 away win at Napoli. His records would count for nothing, however, as at the tail end of the campaign, a torn ACL meant that he would miss out on winning the Coppa Italia. Nevertheless, he was urged to lift the trophy by his team-mates, becoming Roma's most successful captain of all time with five trophy wins.

Totti wasn't able to regain his fitness and form until the end of the 2010/11 season as the coach, Claudio Ranieri, decided that with Totti struggling to find any real rhythm after his injury, he would have to play second fiddle to a younger crop of strikers. This backfired on the coach, who was eventually replaced by Vincenzo Montella, who immediately recalled Totti to kick-start the club's failing season. Totti scored 12 goals in his final 13 matches of that season, but Roma could only manage a sixth-place finish.

Montella had only been called in for a short-term fix and was soon shown the door as not only did the coach change in Rome but the club's owners did too. American owners, headed up by Thomas Di Benedetto, were now running the show and brought over Luis Enrique from Barcelona's B team. This was to help bring a little style to a team that had ultimately reverted to the Italian throwback position of sitting behind the ball for 90 minutes without any real attacking threat.

Another new man at the helm and, yep you guessed it, another position for Totti to revel in. This time, however, and with the years now beginning to catch up with him, he was slotted in as a playmaker. The annual early season struggle for Roma was compounded when Totti was injured in the autumn and missed large chunks of an otherwise uninspiring campaign, which finished with the club floundering in seventh spot and Enrique winging his way back to Catalonia.

Zdenek Zeman was reappointed, 13 years after his previous stint in charge, and like day following night he changed Totti's position, this time back to the inside-left role that he had mastered over a decade before. Unfortunately for Zeman, and with Totti approaching his 36th birthday, neither the coach nor player could replicate the years gone past and, by the close of the 2012/13 season, Zeman again found himself out of a job. Totti had contributed with 12 goals, but it wasn't enough for a team that still seemed so reliant on a player who was in the twilight of his career.

Rudi Garcia replaced the departing Zeman, and guess what? Totti was now playing as a false 9. Garcia's style of play seemed to suit Roma, though, as they immediately began to improve domestically. They finished in a respectable second place in 2013/14, but were so far behind Juve that they needed binoculars to see them in the distance, finishing a whopping 17 points adrift. Then 2014/15 was identical, as again a 17-point deficit was the difference between the team from the capital and the Old Lady of Turin. Totti had only managed 15 goals in two seasons as the sands of time were beginning to drain away for a player who was still so heavily tasked with firing the club to glory. His game time was beginning to become limited in a bid to keep him fresh and extend whatever shelf life he might have left.

In January 2015, Roma trailed 2-0 in the derby. Totti headed in a goal to reduce the arrears before scoring from a tight angle only to not level the match but also to become the top goalscorer in Rome derby history. As if that wasn't enough, he raced behind the goal, grabbed a mobile phone and took a selfie with his fans in the background. Moments like this were what made those supporters worship the ground on which he walked.

It was revealed on the club's website exactly how the celebration unfolded and how the player executed it as beautifully as the equaliser itself. Asroma.com said:

> Totti had come up with the idea for a special celebration should he score a goal in the city derby against local Serie A rival Lazio, according to Sean Foley, who runs the club's digital and social initiatives. From there, the plan was simple: Plant an Iphone6 with goalkeepers coach Guido Nanni, who would be easy for Totti to find should he deliver a score.

And deliver Totti did. His second goal of this Sunday night levelled the match at 2-2 and was a flying volley. Foley told Mashable the following day that the goal celebration was Totti's idea, but manifested through a 'coordinated effort' between the player, the club's digital operatives and, of course, goalkeeping coach Nanni, who held the crucial job of handling Totti the phone.

But the spirit of the celebration was born in 2012, when an American named James Pallotta became AS Roma's president after buying the club. Chief among Pallotta's immediate priorities was: 'Making AS Roma more effective and nimble in a world where soccer fans increasingly interact with and read about their favourite teams and players online.' As Totti would later tell it, a thousand different ideas were running through his head, but one stood out above the rest. He resolved to score and take a selfie in front of the Stadio Olimpico's Curva Sud, capturing the jubilation of Roma's supporters behind him. 'I gave my phone to goalkeeping coach Guido Nanni,' he explained. 'I asked him to take it with him when he went out to the pitch.'

Third time lucky maybe for Garcia and co in the league? No, this time they finished even further adrift after only managing a third-place spot in 2015/16. By now, Totti was reduced to the role of super sub and, as you would expect, revelled in the role bestowed upon him. In April 2016, with Roma trailing to Torino and just two minutes remaining, substitute Totti scored from the penalty spot and then netted the winner deep into injury time. His final six matches of the campaign as a substitute yielded four goals, prompting Roma to extend his contract again for another year, except this time it was going to be the player's last. 'I really wanted this contract, it represents the realisation of my dream,' Totti told asroma. com. 'I always wanted to end my career having only worn one shirt – the Roma one. After speaking with the president, I am even more convinced that, working together, we can achieve great things.'

On his first appearance in the 2016/17 season, with Roma trailing 2-1 to Sampdoria, Totti set up Edin Dzeko to equalise, before slotting home himself to turn the match on its head and win 3-2. The pair linked up superbly during the season, with Dzeko notching 39 times as Roma again battled with Juventus for Italian supremacy. Totti scored the last of his 307 goals for the club in a Coppa Italia win over Cesena, but it wasn't enough, as again Roma played second fiddle to Juve.

Scudetto in 2001 aside, Totti was nearly always the bridesmaid in domestic football, something that rankled with the player as he bowed out in the summer of 2017. 'They call me crazy and can't accept it,' wrote Totti in his book, *Gladiator*, 'Because obviously the World Cup is the pinnacle of any career, but this is more the case for those who win titles every year, like Juventus players, than for those who almost never win. For us, the best thing is the Scudetto, and my biggest gripe is not having won at least a second.'

As the curtain came down on the king of Rome, the plaudits began to flood in, with compliments being showered from both home and abroad. Carlo Ancelotti led the way: 'Totti is immortal and he is a symbol of our sport. I only regret not having worked with him A great player! What a phenomenon.'

11

The Nearly Men

Adverb: Nearly – very close to; almost

THERE HAVE been some top-quality players mentioned in this book, ranging from the more iconic to those that share the cult hero tag. Having explored many other avenues, I've stumbled across others who should be mentioned in despatches and given their time in the sun. There are also players who could arguably be given their own chapter, depending on your team's persuasion, of course. Nonetheless, they've made the cut through the tradesman's entrance, so let's give them the credit they truly deserve.

> *'I told myself before the game, he's made of skin and bones just like everyone else, but I was wrong.' – TARCISIO BURGNICH, WHO MARKED PELÉ IN The 1970 WORLD CUP FINAL*

'If they are good enough, they are old enough,' an old adage from then Manchester United manager Sir Matt Busby. Having nurtured a young group of talent who were to be named 'The

Busby Babes', Sir Matt seemed to know a thing or two about adolescent footballers and their maturity beyond their fledgling years. In Brazil, growing up in the suburbs of São Paolo, was a young teenager by the name of Pelé.

Like all young Brazilian footballers learning their craft, futsal is a huge part of their development and for Pelé this was no different. Little pitches with hardly any room to manoeuvre, encouraging a good first touch and lightning-quick reactions when receiving or playing the ball. Pelé mentioned that playing futsal tournaments with both his own age group and adults helped him develop a rapid thought process that ultimately set him up for the professional game ahead. 'That gave me a lot of confidence,' Pelé said, 'I knew then not to be afraid of whatever might come.' By the age of 15, he had made his first-team debut for Santos and went on to international credit just a year later.

Waldemar de Brito had coached Pelé through his early years and taken the youngster to meet the directors at Santos, prior to signing professional terms, and after a successful trial. Having met with the men from the boardroom, a confident Pelé stated that one day he would be the greatest player in the world, a bold statement from a scraggy-looking teenager. On 7 September 1956, the road to becoming the best began. A goal on his debut in a 7-1 win over Corinthians Santo Andre set the tone for what was to be a quite glittering career.

By the age of 16, Pelé had become the league's leading goalscorer and was called up to the national team. Making his debut in the Maracanã, a goal to open his account wasn't enough to mark a remarkable start to his international career as Argentina managed a 2-1 win to somewhat dampen the mood. The 1958 World Cup in Sweden was on the horizon, but Pelé had suffered a knee injury in the build-up, which seemed to knock the stuffing out of him somewhat. His team-mates pleaded with the coach to include him in the third match of the tournament against Russia, with Pelé having proved his fitness. The coach conceded to player power and included the youngster in his starting XI for match three.

His appearance in the finals meant that the teen was now the youngest player ever to have appeared at the tournament, a record that's since been broken by Norman Whiteside of Northern Ireland in 1982. Brazil roared through to the final, with Pelé having notched a hat-trick in the semi-final win over France. But the fairy tale wasn't over just yet. On 28 June 1958, he scored a brace to help Brazil lift the Jules Rimet Trophy at the expense of hosts, Sweden. The first strike of his double was voted as one of the goals of the tournament, Pelé flicking the ball over the oncoming defender before unleashing a fierce volley past the Swedish goalkeeper. He also finished runner-up for the Golden Boot behind Just Fontaine. Swedish player Sigvard Parling would later comment: 'When Pelé scored the fifth goal in that final, I have to be honest and say I felt like applauding.'

Once the referee had signalled the end of the match, the young Pelé collapsed on the pitch. The emotions and experience had completely overawed him, requiring his team-mate Garrincha to comfort him.

By the time the next World Cup rolled around in 1962, Pelé was widely regarded as the best player on the planet. Unfortunately for Brazil's frontman, a nasty injury during the tournament meant a premature end for him during the knockout stages. Brazil would again go on to win the final and claim a second successive World Cup title. Unfortunately for Pelé and Brazil, a hat-trick of trophy lifts was cut short on English soil in 1966 when those in the iconic yellow shirts were dumped out in the group stage, despite boasting the best player in world football as well as a host of other exceptional talents, including Garrincha, Gilmar and Jairzinho.

Age was finally catching up with Pelé in 1970, but he was asked to remain with the squad for the forthcoming tournament, although all the faces that he had grown up with had now departed. There was a new breed in town. While a couple of the players mentioned previously had retired, fresh names were now on the Seleçáo team sheet. Jairzinho, Rivelino, Gerson, Carlos Alberto Tores and Tostão were part of what was described as arguably the greatest international team of all time. The 1982 Brazil team would clearly run them close, but the massive difference between the two was that the class of 1970 actually managed to get over the line.

Brazil dispatched Czechoslovakia in the opening match, 4-1, with Pelé scoring and coming close to a second after lobbing the opposition goalkeeper with an audacious effort from the halfway line. In their second match, against world champions England, Pelé thought he had added to his tally, but as his header looked to fly into the bottom corner, Three Lions custodian, Gordon Banks, flew across his goal to somehow tip the effort over his crossbar. Pelé recalled that he was already shouting 'Goal' when he headed the ball. It was an iconic save and is frequently discussed as the 'save of the century'. However, Brazil finally broke England hearts and won the match 1-0.

Romania were up next and they too were put to the sword as Pelé notched a brace in a topsy-turvy match that ended 3-2 to the Seleçáo. Fellow South Americans Peru awaited in the quarter-final. By now, Brazil were beginning to purr and were in no mood to be messing around. The Peruvians were sent back home licking their wounds after a 4-2 defeat.

There was another all-South American tie in the semi-final, this time Brazil's World Cup nemesis Uruguay. Despite Brazil easing through to their third World Cup final in four years with a 3-1 win, the match will always be remembered for one of the more iconic moments of Pelé's career. Tostão played a through ball for Pelé, which was slightly overhit. Uruguay's goalkeeper Ladislao Mazurkiewicz rushed off his line to attempt to reach the ball before the onrushing forward. Pelé got there first and hoodwinked Mazurkiewicz with a manoeuvre by not actually touching the ball, leaving it to roll to the goalkeeper's left, while Pelé went to the goalkeeper's right. With the keeper following the man rather than the ball, Pelé ran around the goalkeeper to retrieve the ball and took a shot while turning towards the goal, angling his body on the half-turn to ensure the effort hit the target. The pace of the run and shot seemed to be too much and the ball drifted agonisingly wide of the far post. The passage of play summed up Pelé's career beautifully. Thinking outside the box and not acting in a conventional manner as a footballer were what set him apart from the mere mortals of the game.

Italy joined Brazil in the final, but were no match for the yellow machine as they powered their way to a 4-1 victory, claiming yet another Jules Rimet Trophy. This time they were allowed to keep it. Pelé opened the scoring after outjumping Italian defender Tarcisio Burgnich, his marker throughout the final, who was quoted as saying, 'I told myself before the game, he's made of skin and bones just like everyone else – but I was wrong.'

Pelé spent the majority of his career in his native Brazil playing for Santos, where he won six league championships as well as back-to-back Copa Libertadores in 1962 and 1963. He won numerous accolades, including golden boots, golden balls, Ballon d'Or, Player of the Century, FIFA World Cup player and many, many more. His goal tally at club level reads a ridiculous 1,279 goals in 1,363 matches, although this statistic includes friendlies, which has both raised eyebrows and caused confusion. In his 92 matches for Brazil, Pelé found the back of the net 77 times and he never lost a match in which he and his team-mate Garrincha played.

Barney Ronay, chief sportswriter for *The Guardian*, described Pelé: 'With nothing but talent to guide him, the boy from Minas Gerais became the first black global sporting superstar, and a source of genuine uplift and inspiration.' Pelé is often in the conversation about the greatest player in the world ever, but I'll let you ponder on that.

'He'll take some pleasure from that, Brian Carey. He and Steve Bull have been having it off all afternoon.' – **Ron Atkinson**

Steve Bull made his way to the professional footballing world via the non-league pyramid. Bully, who was born in Tipton, West Midlands, signed for his hometown club in 1981. After leaving school, he flirted with a few factory jobs to start the money coming in as he tried to make his way in the hustle and bustle of part-time football. Fortunately for Bull, the manager of Tipton Town was also a scout for West Bromwich Albion.

Sid Day recommended his young forward to the Baggies and Bull was offered a trial before signing for First Division Albion in 1985. It was only to be a short but sweet stay at The Hawthorns as Bull's future would eventually lie elsewhere, but he wasn't to know that just yet. Bully made only a couple of appearances in the top flight, making his professional debut in a 1-0 defeat away at Queens Park Rangers. WBA were relegated that season and Bull's fleeting moments in England's top tier were over and to be his last. Little did the prolific forward know that in his 16-year career, he would never return.

His record of three goals in nine matches wasn't enough to force him into the manager's plans on a regular basis and Bull soon found himself moving across the Black Country to neighbours Wolverhampton Wanderers. Talking to Wolves. co.uk, Bull said:

> Ron Saunders came to me and said he'd had an offer from Wolves, and I said: 'Wolves, where are they?' I looked at the table and they were fourth from bottom, going into liquidation, and I pleaded with him for 10 minutes to keep me at Albion – I know Wolves fans won't want to hear that, but I wanted to play for the Albion. But me and Andy Thompson took a trip down the road, because we just wanted to play football, we signed that day and the rest is history.

Despite finding himself at a team in the bottom division and nearly bankrupt, Steve Bull went on to score an absolute shed-load of goals for the Wolves. His record of 306 goals in 561 matches will probably stand the test of time at Molineux. During his first full season at the club, he inspired them to win the Fourth Division, with Bull netting a club record 52 goals in all competitions. He and his team-mates went one better the following campaign as again Bully spearheaded another title-winning team, with Wolves claiming back-to-back promotion titles, although he only scored 50 times!

On 29 May 1988, Bull was also part of a team that claimed the Football League Trophy with a 2-0 win over Burnley. The striker's appearance at Wembley for Wolves was to be his only one at club level, although not for his country as he had been making huge waves outside the top tier, which hadn't gone unnoticed by the England manager, Bobby Robson. The Wolves forward was called up for his country for the World Cup qualifiers in 1989, having impressed Robson, who clearly felt that he had something to add to his squad.

Bull was still technically a Third Division player when he won his first international cap at the end of the 1988/89 campaign, as Wolves hadn't yet played in the Second Division following their promotion. He remains the last player to be capped by England from outside the top two tiers and his record for the Three Lions is four goals in 13 caps.

In his quest to reach the newly formed Premier League, Bull faced play-off heartache twice in three years as Wolves succumbed to semi-final defeat in both 1995 and 1997, losing to Bolton Wanderers and Swindon Town respectively. Knee injuries were starting to take their toll on the frontman, whose chances of reaching the top league were now beginning to fade into the distance. Eventually, in 1999, Bull decided to call time on his fight to regain regular fitness and his days at Wolverhampton Wanderers were over.

When asked about his finest match, Bull replied:

My greatest game for Wolves came away at Newcastle on New Year's Day 1990. We went up to Newcastle on New Year's Eve on the Hills coaches and I think the 3,000 Wolves fans went up on Monarch Airlines – we knew where the money was! The night before we played a few games of cards and the gaffer told us he wanted us in bed by five past 12, wished us Happy New Year and said we could have a couple of halves. I remember calling the wife later that night telling her I loved her – I'd only had 14 halves! We woke up the next morning smelling of drink before ending the first-half drawing 0-0. But I never knew what hit me in the second-half, I scored four goals and we won 4-1. Coming off the pitch I thought I'd never play as well as that again – and it came under the influence.

*'The referee, internationally experienced Clive
Thomas, told him that was the best he had
ever seen, even better than Pelé and Johan
Cruyff. "Really?" replied Friday. "You should
come down here more often, I do that every
week."'* – **Robin Friday**

The greatest footballer you never saw. This is not only the
title of the biography of Robin Friday, but also a statement of
truth. The book was brilliantly written by Oasis bass guitarist,
Paul McGuigan. If you have or haven't heard of the enigmatic
forward with a colourful background, then you should take a
look a little closer into the man Friday. Born in Acton, west
London, as one of twins, Friday entered the world in 1952. His
early years as a footballer were shared between a few London
clubs, with Crystal Palace, Queens Park Rangers and Chelsea
all giving the youngster a run in youth football. Friday's laid-
back attitude and his reluctance to be disciplined cost him a
place at all of those clubs.

At 15, Friday left school and became an apprentice
plasterer. His other hobbies had begun to overtake his love for
football, and his lust for music, drinking and then drugs soon
wound him up in borstal. On his release, Friday signed for his
friend's team in the Isthmian League, where he made his debut
for Walthamstow Avenue in 1972, earning £10 a week. He
then moved on to Hayes, where his record of 46 goals in 67
matches affected the attention of Fourth Division clubs, most
notably Reading.

In January 1974, Friday signed for the Royals for £750.
Charlie Hurley, the Reading manager, had heard glowing
reports on the youngster and had visited Hayes on numerous
occasions to watch Friday play before eventually bringing him

to Elm Park. Upon his arrival, his manager said, 'In his very first training session, they were playing a six-a-side game and Robin went around trying to kick as many of the established Reading players as he could. He must have put two or three out of the game. I had to call him off.'

With Reading struggling after 14 matches without a win, Hurley decided to throw in his young forward. Friday's raw ability made him very popular among Reading fans. The *Reading Evening Post* report of Reading's 4–1 victory over Exeter City on 10 February 1974, Friday's first match as a professional, described his performance as 'sheer magic' as he notched a brace.

The match report also called his first goal of the day 'glorious'. It read: 'He collected the ball wide on the left wing, took it past four Exeter defenders and then fired the ball low and hard into the opposite corner from the edge of the penalty area.'

During his first season at Reading, Friday was scouted by First Division Arsenal, as his goals were the talking point of the country. It was during the 1975/76 season, in a match against Tranmere Rovers, with World Cup referee Clive Thomas officiating matters, that Friday really put on a show. It was described in the book, *The Greatest Footballer You Never Saw*:

> Right-back Gary Peters, upon receiving the ball from goalkeeper Steve Death, arrowed a long ball up the field in the direction of Friday, who, upon leaping in the air and bringing the ball down with his chest, smashed a thirty yard rocket over his shoulder into the top right-hand corner of the net, causing referee Thomas, a man who had been on the same pitch as Johan Cruyff no less, to put his hands over his head in disbelief at what he'd seen.

Friday was dubbed the lower league George Best as his career mirrored that of the Manchester United legend, albeit on a less glamorous scale. While Best had lit up Old Trafford and other top footballing amphitheatres across Europe, Robin was strutting his silky skills in a showman-like fashion at less enviable venues. Friday loved a drink, as well as some other recreational activities that would in the end hamper his performances. His rap sheet at Reading consisted of the following:

- Consuming large quantities of American Colt 45 liquor as a tipple of choice
- Being barred from one pub on ten occasions
- Entering a nightclub wearing a trench-coat and hobnail boots while being completely naked underneath, and removing said trench-coat
- Performing 'the elephant', a charming dance routine that involved turning his pockets inside-out and letting his John hang out of his fly
- Listening to heavy metal, irrespective of what time of the day or night, while tripping balls on LSD
- Deciding to join a hippie commune prior to pre-season training without informing anyone
- Bringing a swan into a hotel bar
- Attempting to steal stone angels from a graveyard, the only incident for which he received a sharp scolding

Despite winning promotion with Reading from the Fourth Division in 1976 and winning the Reading Player of the Year award during his two seasons with the club, with his off-field problems beginning to mount and manager Hurley beginning to lose patience, Friday was sold to Cardiff City, ending a near three-year love affair with the Reading supporters who, incidentally, have since voted him their greatest player of all time. His 46 goals in 121 matches prompted the Blue Birds to part with £28,000 for his services.

On arrival at Cardiff Central railway station, Friday was arrested by the British Transport Police for having travelled from Reading with only a platform ticket. Manager Andrews bailed his new player out of police custody and took him to Ninian Park to sign his contract. Despite the unorthodox manner of Friday's arrival, and although he knew there 'had to be something wrong with him', the Cardiff manager was still happy with his new addition, describing his purchase as an absolute steal.

Friday lined up for his new club against a Fulham team that included World Cup winner Bobby Moore. Friday terrorised Moore and finished the match by squeezing the ex-England captain's testicles, as well as walking off the pitch after scoring two goals. He was instantly loved by the Cardiff fans for his dynamic displays, although by the time Friday had reached the Welsh capital, his drug use was also showing signs of reaching peak levels.

His manager Andrews was also struggling to get the best out of the forward, and Friday's swansong before his departure from Cardiff was a red card in a match against Brighton and Hove Albion. Friday was marked during the match by Mark Lawrenson, who frustrated the Cardiff forward so much with his close attention that Friday waited for Lawrenson to attempt a slide tackle and then kicked him in the face. The forward was instantly shown a red card. Friday left the ground with the match still going on. According to legend, before leaving he broke into the Brighton dressing room and defecated in Lawrenson's kit bag.

Friday retired from professional football at the age of just 25. His career was littered with off-field incidents, but anyone who had the pleasure of seeing him play on a Saturday afternoon would tell you he was simply sensational on the field.

In 2010, Football365 placed him eighth in their most wasted talent poll. Friday passed away in 1990 after suffering a heart attack, which was rumoured to be drug-related.

Despite his wild ways, Friday was still worthy of winning the title of 'Player of the Millennium' from Reading supporters in 1999. He was also voted the top 'all-time cult hero' for both Reading and Cardiff in a 2004 BBC poll. Jimmy Andrews, his manager at Cardiff, later called Friday 'the complete centre-forward' and placed him on a par with Alan Shearer. That man Friday. Rest in peace, Robin.

> *"Before Stoichkov came, we had a team of very nice people," he said. "But you can't just have a team of very nice people. You need someone like Stoichkov who is aggressive in a positive way. He goes for the ball and when he gets the ball he shoots at goal."* – *Johan Cruyff*

Barcelona were finding it difficult to keep up with the Joneses in Spain, most noticeably their arch-enemies in Madrid. Los Blancos were claiming title after title in the Spanish capital, leaving those in Catalonia to pick up the pieces in domestic cup competitions. Johan Cruyff had now taken over the reins in Barcelona and was given the task of closing the gap on their rivals. Barcelona hadn't claimed a La Liga title in six years, so something had to give, as a Copa del Rey and European Cup Winners' Cup were still not enough to appease those who frequented the Camp Nou.

Far away in Eastern Europe was a young forward plying his trade in his native Bulgaria. Hristo Stoichkov had already made a name for himself, and not just for his goalscoring prowess at CSKA Sofia. Signed from a third tier team in 1985, Stoichkov made an instant impact on the pitch both with his ability and his temper. Playing as a striker, he could also link the play with a brilliant ability to create assists for this team-mates, but he had a very short fuse.

While playing in the 1985 Bulgarian cup final, a mass brawl ensued as the intense rivalry between the two Sofia clubs led to fighting on the pitch and even an attack on a referee. Stoichkov was later banned for life, which coincided with his call-up to military service. The ban was overturned on appeal, but he still missed the whole of the 1985/86 campaign. Writing in his biography, Stoichkov said:

> After the final whistle, Levski's players gathered around Asparuh Yasenov [the referee]. Players like Borislav Mihaylov – national team's keeper, Nasko Sirakov – former national player and footballer for [Real] Zaragoza and Espanyol, (players who should act like professionals) were all cursing, hitting, threatening, and pushing him [the referee] while we were celebrating in front our ecstatic fans. At the age of 19, I won my first cup during my first season with the club I love – the team of the army.

On return from his ban, Stoichkov started to find the net on a regular basis and his 81 goals in 119 matches reaped the rewards of three Bulgarian league titles, four Bulgarian league cups and the Bulgarian super cup. In his final season in Sofia, the forward netted 38 times in just 30 matches, catching the attention of Cruyff and Barcelona. With a fee of around £2.7m agreed, the explosive striker was finding his way to Catalonia.

Stoichkov's first season with Barcelona was one of mixed emotions. His temper was still on a knife-edge and, in the

Spanish Super Cup, he was red-carded for stamping on the referee's foot. *Marca* wrote:

> Famous Spanish referee Urizar Azpitarte took charge of 15 'Clásicos' in his time. And one that he's sure to remember was a Spanish Super Cup. After Johan Cruyff and Hristo Stoichkov were sent off for protesting, the Bulgarian lost control and stamped on the referee's foot. Stoichkov was 'only' away from the pitch for 81 days though. His ban could have been extended to six months, but the extension of the ban by an appeal committee was not registered correctly and was thus not valid.

Now, while I'm clearly not painting the best picture of this left-footed wizard, it's only fair that I show how for all the bad in this beast of a player's reputation, there's also the beauty. I mean they're only human after all; they just want to win. Cruyff commented: 'If there are star players who are not aggressive, how can you have an aggressive team? Impossible.' Despite the ban, Stoichkov notched on 22 occasions in the 1990/91 season, bringing the La Liga title back to the Camp Nou.

Barcelona would go on to win four straight championships as well as the Copa del Rey, Spanish Super Cup, European Super Cup and Cup Winners' Cup, but, most important, was the European Cup success in 1992, Barcelona's maiden victory in the competition.

Stoichkov's link-up play with Brazilian striker Romário was out of this world. They were absolutely ripping it up together, with 56 goals scored between the pair in another carnival season. Football writer Sid Lowe said, 'That season [1993/94] Romário and Stoichkov were a force of nature, blowing everyone and everything to bits.'

With the wind behind Stoichkov, the Bulgarian and his national team-mates headed off to the US for the 1994 World Cup. With this footballing nation having never made it past the last 16 before, hope more than expectation was placed on the shoulders of the man dubbed El Pistelero (The Gunslinger) and, my word, did he gun down plenty of defences in his time. Despite losing the opening match of the tournament to eventual group winners Nigeria, the 3-0 defeat did nothing but ignite the fire inside Stoichkov and co.

Heading into the second match of the group, the Lions needed a response and, boy, was it impressive, with a 4-0 victory over Greece. Stoichkov netted with a brace of penalties. The turnaround was complete when Bulgaria turned over one of the tournament favourites in Argentina with a superb performance and a 2-0 win. It was an ill-tempered match that saw nine yellow cards, plus a red for Bulgaria's Tsanko Tsvetanov. Stoichkov again found the net after racing on to a through ball and prodding past the onrushing goalkeeper.

Bulgaria had qualified for the last 16, where they faced a Mexico team that had thwarted them at the same stage in the 1986 tournament. After just six minutes, Stoichkov raced on to a through ball down the left flank and angled a fierce drive past the Mexican keeper. Unfortunately, the match ended level, but the Bulgarians managed to scrape into the quarter-finals, where they faced the holders Germany.

Germany took the lead just after the start of the second half, then with just a quarter of an hour left on the clock, Stoichkov drove a free kick from the right-hand side of the area straight into the top corner. The keeper just waved it past. 1-1. Could they? Just moments later and diving header from Yordan Letchkov had completed a dramatic turnaround as Bulgaria won 2-1.

Into the final four, where Bulgaria met Italy who, in Roberto Baggio, had one of the most lethal finishers in the world. He notched twice in the first half and by then the match was gone. Stoichkov scored his sixth goal of the competition but it wasn't enough for the Lions, who eventually finished fourth in the tournament. It was a truly inspiring performance from the striker, who, along with Letchkov, had dragged his team-mates to the brink of international glory.

Stoichkov received the Ballon d'Or in 1994, but for some strange reason, this star lost some of his shine post-USA '94. His goalscoring rate had slowed in the 1994/95 season and Cruyff had seen fit to sell one of his prize assets across the border into Italy. The Bulgarian headed off to Parma, but his spell with the I Gialloblu was both short and unsuccessful. A return to Barcelona looked to ignite his prowess, but despite claiming another La Liga title in 1996/97, Stoichkov couldn't quite reach the heights of his previous stint in Catalonia.

In his two spells with Barcelona, Stoichkov scored 117 times in 255 matches. This also included an abundance of titles as well as red cards. He played the game with a knife between his teeth, which for the most part bore some of the sweetest fruit. His red cards may have blotted his copybook, but that was the way he played. Fleeting appearances in Japan, Saudi Arabia and in the MLS brought an end to the colourful career of Stoichkov, who for the most part will be fondly remembered for his devastating partnership with Romário in Johan Cruyff's dream team.

*'Zinedine Zidane. What he could do with a football is a dream for most of us.' – **Xabi Alonso***

'The match you played last night was full of talent and professionalism. I know that you are sad and disappointed but what I want to tell you is that the whole country is extremely proud of you. You have honoured the country with your exceptional qualities and your fantastic fighting spirit, which was your strength in difficult times, but also in winning times.' Compassionate words from Jacques Chirac, President of France in 2006, just hours after Zinedine Zidane had seen red in the 2006 World Cup Final defeat to Italy. His early shower would signal the end of the career of a player who had won the lot ... but how did we get here?

Having shone in the youth set-ups in his native France, Zidane was finally signed by AS Cannes. 'He'd go past one, two, three, five, six players – it was sublime. His feet spoke with the ball,' said Jean Varraud, the man who was credited with unearthing this precocious talent. In 1991/92, ZZ helped Cannes to their highest league position and a UEFA Cup berth before flying the nest to Bordeaux. It was there that the flamboyant midfielder honed his talent for four years, scoring an impressive 39 goals in 175 matches from midfield. Bordeaux were unlucky to be beaten in the 1995/96 UEFA Cup final but the appearance in the showpiece was the catalyst for the young midfielder.

The story goes that prior to Zidane signing for Juventus in 1996, both Blackburn Rovers and Newcastle United had opportunities to bring the player to the Premier League. Jack Walker, the then owner of Blackburn Rovers, quipped, 'Why do we need Zidane when we have Tim Sherwood?' and Kevin Keegan at Newcastle was unsure that Zidane could hack it in the rough and tumble of the English top tier. Whoops. But then I guess hindsight is a wonderful thing, eh. It wasn't just his performances in France but also for the national team that were starting to prod the footballing hierarchy. Champions League holders Juventus weren't messing about and decided to splash around £3.15m for the midfielder.

The Old Lady had some special players in and around their squad at the time, including midfield maestro Edgar Davids. 'He is a special player,' said Davids. 'He creates space where there is none. No matter where he gets the ball or how it comes to him, he can get out of trouble. His imagination and his technique are amazing.' It was during his four-year stint in Italy that Zidane began to capture the imagination of the watching world, particularly in England, as Manchester United seemed to draw Juventus nearly every season in this period.

In his first season in Italy, Zidane contributed to a Scudetto and an Intercontinental Cup win as well as claiming the Serie A Foreign Footballer of the Year. The following campaign, Zidane and co reached the 1997 Champions League final, but were beaten 3-1 by a very stubborn Borussia Dortmund team. Scotland's Paul Lambert had paid particular attention to the Frenchman and nullified his threat. The following season, though, was really the start of the success for ZZ.

Zidane's seven goals in 32 matches helped Juventus to back-to-back Scudettos and his skill and trickery had helped them reach a third consecutive Champions League final. But, like the previous one, Zidane would have to settle for the runners-up podium as Real Madrid ran out 1-0 winners on the night. The Frenchman must have been cursing his luck as he had joined the Champions League winners only for his next two appearances to end in defeat.

After a bittersweet end to the campaign, Zidane headed back home to France for the 1998 World Cup finals. He was in imperious form as he helped his team-mates to three out of three in the group stages with wins over South Africa, Saudi Arabia and Denmark. Into the last 16, it was an extra-time win over Paraguay that meant the hosts would meet a tough Italian team in the quarter-finals. Many of Zidane's club-mates and players he would have faced on a weekly basis were desperate to put one over on the French, who hadn't really been up against too much competition thus far.

A tough match ended 0-0, which meant the lottery of penalties. Zidane stepped up first and scored and, with Albertini and Di Biagio both failing to convert, France were through to the final four. Despite falling behind to Croatia in the semi-final, France hit back to win 2-1 and go through to the showpiece in the Stade de France, where they would face the much fancied current holders, Brazil.

A sidenote to this story is that, in Ronaldo, Brazil had arguably the best player on the planet at that time in their ranks. What was to follow could have possibly won France the cup prior to kick-off as Ronaldo was ruled out with a mystery injury, which shrouded the final in controversy, both before and after the match. Zidane didn't care for the sideshow and, when the midfielder nodded in twice from corners in the first half, the writing was on the wall for the boys from Brazil. France eventually won 3-0 to run out world champions. The pinnacle for any footballer. Zidane was an instant national hero and was handed the Legion of Honour. He also won the Ballon d'Or for 1998, crowning a fantastic calendar year.

Euro 2000 just two years later gave Zidane another chance to wow the watching world, which he certainly did. France again were victorious and this was mainly due to the footballing talent of the midfielder. UEFA's website declared:

> In Belgium and the Netherlands, Zidane dominated a major championship in a way no individual had managed since Diego Maradona in 1986. From the opening game against Denmark to the final against Italy, 'Zizou' shone brightly, casting a spell on his opponents with clever flicks, mesmerising stepovers, slaloming runs and masterful vision.

Zidane's curling free kick in the quarter-final win over Spain was followed by the golden goal in the semi-final to drag France to a showpiece final for the second time in two years. So now the player could add European champion to his world champion tag. Zidane was also named the player of the tournament, just to add to his ever-growing trophy haul.

The problem with becoming one of the greatest players on the planet, though, is that you start to become a marked man, as Hamburger SV player Jochen Kientz found out to his cost. In 2000/01, Zidane was about to showcase the move that would ultimately end his career. In a Champions League match, ZZ was shown red for headbutting his opponent. His ban contributed to Juventus failing to reach the knockout stages of the competition, the first time in over a decade. They were also pipped at the post in Serie A too, losing out to Roma in the title race. This was the first campaign that the midfielder hadn't been spraying around champagne at the end of the season.

By now, Zidane was on the lips of every team in the world, but not all could afford the 150 billion Italian Lire he cost, around £75m. That's exactly what Real Madrid had to pay to prise the player from Turin to the Spanish capital. It was part of the club's Galactico era and Zidane was certainly deserving of the name. In his first season, he helped Madrid reach the 2002 Champions League final, where not only did he make it third time lucky with a 2-1 win, but also scored arguably one of the greatest goals in the final itself, a volley with his left foot that arced over the Bayer Leverkusen goalkeeper from the edge of the area, as the ball dropped towards his shoulder. Fantastic.

Rory Smith, writing for *The Telegraph*, stated:

> Zinedine Zidane, 18 yards out, watching and waiting, adjusts his body and, in one, smooth movement, pirouettes and catches it full on the volley with his left

foot. It flies past Hans-Jorg Butt. It was the moment
of Zidane's apotheosis, more so than the 1998 World
Cup Final, because of the moment's grace and beauty,
because of his control of everything around him. He
was Bruce Lee in slow motion while kung-fu chaos
reigned around.

A year later, Zidane added the La Liga title to his collection,
although this was to be his only league success gained in Spain,
despite the huge array of talent surrounding the Frenchman at
the time. Two Spanish Super Cups, Intercontinental Cup and
Super Cup aren't to be sniffed at when you sit down and tot
up your winnings, although I'm pretty sure the player would
have preferred to have lifted the championship on a few more
occasions. But then I guess no player or team has a divine right
to win anything, regardless of their status in the game.

In the summer of 2005, Zidane declared that this would
be his final campaign before hanging up his boots. Again,
Madrid could only play second fiddle in La Liga, but in the
final match of the season, the 80,000 fans in the Bernabéu held
up a banner saying, 'Thanks for the Magic'. Zidane scored in
an entertaining 3-3 draw with Villareal. I mean, would he have
really had it any other way?

ZZ had already retired from the national team in 2004, but
with a raft of experienced players all calling it a day before the
2006 World Cup in Germany, a last-minute rallying call was
sent out to Zidane, who not only performed a U-turn to come
back and play but was also installed as captain. The beginning
of the tournament was stop-start, as a one-match ban meant
that Zidane missed the third match in the group, although
France qualified for the knockout rounds.

France faced Spain in the last 16, where a goal and an
assist from Zidane enabled them to make their way to the

quarter-finals to face Brazil. ZZ, again turning on the style, assisted Henry to notch the winner and set up another semi-final against the Portuguese. As six years previously, Zidane's spot kick was enough to send France through to the final. How fitting that a player with so much talent, in the final match of his career, should finish on the high of the World Cup Final. Oh ...

With just six minutes showing on the clock, France were awarded a penalty and, in true Zinedine Zidane style, on the biggest stage of all against one of the game's greatest goalkeepers in Gianluigi Buffon, he stepped up and, in full Panenka style, dinked the ball straight down the middle, clipping the underside of the crossbar on its way in. Italy equalised and neither team was able to break the deadlock. In extra time, with the final heading towards penalties, a scuffle in the penalty area caused one of the most infamous football moments in the 21st century.

As the ball was cleared, Zidane and Marco Materazzi seemed to tussle, but both jogged out of the area. As ZZ began to make his way back towards his own goal, the midfielder, playing his last match, spun round and planted a headbutt straight into the chest of the Italian defender, who fell to the ground. A red card was flashed at Zidane. Italy went on to win on penalties and ultimately spoil the fairy tale ending, but it was a quite bizarre way for Zidane to bring the curtain down on his career.

Marco Materazzi spoke about the incident:

> There had been a bit of contact between us in the area. He had scored France's goal in the first half and our coach [Marcello Lippi] told me to mark him. After that first brush between us, I apologised but he reacted badly. After the third clash, I frowned and

he retorted: 'I'll give you my shirt later.' I replied that
I'd rather have his sister than his shirt.

Let's not forget that, prior to this, Zidane had mesmerised the
footballing world with his superb first touch, silky skills and
cool-as-ice finishing. His managerial career hasn't begun too
badly either. In 2014, Zidane was named the Real Madrid
Castilla coach before making the step up to the first team
in 2016. He would go on to claim a hat-trick of Champions
League trophy wins from 2016–18, as well as two La Liga titles
in 2016/17 and 2019/20.

Zidane's record at playing level sits at 695 matches and 125
goals, with many being important match-winning finishes.
His record for France was 108 appearances and 31 goals. It
made him a supreme footballer who wowed supporters all
over the world.

'I told Martin Edwards (then Manchester
United chairman) when he signed Bryan
Robson: "It's not even a risk. He's solid gold."'
– Ron Atkinson

When Manchester United paid a British record fee for
midfielder Bryan Robson from West Bromwich Albion on 1
October 1981, boss Ron Atkinson knew that he had signed an
absolute winner. Big Ron had managed Robson a few years
previously at WBA before the manager left The Hawthorns
to take over at Old Trafford, following the departure of Dave
Sexton. Ron knew that, despite the hefty £1.5m price tag, he
still had a bargain on his hands. He had already bought Remi
Moses from WBA for £600,000 in September 1981. Before
he signed Robbo later that year, Big Ron sought the advice

of Bill Shankly, asking the Liverpool legend how much he should pay for him. The transfer fee was deemed a very good price for a young player. Robbo was 24, but early in his career had already broken his left leg twice and his right ankle once. Shankly's advice was short and sweet: 'Whatever it takes, son, whatever it takes.'

Unlike the extravagant unveiling of players in the modern age, which is now carried out through social media outlets, Robson's was something a little less billboard. A wooden desk was placed by the halfway line of the Old Trafford pitch and Robbo put pen to paper in front of his new supporters prior to the match against Wolverhampton Wanderers. Robson recalled:

> I left The Hawthorns with mixed feelings. West Brom had been great to me from the day I first went to the club. I made lifelong friends there. If I hadn't had ambitions to win trophies, it would have been a fantastic place to spend the rest of my career. The local press, who had championed my cause to play for England, were now hammering me. I was dubbed a 'Judas', a 'money grabber' and much, much worse. That hurt because I felt I had played my part for the club, never given less than 100 per cent, and I still didn't even know what my salary at United would be.

Manchester United hadn't won a league title since 1967 and Robson was seen as an integral part of Big Ron's new-look team to help achieve that. His debut, just days after signing, was in the Manchester derby. (Robson was handed the No. 7 shirt, which he would wear for United throughout his career, until squad numbers were issued in 1994 and he was handed No. 12 as Eric Cantona had been passed No. 7) due to his emergence in the team and Robson's advancing years.

Robson's first goal came a month later in a 5-1 victory over Sunderland at Roker Park. His inaugural campaign yielded five goals in 32 appearances. That summer he scored the fastest-ever goal at a World Cup finals when he notched against France in just 27 seconds. The record stood until it was broken by Turkey player, Hakan Sükür, whose strike after just ten seconds in the 2002 World Cup ended Robbo's proud record.

On his return to United, Robson's influence on the pitch was growing. His omission through injury from the League Cup final in 1983 played a huge part in United's 2-1 defeat to Liverpool, and that injury picked up in the semi-final against Arsenal looked to have curtailed his season until, through grit and determination, he battled back to fitness in time for the FA Cup Final against Brighton and Hove Albion.

United huffed and puffed against the Seagulls and were lucky to escape Wembley with a 2-2 draw. United and Robson weren't messing about in the replay, with United's No. 7 notching twice and even turning down the chance of a hat-trick when handed the chance of taking a penalty. Instead, he gave the ball to United's usual penalty taker, Arnold Muhren. Robson led the team up the Wembley steps after a 4-0 victory to hoist aloft the FA Cup.

With United claiming the trophy, the following season brought European football to Old Trafford in the form of the Cup Winners' Cup. In probably the most iconic match of Robson's stint in Manchester, United found themselves trailing 2-0 after their first leg defeat in Barcelona. The Catalans boasted Diego Maradona and Bernd Schuster in their ranks and had one foot in the semi-final after their display in the Camp Nou. Robson, though, had other ideas. Reports from fans and journalists who were at Old Trafford that night suggest that he carried the entire team on his back, which was ironic as he was carried off the pitch at the full-time whistle after scoring twice and securing United a spot in the last four, dragging the team through to a 3-2 aggregate win.

Robson began the fightback after 22 minutes when he connected with a diving header from a Ray Wilkins corner. Five minutes after the break, he sent the majority of the 58,350 crowd into raptures by slamming home from close range after Javier Urruticoechea fumbled a Wilkins cross. The tie was level on aggregate, but there was only going to be one winner. As United poured forwards, Frank Stapleton latched on to a Norman Whiteside knockdown and lashed the ball into the net from an acute angle. They say the roof at Old Trafford nearly blew off, which probably explains why there are said to be so many leaks in it today, although these reports are unproven.

Unfortunately for Robson and United, the midfielder, who was now dubbed 'Captain Marvel', was injured for the semi-final tie against Italian powerhouse Juventus, who sent United packing thanks to an inspired Michel Platini. Robson very nearly signed for the Old Lady but instead pledged his future to Big Ron and the supporters at Old Trafford.

The league title was on the wish list in M16, but during the 1980s under Atkinson, United were more of a cup team as they were too erratic over the course of a 40-odd match campaign. The matches United lost would invariably be due to Robson's absence, with the midfielder missing large parts of seasons due to the wear and tear caused by his all-action performances. Brian Clough said of the England captain:

> When Robson plays football, he must expect to get hurt, because that's him. When he sees a ball, irrespective of where it is on a football field, he automatically goes for it. Afterwards, he sometimes says, 'I don't really know why I went for it.' And he'll be asking that when he's lying in the treatment room.

But that is Robson, and that is the end of the story with him.

During the 1984/85 campaign, Robson's performance against Liverpool in the FA Cup semi-final cemented even further his status in the hearts of the United supporters. After a 2-2 draw in the first match at Goodison Park, the replay at Maine Road didn't start particularly well as Liverpool took an early lead. Robson recalled:

> The atmosphere at Maine Road was great, but it was a bad start for us against a Liverpool team who were dominant at the time. I always enjoyed playing at Maine Road though, because to me it always seemed to be a big pitch. I don't actually know whether it was. For the United fans, it was extra special because Liverpool had gone in front and it was extra special for us because we came back and I was fortunate enough to score.

Robson rates his goal as one of his greatest and, after seeing it played back, added: 'It was one of the best goals I ever scored for United. It was a great moment with the fans all mobbing me at the end.' Not for the first time, or the last, Bryan. At Wembley, Robson this time led a ten-man United to victory over league champions Everton. Despite having Kevin Moran sent off, United's 1-0 victory ensured Robson again tasted champagne.

But the final victory was another false dawn. In the league in 1985/86, United began on the crest of a wave and, after ten matches, were sitting proudly at the top of the table after a perfect start. Then, as the clocks changed to signal the end of British Summer Time, the wheels began to fall off. Robson injured his shoulder in February 1986 and missed the remainder of the season, battling back for the World Cup to be held in Mexico that summer. United eventually finished in a disappointing fourth place. And the disappointment didn't finish there for Robson, as again the dislocated shoulder suffered in the winter months reared its ugly head during the World Cup finals.

With Robson missing the opening of the 1986/87 season, United's form faltered and, by November, they had parted company with Robson's friend and manager, Ron Atkinson. Alex Ferguson took the reins, with the objective still the same, to try to close the gap on Everton and Liverpool and bring a league championship to Manchester United. Despite Robson staying reasonably injury free, United's league form was inconsistent under Ferguson, as the Scot set about making a mark on the squad with his own ideas. The league positions fluctuated from a mid-table finish, to runners-up, back to mid-table again.

In 1990, and with Ferguson's time seemingly up at the club, United embarked on a cup run that led to a semi-final tie at Maine Road against Oldham Athletic. The match was a real advert for football, a titanic tussle ending in a 3-3 draw after 120 minutes. Oldham had taken an early lead and, with United struggling to find any rhythm, they looked to their captain for inspiration. *The Guardian* explained the moment that Robson equalised beautifully:

> If you want a job done properly, do it yourself. Having watched his team-mates blunder around for half an hour, Bryan Robson has dragged them level! After a game of pinball in the Oldham half, Bruce slid in decisively near the halfway line to beat Marshall to a loose ball. It ran through to Webb, who took a touch and angled a soft, early pass into the space

behind the defence. Robson, who was on his arse a split second earlier after a late tackle from Milligan, marauded through and forced a right-footed shot through Hallworth.

The report continued with more praise for Captain Marvel:

> This is the fourth FA Cup semi-final in a row in which Robson has scored – and it says a lot about his personality that three of those were equalisers. How many times is he going to pull United out of the malodorous stuff? He's nowhere near fully fit, but here he is, bending yet another big match to his will. The word 'hero' doesn't begin to do him justice.

On to the replay, where a hard-fought display was enough to send United through 2-1 after another 120 minutes of football had been played out. Crystal Palace were waiting for Robson and co in the final at Wembley, having heroically defeated Liverpool 4-3 in the other semi-final. Palace took an early lead, before Robson again levelled, this time with a header at the far post, beating the diving Nigel Martyn. Replays were a theme for the Red Devils as a 3-3 draw meant that the two teams would have to face off again on the following Thursday night.

A single Lee Martin strike was enough for Robson to lift his third FA Cup in the space of just seven seasons. The silver lining to this particular cloud was that English clubs were again allowed to participate in European competition following the five-year ban after the Heysel disaster on 29 May 1985, where 39 football fans lost their lives due to a horrific incident in the stadium.

Another summer and another World Cup in which Robson would pull up lame. This time it was Italia '90, but an Achilles injury meant that the Manchester United and England captain missed both the finals in Italy and half of the 1990/91 domestic campaign. By the time he returned, United had reached a League Cup Final against Sheffield Wednesday, but even the prowess of Captain Marvel couldn't help United overcome the Owls at Wembley, where they lost 1-0 to a John Sheridan strike.

Despite the heartache of losing in the final, Robson was finding his fitness just in time to help his team-mates reach the final of the European Cup Winners' Cup. This was bittersweet for the skipper, who had missed his last tilt at the semi-final stage due to injury. This time around, Johan Cruyff's Barcelona lay in wait. In Rotterdam on 15 May 1991, United and Robson headed into their first European final since their 1968 European Cup triumph.

The Barcelona team was littered with stars and United were classed as the underdogs in the tie, which suited Ferguson and his captain just fine. After a goalless first half, United were awarded a free kick, which Robson chipped into the box. Steve Bruce rose at the far post to head the ball back across goal and inside the far corner. Mark Hughes, who had previously had a short but seemingly unsuccessful spell at Barça, prodded in to make sure the ball crossed the line.

There may have been controversy over who scored the opening goal, but there was no denying who scored the second as again Robson found himself with the ball just inside the Barcelona half and played a delightful through pass with the outside of his left foot. The ball found its way through the channel between centre-back and left full-back, landing at the feet of Hughes, who controlled the ball instantly. The Barcelona keeper raced from his area to meet the United forward, who, with calmness personified, danced around the Catalan custodian and arrowed a shot into the far bottom corner. United held on for a 2-1 win and Robson was tasting his first European success.

As well as his footballing prowess, Robson would also look out for the youth players who were breaking into the first team, part of his role as club captain. Most notable was Ryan Giggs, who admits Robbo was his minder when he was first coming through at United. He later recalled in an interview with *The Telegraph*:

> This Sheffield United right-back was kicking me in one game, giving me a few verbals and it affected me a little bit. I said to Robbo, 'That right-back's just said he's going to break my legs.' Robbo said, 'Did he? You come and play centre-midfield. I'm going to play left wing for ten minutes.' We swapped positions. Robbo soon came back. 'Aye, you're all right now, go back over.' Problem solved! I had this mentality that if Robson was playing we'd never lose. We usually won. He had that authority. He'd tell me when I was not passing enough or dribbling too much. Him and Brucey [Steve Bruce] were brilliant for me.

Even while acting as his on-field bodyguard, Robson would still find time to educate Giggs in the ways of the changing room and none more so than when the young winger was shown how not to overstep the mark too soon. Speaking to ManUtd.com, Giggs said:

> Oh, yeah … I got stitched up. My memories of that … the first thing that comes to mind is the gaffer's red face, looking at me and wanting to throw me out the window! I had said to Bryan Robson, 'Robbo, everyone's got a club car apart from me and I've

played 25 games in the first team now.' He said, 'Yeah, I think you should go and ask the manager. Tell him you've played 25 games and ask him to give you a car.' Robbo had never taken the mick out of me or done any practical jokes, so I trusted him. So, I've gone knocking on the door and I've said to the manager, 'Listen, boss, I've played 25 games now, I think I'm fairly established. What about a club car?' Halfway through the sentence I could see his face changing, and as soon as I said 'club car', I could see his face was red and he just started swearing at me. He said, 'Club car? You won't even get a club bike. Get out of this office now, before I throw you out!' As I opened the door, half the first team were outside – they had been listening in, looking for a reaction. You live and learn!

Robson wasn't getting any younger and, with injuries beginning to take their toll on the action man's body, he found his appearances beginning to diminish. Eric Cantona had been signed from Leeds United and had taken over the mantle of the No. 7 shirt, although with Robson giving with one hand, he was taking with another, as with Cantona's help he would walk away with his first league championship medal at the tenth time of asking. United broke their 26-year hoodoo and finally climbed back to the top of English football, with Robson scoring his only goal of the campaign in a win over Wimbledon on the final day of the season.

With his career seemingly reaching a sunset moment, Robbo was looking to head into coaching and management. During his final season at United, he still managed to score his obligatory semi-final goal, again against Oldham in the FA Cup replay, playing his part in the squad that won a Premier League and FA Cup double. His 99 goals in 461 appearances cements him as one of the greatest players ever to play for Manchester United. Robson essentially dragged both Ron Atkinson and Alex Ferguson's United sides kicking and screaming through the 1980s.

Robson eventually left to pursue his coaching career and headed north to Middlesbrough to become their player-manager, as well as assistant to Terry Venables in the England set-up. I briefly spoke to ex-Manchester United player Alan Tongue, who was at the club while Robson was strutting his stuff. When asked how to describe the skipper, Tongue said, 'A supreme footballer. Could do it all. Good first touch, pass short and long, tackle, score goals, good in the air, great engine, courageous and a leader of men. Solid gold.'

12

The Pretenders

Noun: Pretender – A person who claims or
aspires to a title or position

THERE ARE so many players that could have shoehorned their way into these chapters. Players from all different eras. Gareth Bale was close for the way he single-handedly carried his Tottenham Hotspur team from 2010 to 2013 before heading off to Real Madrid to collect an armful of La Liga and Champions League trophies, including a memorable overhead kick in the 2018 final against Liverpool. 'When Gareth picks up the ball and turns and runs at you, he is unplayable,' said his former manager, Harry Redknapp.

Alan Shearer also made a case with his goalscoring prowess at both Blackburn Rovers and Newcastle United, catapulting him to the top of the all-time Premier League goalscoring charts with a whopping 260 goals. His early years contributed to a Blackburn Rovers title win in 1994/95, toppling Sir Alex Ferguson and his Manchester United team. Shearer then found himself off to his boyhood club, Newcastle United. He helped the Magpies to two consecutive FA Cup Finals in 1998 and 1999, although both were lost 2-0, to Arsenal and Manchester

United respectively. Ex-Blackburn Rovers strike partner Kevin Gallacher said, 'I wouldn't say he was the most talented centre-forward in the world, he wouldn't go and take a centre-half on and do six stepovers and a dummy to the side. It was more straightforward, he would gain that half a yard, shoot and score the goal. That's all he had to do, it was so simple, A to B, and that was Alan. He was the best at it.'

When Kenny Dalglish moved south of the border to Liverpool from Celtic, little did anyone know at the time just how good the Scottish forward would turn out to be for the Red men. Dalglish had already collected four Scottish titles and half-a-dozen cup medals during his time at Parkhead and wasted little time settling in at Anfield.

Ronnie Moran described the forward perfectly: 'Kenny wasn't the quickest of movers, but he was 20 yards quicker than anybody else with his football brain and he would be in position before any defender knew what was happening. I've always said the best signing that Liverpool ever made was Kenny Dalglish.' Six First Division titles, one FA Cup, four League Cups and three European Cups later, everyone knew exactly what all the fuss was about. Oh, and the 345 goals in 850 appearances helped.

There could be a case for Wayne Rooney to hold his own segment in these chapters after completing a double record for both Manchester United and England. Bobby Charlton must have been secretly sick of the sight of Rooney, as the talented forward broke both of the World Cup winner's goalscoring records. I think the thing that sets Rooney apart from the others is similar to the Ian Rush scenario, in that both players were unbelievable in front of goal but were also surrounded by so many talented players.

Rooney's record for Manchester United was 253 goals in 559 matches, with the record-breaking strike coming from a wide free kick that looped over the Stoke City keeper and into the net. His record-breaking goal for his country was a penalty against Switzerland at Wembley. Rooney scored 53 times for his country in 120 caps.

He's also scored some memorable goals, with his two most notable coming in the Premier League. One was a fine volley against Newcastle United while arguing with the referee, when he then ran on to a loose ball dropping out of the sky and, in pure anger, smashed a volley past Shay Given. The other, and possibly the one shown the most, was the stunning overhead kick in the Manchester derby. This was against the backdrop of handing in a transfer request, which was soon withdrawn.

Rooney scored great goals but there was a huge dip from the early years' performances once the team of Ronaldo and Tevez was broken up. He looked a world beater when he burst on to the scene, but maybe it was a case of a little too much too soon for the man who was like a raging bull on the pitch. His record speaks for itself but, speaking personally, he wouldn't get into my all-time Manchester United or England teams.

Ian Rush scored over 300 goals for Liverpool across two spells, which catapulted him into the hearts of the red half of Merseyside. In fact, his 346 goals in 660 matches helped the Red men to a host of titles on both domestic and European shores. Stereotypical penalty box poacher, Rush had an uncanny knack of being in the right place at the right time.

Adel Taraabt was signed in the summer of 2015 by Queens Park Rangers after an initial loan spell that saw him light up west London with his skills and finishing, including an absolute belter against Preston North End. This prompted the Rs to pay Tottenham Hotspur a cool £1m for his services, an absolute bargain for a player who was about to turn water into wine.

QPR had finished 13th in the Championship at the end of the 2009/10 campaign. Manager Neil Warnock knew he had a special player on his hands and told the senior players that, although he wouldn't be doing the dirty work around the pitch, he would certainly win them matches. After watching Taarabt take Scunthorpe to the cleaners, Warnock giddily told reporters, 'I've never seen anybody with ability like his. At 61, I've never seen anyone like him in my life.'

Playing as an attacking midfielder, Taarabt's 19 goals lifted QPR into the Premier League. Some say he was the most talented player ever to have played outside the top division, but I think there could be a standing case for quite a few participants. Warnock certainly knew how to make him tick, in fact he told his players in no uncertain terms how the team was going to function with him in the side. After Taraabt had been dispossessed deep in his own half, which led to a goal, Warnock decided to put a new system in place. Taarabt said that if any of his team-mates passed to him in their own half they'd get fined by Warnock! But if any of his team-mates didn't pass to him in the opposition's half, Warnock would also fine them. It clearly worked, as not only did he fire them into English football's top tier, but they also won the Championship title.

Juan Román Riquelme was an Argentine midfielder who started his career in his native land, plying his trade with Boca Juniors. He played in the No. 10 role made famous by his predecessor Diego Maradona. Since the great man had retired, there was a clamour to find the next '10'. Many tried and failed. Juan Sebastián Verón, Ariel Ortega, Pablo Aimar and Javier Saviola all threw their hats into the ring until Riquelme arrived to fill the void. During his time at Boca, he won three Argentinian league titles in a row from 1998 to 2000, as well as two Copa Libertadores in 2000 and 2001.

Riquelme then signed for Barcelona, before moving on to Villarreal, where he became a cult hero in Spain for his nonchalant play, disregarding any opposition, whether they had a big reputation or not. At the end of his first season with the club in 2004, *Marca* announced him as their 'Most Artistic Player'. His 51 goals in 180 matches coincided with the rise of the Yellow Submarine, who were in the top tier of Spanish football for the first time in their history and not only qualified for the Champions League but also managed to reach the semi-final in 2006.

After his spell in Spain ended, Riquelme headed back to Boca. In his second stint at the club, he managed to secure another two titles in 2008 and 2011, as well as a third Copa Libertadores in 2007.

In more than 500 matches at club level, Riquelme found the net on 145 occasions. His strike rate for his country was equally good; he scored an impressive 17 times in 51 appearances. planetfootball.com wrote some words to describe the playmaker:

> Juan Roman Riquelme was caught somewhere in between. Arguably the purest example of the No.10, his languid style and silken touch enraptured at times and infuriated at others. A master of space and angles, unlocking tightly-packed defences and toying with the opposition, in many ways he was a player strangely out of step with modern football – a throwback to a slower-paced and less physically demanding era. Like Maradona before him, Riquelme went from Argentinos Juniors to Barcelona via Boca Juniors. And the beginning of the latter's career was symbolically entwined with the ending of the former's.

Ronaldinho Gaucho is arguably one of the most skilful players that I've ever seen play football. While the older generation could argue that George Best would take that accolade, unfortunately I wasn't old enough to witness the magic that Best could conjure on a Saturday afternoon. Ronaldinho, on the other hand, from the moment he left PSG in the 2003/04 season to sign for Barcelona, was an absolute wizard on the pitch. I was lucky to witness it, but not sure I could conjure up the superlatives to throw at him.

The Brazilian rocked up at Barça at a time when, yet again, the power had shifted back to the Galacticos over in the capital. Messi was still in La Masia, learning his trade, although he did acknowledge in later years the fact that it was Ronaldinho who put the Catalans back on the map. 'Ronaldinho was responsible for the change in Barça. It was a bad time and the change that came about with his arrival was amazing,' said Messi.

Ronaldinho's five seasons at Barcelona brought 94 goals in 204 matches. He was at the peak of his powers on the pitch, bringing back the La Liga title in 2004/05 and retaining it in 2005/06. There was also a Champions League win in 2006 against Arsenal. And let's not forget his memorable goal in the same competition at Chelsea in 2005, when he stood on the edge of the Blues' penalty area with a wall of defensive players in front of him and, with seemingly nowhere to go and very little back-lift, bent the ball around two players with the outside of both foot and toe to nestle inside Petr Čech's post.

He remains only one of two players ever to have received a standing ovation at the Bernabéu, from the home supporters that is. Diego Maradona was the first and, on 19 November 2005, Ronaldinho scored the second of his two goals that evening and the fans applauded him. His coach Frank Rijkaard spoke after the match to the press, who were shocked at the fact the home fans had given such high praise to an opponent, especially during an El Clásico: 'He transmits a lot of joy and pleasure playing the game, and he has individual skills that are of such a high level that everybody in the world adores him.'

With Pep Guardiola taking the hotseat from Rijkaard at Barcelona and Lionel Messi breaking into the team, Ronaldinho was sold to AC Milan in 2008. He endeared himself to the home supporters straight away by scoring the winner in the Milan derby, but his partying ways were beginning to catch up with him, with one media outlet claiming that Milan should cash in on their man before it was too late.

A change in manager for the 2009/10 campaign brought about a change in attitude from the player as Brazilian Leonardo replaced the departing Carlo Ancelotti. It seemed to reap rewards, as moving Ronaldinho out of the centre of the pitch seemed to give him even more creative licence. As if he actually needed any more. He scored his first Milan hat-trick in a win over Siena, which was a penalty, a glancing header and a 20-yard strike into the top right-hand corner. *The Estado De São Paulo* newspaper declared: 'Ronaldinho revives his golden years.'

By the time the Brazilian headed back to his homeland, his best days were, unfortunately, behind him. As mentioned earlier, Best was considered by a generation to be the most skilful, as was maybe Maradona after him. It's great to compare the players as it gives us plenty of talking points down the pub or round a table at Christmas. One thing is for sure, for anyone who had the privilege of seeing Ronaldinho in his pomp, my word, you were absolutely spoilt. Some of his tricks were as dirty as a miner's helmet.

During the mid-1980s, Michel Platini was virtually unplayable at times. During the period between 1983 and 1987, he spearheaded a Juventus team to multiple titles, as well as having success with the French national team. His knack of scoring important goals enabled his team to sweep the floor with the opposition. Throughout this period, Platini notched 103 times in 222 appearances for the Old Lady of Turin, as well as 41 goals in 71 matches while on international duty. His honours included two Serie A titles, the Coppa Italia, European Cup and the Cup Winners' Cup, as well as single-handedly dragging France through the 1984 European Championships, winning both the player of the tournament and the Golden Boot.

Sticking with the Juventus player vibe, Andrea Pirlo is thrown into the mix. Having made his breakthrough into the Brescia first team at the tender age of 16, Pirlo soon found his talents taking him to Inter Milan. His fledgling career looked to stall at Inter before he crossed the San Siro divide to big brother AC Milan, under Carlo Ancelotti. It was with the Rossoneri that Pirlo would flourish in a deeper playmaking role. His ability to dictate the tempo of a match and his eye-of-the-needle passing brought him the nickname 'L'architetto' (the Architect).

Milan embarked on another golden era with Pirlo pulling the strings. After a decade in the fashion capital of Italy, Pirlo had chalked up two Scudettos, two Champions Leagues, the Coppa Italia, and the Supercoppa Italiana, as well as helping Italy to the 2006 World Cup. The man was laid back, in fact so laid back he was practically horizontal. When quizzed about nerves prior to the biggest match of his career, the unruffled midfielder replied, 'I don't feel pressure ... I don't give a toss about it. I spent the afternoon of Sunday, 9 July 2006 in Berlin sleeping and playing the PlayStation. In the evening I went out and won the World Cup.'

Like an Italian fine wine, Pirlo simply got better with age. A mutual decision not to extend his contract with Milan in 2011 meant that the midfielder was a free agent. Juventus, whose model in the last two decades has been to attract top talent without having to pay a transfer fee, swooped. Goalkeeper Gianluigi Buffon was excited about the potential signing. 'When Andrea told me that he was joining us, the first thing I thought was: "God exists". A player of his level and ability, not to mention that he was free, I think it was the signing of the century!'

Pirlo continued his slick passing game and, during his four seasons at Juventus, he won four league titles, a Coppa Italia and a Supercoppa Italiana. He also appeared in the Italy team that lost in the final of the 2012 European Championship. Despite three man-of-the-match awards in the tournament, Pirlo was helpless to stop a rampant Spain from taking home the trophy.

The superlatives for Pirlo came from across the world. Italian legend Roberto Baggio said, 'His vision, what he can do with the ball, and what he's able to create, make him a true superstar. Andrea has something which you don't see very often.' Barcelona's Xavi continued the praise: 'A footballer in capital letters, spectacular. There is no player in the world right now that shares Pirlo's talent. We played at all levels before finally meeting as professionals, when he was playing for Italy, Milan, and Juventus. I have always been a fan and admirer of Pirlo.'

Matt Le Tissier was a cult hero on the south coast of England, where he spent almost his entire career playing for his boyhood club, Southampton. Signed on YTS forms in 1985, Le Tissier made his First Division debut for the club in a 4-3 defeat to Norwich City in 1986/87. The attacking midfielder, who had a keen eye for goal, scored his first two goals in a 4-1 League Cup win over Ron Atkinson's Manchester United, the final match before Big Ron's sacking.

Le Tissier fired in over 20 goals in the 1989/90 campaign, which brought the playmaker the PFA Young Player of the Year award and helped the Saints to a seventh-place finish in the table. 'Le God' shunned interest from clubs such as Tottenham, Chelsea and even Liverpool to stay at his beloved Southampton. He lit up The Dell every other weekend with his performances, even if the Saints didn't always go marching in, as Southampton found the early Premier League years a struggle.

Despite their yearly scrapes with the bottom three, Le Tissier hosted his own goal of the season competition each week. If you were to show kids a showreel of his goals, they would probably think he was one of the greatest players of all time. I can barely remember him scoring a tap-in. His penalty record wasn't bad either. 'Le God' scored 47 of 48 spot kicks, with only Nottingham Forest's Mark Crossley denying a perfect record. Now that's a pub quiz question if ever I saw one.

Le Tissier's two goals against Newcastle in October 1993 were pivotal for the player, who had seemingly been bombed out by his manager. Returning to the team, Le Tissier scored not one absolute banger but two in a 2-1 win over the Magpies. A long ball up from defence was headed towards Le Tissier by Iain Dowie, although it was just a tad behind the playmaker. However, 'Le God' stuck out a leg and managed to flick the ball back into his own path, which tempted Barry Venison towards the ball. His lunge allowed the Southampton man to flick it past him, enticing Kevin Scott to attempt to cover for his stranded team-mate. The third touch, the most important one, was far more controlled, as he lifted the ball over Scott's head, creating a one on one with the goalkeeper. Many would have smashed the volley as hard as they could towards goal, but not Le Tissier. He composed himself and calmly side-footed the ball past Newcastle keeper Mike Hooper, who just sat on his bum, stranded and bedazzled. It was a goal of pure beauty. Moments later, Le Tissier was at it again. A failed clearance from the Newcastle defence fell to Neil Maddison, lurking just outside the penalty box. The midfielder headed the ball across to the left, on to Le Tissier's knee. He flicked it up and unleashed a fierce volley into the top corner for a truly outstanding finish. Le Tissier reflected on his goals:

> That game against Newcastle is one that gets brought up a lot even now, because the two goals in that game were both pretty decent goals. The first one was my second-favourite goal of my entire career, and the winning goal was in the top 10 too. It looked like I might have been subbed, Paul Moody was warming up just before I scored the first goal, and as I scored it the camera panned back to the dugouts and I could lip-read the manager looking at him and saying 'sit down, Moods'. He'd been playing in my place for the games I was out.

Le Tissier's number-one ranked goal was the 1994/95 *Match of the Day* goal of the season. In a match away at Blackburn Rovers, he received the ball just inside the Blackburn half, turned to face the goal, jinxed past two central midfielders, before unleashing an amazing 40-yard looping strike into Tim Flowers' top right-hand corner. The shot was like a hybrid of lob and tracer bullet as it arrowed into the stanchion.

Also, his chip over Peter Schmeichel in 1996 was absolutely delicious. Receiving the ball outside the penalty area with his back to goal, Le Tissier turned to face both Gary Pallister and David May. He weaved in between them and delivered a delightful chip past the United keeper, clipping the underside of the crossbar.

Le Tissier may not have won honours like others mentioned in this book but his worth to Southampton was priceless. His goals kept them treading water in a league that was littered with stars, even if the Saints couldn't match other clubs financially. He scored 209 times in 540 matches, and most of them you could watch over and over again. His international career was very short, he only made eight appearances for the Three Lions, as he was constantly overlooked by first Terry Venables and then Glenn Hoddle.

In April 2000, Le Tissier scored a penalty to reach the Premier League's 100 club, the first midfielder to do so at the time. His final goal for Southampton was to be his most unique, as in May 2001 he scored the final goal in the last match to be played at The Dell before the Saints moved on to pastures new. It was written in the stars that their mercurial talent would be the player to provide the headlines, coming off the bench to score the winner against Arsenal.

World Cup winner and ex-Saints boss Alan Ball knew exactly how to get the best out of the player. 'Do what you're good at. Don't bother defending, because we know you're rubbish at that, but when we are defending, get yourself in a position where, when we get the ball, we can pass to you.'

Zlatan Ibrahimović is like marmite, you either love him or hate him. Since bursting on to the scene as a youngster at Malmö in his native land, the Swede has been a divisive figure in the game among supporters, managers and even team-mates. His talents took him to the Netherlands, where he featured in an Ajax team that claimed the Eredivisie title in his first campaign at the club. He announced himself to the world with a goal against NAC Bred in 2004, when he left about six defenders with twisted blood before slotting the ball past the goalkeeper. The finish was voted the Eurosport goal of the season and alerted clubs to his existence. Having won two Dutch league titles and scored 48 goals in 110 matches, Zlatan found himself at the beginning of a magical mystery tour around Europe.

Juventus forked out a sum of around £15m for the services of the striker and were rewarded with 16 goals that led them to a Scudetto in 2004/05. His following season wasn't as fruitful as he was moved out of his favoured central role and into a wider attacking position. Ibrahimović wasn't impressed with the switch. Neither were the supporters in Turin, who saw a poor run of form from the Swede.

By the end of the season, Juventus had been stripped of their last two titles and were relegated to Serie B in the Calciopoli Scandal, in which the club was investigated for match-fixing. Juventus were relegated and officials put forward a request to the playing squad to stay, but with Ibrahimović's stock rising, he looked for a move away from the club. He didn't have to move very far. From Turin to Milan, in fact.

Inter Milan was Ibra's next destination, with I Nerazzurri, where he would yet again find the net for a team that went on to win the title for three consecutive seasons. By the time the Swede had lifted a hat-trick of Scuddettos in May 2009, one of the biggest clubs in the world had been alerted to his talents. Ibrahimović's record of 92 goals in 208 matches while playing in Italy was up there with the very best on the planet.

Barcelona were keen to bring the forward over to Spain in the summer of 2009 and paid just shy of £60m for the privilege. Pep Guardiola was building a team and had just won the Champions League in his first season in charge. He was looking for a forward who could link up the play between his galaxy of stars. Ibra was in football heaven, or so he thought. 'I was probably with the best team in history. Their football was beautiful. When I prepared for a game, I knew I had won even before we started. I looked at the players around me and saw Messi and Iniesta and Xavi and Puyol and Piqué and Dani Alves and Busquets. Unbelievable! It was football from another planet and I loved it. It was technically perfect.'

Despite notching 26 goals in 42 matches and helping the Catalans secure the 2009/10 La Liga title, the UEFA Super Cup, Supercopa de España and the FIFA World Club Cup, Guardiola and Ibrahimović didn't see eye to eye. In the Swede's autobiography, *I am Zlatan*, he said, 'It started well but then Messi started to talk. He wanted to play in the middle, not on the wing, so the system changed from 4–3–3 to 4–5–1. I was sacrificed and no longer had the freedom on the pitch I need to succeed.' He also told his manager, 'You bought a Ferrari, but you drive it like a Fiat.'

With heads butting, Ibra was shipped out of Catalonia after just one season and found himself back in Milan, this time on the other side of the divide with AC Milan. His 56 goals in 85 matches brought him another Scudetto, a quite astonishing achievement considering he had won it with three different clubs in each of his first seasons. He was adored at the San Siro, but with PSG now being owned by the Qatar Sports Investors, they were willing to do whatever it took to bring the cream of Europe to the French capital.

Zlatan was on the move again and spent four seasons with the Parisians, where he scored an impressive 156 goals in 180 matches. This heralded a period of dominance in French football, with Ibra and his team-mates claiming four Ligue 1 titles as well as eight domestic cup wins. He also broke the club's record for most goals, which has since been broken again by Edinson Cavani. Jean Pierre Papin claimed, 'We haven't had a goalscorer like him in France for a long time. He is on a different planet to anyone else.'

In 2016, Zlatan finally made his way to England, where his debut season with Manchester United brought goals and trophies, including scoring the winning goal in the League Cup final in 2017. Unfortunately for Ibra, a knee injury ruled him out of United's Europa League win over Ajax. He scored

28 goals in 48 appearances, but with an ACL injury looking to curtail his career, Zlatan had an extended spell on the sidelines.

As Ibra does, he defies physics. He not only got himself fit but also found his form again after a move to LA Galaxy in 2018. In 58 matches for the Galaxy, he found the net on 50 occasions. He stayed on the west coast of the US for two seasons before another move, to the club where at the time of writing he currently resides, AC Milan. His return to the club in 2019 has so far provided 36 goals in 66 matches, but the 2021/22 campaign is still going strong. His last piece of silverware was the Europa League in in 2017, but personal accolades have continued for the mercurial frontman.

Zlatan's strike rate for his country is a goal every other match, and his record of 62 goals in 120 appearances is most definitely not to be sniffed at. His club record is 510 goals in 854 matches and counting. He still holds the record for the only player to have scored in De Klassieker in the Netherlands, Derby della Madonnina and Derby d'Italia in Italy, El Clásico and Derbi Barceloní in Spain, Le Classique in France, the Manchester derby in England, and the El Tráfico and California Clásico in the US. He's also the only player to score in the UEFA Champions League with six teams: Ajax, Juventus, Inter Milan, Barcelona, AC Milan and PSG.

Another player who was so close to making the cut and could arguably have had his own segment in the book was George Best. The 'Fifth Beatle' was an absolute class act during his career, which mainly involved playing for Manchester United before embarking on a world tour, showcasing his exceptional talents to the masses. His footballing prowess took him halfway across the globe, from Northern Ireland to Manchester and then on to the US.

Spotted at the age of 15 in Northern Ireland by a Manchester United scout, Best was whisked over the Irish Sea to Salford to meet Sir Matt Busby. The scout's telegram to the boss prior to his arrival read: 'I have found you a genius'. By the age of 17, Best was making his debut for the Red Devils and he never looked back. His first appearance in a red shirt was on 17 September 1963. He was seen as an integral part of the rebuild after the tragedy of the Munich Air disaster, which cruelly took the lives of half of Sir Matt's squad.

The charismatic winger helped United claim a league title in 1964/65, meaning a first appearance on European soil beckoned for the fledgling star. United faced a Benfica team that boasted a wealth of stars, including Eusébio and Coluna. Jon Carter, reporting for ESPN, described Best and his demeanour beautifully

> Before the game, manager Matt Busby had told his wingers, Best and Connelly, to stay deep for the first 20 minutes. Keep it tight and quieten the crowd. But George Best was only 19, too young for such caution. All he heard was 'blah, blah, blah'. When the game started, he grabbed it by the scruff. 'Watch this, Eusebio. And Coluna, Simoes, Torres, Germano, Jose Augusto. I'm George Best, and this is how it's done.'

United claimed another league title in 1966/67, which culminated in Best's most memorable moment playing for United. They were embarking on another journey into the footballing unknown of Europe's elite, reaching the 1968 European Cup Final, which was staged at Wembley. Even though United were on 'home' soil, the lads from Old Trafford played in their blue third kit. Best would again shine on the biggest stage of all, scoring the second goal by rounding the opposition goalkeeper in a 4-1 win over Benfica.

This was the pinnacle for George, and the reason he never quite got the accolades he probably deserves in this book was due to the fact he was surrounded by world-class players in Bobby Charlton, Denis Law and Nobby Stiles. Class, nonetheless. His interviews with the press were nearly as worthy as his performances on the pitch. On one occasion, when stopped by a reporter and quizzed, Best replied, 'If you'd given me the choice of going out and beating four men and smashing a goal in from thirty yards against Liverpool or going to bed with Miss World, it would have been a difficult choice. Luckily, I had both.'

As the banner hanging at Old Trafford states: 'Pelé good, Maradona better ... George Best'.

And last but not least ...

Paul 'Gazza' Gascoigne. One of the most talented footballers that this country has ever produced and arguably the greatest of my generation. His skills were so sublime and, on his day, he could dribble round players like they weren't even there. At times while on the pitch it looked like the ball was superglued to his toe. Despite some of the other players in this book achieving more success during their careers, as well as carrying their respective teams to glory, Gascoigne was something a little different in terms of his ability.

The most prolific period of his career in regard to honours was while playing for Glasgow Rangers, trophy-wise anyway. Gazza's first two seasons in Scotland produced two league titles, a Scottish Cup and League Cup. Team-mate Brian Laudrup, some player himself, adored playing alongside the English midfielder and was lavish in his praise: 'In his prime he was one of the best players in the world. He glided with the ball in a way that made him virtually untouchable for opponents.'

The north-east of England was home for Gascoigne growing up, Newcastle to be precise, with the Geordie captaining Newcastle United's youth teams before breaking into the first team at the age of 18 in 1985. Anyone associated with the club knew the extent of Gascoigne's talent, with Newcastle's all-time top scorer from that time, Jackie Milburn, describing him as one of the best players in the world after a standout performance at Plough Lane, Wimbledon. No easy place to play, especially with Gascoigne's career still in its infancy.

Newcastle United weren't as financially sound back then as they are in the modern day, so, with money tight, they looked at cashing in on their prized asset. Tottenham Hotspur were showing plenty of interest, as well as Alex Ferguson, who at that time was attempting to build a new-look Manchester United team. Gascoigne had promised Alex Ferguson that he would sign for United, so, with this in mind, Ferguson set off on his holiday to Malta, fully expecting the club to bring in Gascoigne. During his trip, he received the news that Gazza had made a U-turn and signed for Tottenham Hotspur for a record British fee of £2.2m.

Spurs boss Terry Venables was the perfect manager for Gascoigne. He knew just how much rope to give the player in terms of his off-field antics, which were beginning to become more prominent as Gascoigne's stature in the game grew. But there was a reason why the Spurs boss let Gazza have the run of the place. 'When Gazza came to the training ground for the first time, he got the ball, went round eight players and smashed the ball into the net,' said Venables. 'Just to see him play like that made the hair stand up on the back of your neck. Everybody stood there and applauded him.'

With the cheeky Geordie beginning to rip it up in the capital, Bobby Robson had begun to take note. The England manager had seen this young talent and, with the World Cup in Italy just months away, decided to take a punt on him in the build-up to the competition. He already knew that Gascoigne could be an England player but there were a few stumbling blocks, most notably his size. Gazza recalls: 'When I played for the Under-19s, I remember he came in and said one day, "You will play for England if you keep off the Mars bars!" That was his words to us … "keep off the Mars bars, lose some weight and I will pick you for England."'

Three years later, when Gascoigne was selected to play against the Czech Republic at Wembley in only his second start for the Three Lions, Robson told him, 'This is your chance against the Czech Republic. Play well and I'm going to pick you for the World Cup.' Gascoigne said, 'I set up three and scored one, and I always remember him saying [wags finger, imitating Bobby], "That was fantastic!"' Gascoigne's relationship with Bobby Robson was more like father and son than manager and player. Gazza would have Robson pulling his hair out with his antics but ultimately the manager knew that, given enough inches, Gascoigne would take a mile on the pitch come matchday.

In the lead-up to Italia '90, during a World Cup qualifier, England captain Terry Butcher was escorted off the field by Gascoigne after a serious head injury against Sweden. The match had ended and England had all but secured qualification to the tournament in Italy the following summer. Butcher, covered from head to toe in blood, marched off the pitch with every inch of his Three Lions shirt painted in claret. Speaking to the press after the match, Gazza said, 'I asked Terry, "Are you okay?" He just said, "Fuck, Gazza, I feel nothing, this is England, this is my house and no fucker comes into my house and takes anything." Sir Bobby Robson grabbed me and said, "That's what it means to play for your country."'

Gascoigne wanted to be a part of that. He was eventually selected for the squad to head to Italy and it was there that he introduced himself to the world. In England's second group match against the Netherlands, the European Champions, Gascoigne handed out a masterclass to the Dutch, most notably a 'Cruyff turn' against Ronald Koeman, which delighted the watching world.

Gazza was instrumental in a midfield that was both solid, yet spectacular. His last-minute assist for David Platt in the last-16 round was delightful. With England and Belgium looking to head to a penalty shoot-out, Gascoigne embarked on a run through the centre of the pitch. The midfielder was fouled and placed the ball down, a good 35–40 yards away from goal. Robson, screaming at Gazza to chip it into the box, wasn't having the last chance of the match being wasted by a speculative effort from closer to the halfway line than the goal. Instead, he delivered a beautiful ball into the penalty area and, with the ball dropping over his shoulder, David Platt arced an amazing volley back over the keeper and into the far corner.

England dispatched a plucky Cameroon in the quarter-final before meeting West Germany in the last four in Turin. Before the match, Bobby Robson pulled his maverick midfielder aside and said, 'Today, you are playing against Lothar Matthaeus, the best midfield player in the world.' Gazza looked at him, slightly puzzled, and quipped, 'Sorry, Gaffer. I am the best midfield player in the world.' It was moments like that that made people fall in love with both the player and the man. His sheer confidence in his own ability was not to be confused with arrogance by any stretch of the imagination. His innocence was part of his charm.

The match was lively, with a place in the World Cup Final at stake. Gazza was having the game of his life in a tie that had seen a deflected West Germany free kick loop over the helpless

Peter Shilton and a fine equaliser from Gary Lineker, but the match seemed to be edging away from England. In extra time, with the scores locked at 1-1, Gazza, ever enthusiastic, overreached for a tackle in the 98th minute, bringing down West Germany's Thomas Berthold. The referee reached for his pocket and showed the Three Lions midfielder a yellow card, his second booking of the tournament, which meant he would be suspended for the final, should England get there. They didn't. Penalty shoot-out heartache followed for Bobby Robson and his charges, but Gascoigne had already endured heartache of his own. In Gazza's book, *Glorious: My World, Football and Me*, the midfielder recalled:

> Suddenly I can't hear anything. The world just stops apart from the bloke in black. My eyes follow his hand, to the pocket, then out with the card. There it is, raised above my head. I looked at the crowd, I looked at Lineker, and I couldn't hold it back. At that moment I just wanted to be left alone. I didn't want to talk to anyone or see anyone. My bottom lip was like a helicopter pad. I was devastated.

Bobby Robson said, after the penalty shoot-out defeat:

> My heart sank the moment the referee took out the yellow card. My heart hit my shoes. Because I realised instantly, that was the final for Paul Gascoigne, out. And that's a tragedy – for him, me, the team, the country, the whole of football. Because he was so good, and he was superb in this particular match. The bigger the game, the better he got.

Gazza continued:

When I was crying, when I got booked, it wasn't cos I was going to miss the final – it was cos I loved it so much I thought it was the end of my career. But Sir Bobby just went at the end of the game: 'You've done yourself proud; you've done your family proud; you've done the country proud – be proud of yourself.'

Gazza's family was waiting for him back in North London. Well, his Spurs one anyway. He grew into being a Tottenham player. His link-up play with Gary Lineker was one of the main reasons that, during this stint in north London, Gascoigne had Spurs on an upward trajectory, never more so than when helping them to the FA Cup Final in 1991. Tottenham faced arch-rivals Arsenal in the semi-final at Wembley, with Gascoigne scoring what was to be voted the 1990/91 goal of the season. With Spurs having a free kick about 35 yards out from goal, Gascoigne placed the ball on the turf, dead centre of the pitch. Arsenal, seeing how far out the free kick was, only placed Paul Davis and Michael Thomas in a two-man wall. Gazza strode forward and arrowed the ball into the top right-hand corner of the net. To make the goal even better, it was David Seamen's side. The Arsenal keeper could only wave it into the goal as he made a despairing dive to try to keep out the rocket.

A 3-1 victory in the semi-final over their north London rivals was more than enough to catapult Gazza into the folklore of the fans. He scored all types of goals in all types of competitions. One of the more memorable goals of that campaign was in a Rumbelows League Cup tie at White Hart Lane against Hartlepool United. Gazza managed to score four times in the match, with the showstopper a jinking run through the heart of the Monkey Hangers' backline, before a left-footed shot nestled in the keeper's far corner.

The midfielder had been named in the PFA Team of the Year and had caught the attention of Lazio in Rome. His heroics in Italia '90 and sterling performances in the 1990/91 season had led the Romans to bid a record-breaking £8.5m. With Spurs in a little bit of a pickle financially, they were advised to cash in on their top asset to ensure that the club's finances would be put on an even keel. Terry Venables accepted the decision, but he certainly didn't agree with it: 'I'm very pleased for Paul but it's like watching your mother-in-law drive off a cliff in your brand-new car.'

With the transfer agreed in principle, Tottenham faced Brian Clough's Nottingham Forest in the FA Cup Final. Gascoigne was pumped up for the occasion, maybe a little too pumped, as his over-exuberance would ultimately prove to be his downfall. A few weeks prior to the final, Gascoigne was providing the fans with tears of joy. This time around, and after only 17 minutes on the clock, Gascoigne was providing his own tears, as a terribly timed tackle on full-back Gary Charles left Gazza crumpled on the pitch. Spurs physio John Sheridan raced on to the pitch to assess the damage and it didn't look good. Gascoigne was in visible pain and discomfort and was lifted up on to his feet.

Stuart Pearce placed the ball on the Wembley turf and fired in a free kick to put Forest a goal up. Gascoigne, like a puppet whose strings had been cut, collapsed back on to the turf and the midfielder's race was run. Sheridan, writing in his book, *The Limping Physio*, said: 'Gazza just said to me, "John, how long am I going to be out?" I said, "I don't know, but we'll get you fit." We both had tears in our eyes. I was sure it was the ACL, but I just said, "You've got a bad injury."' Sheridan himself had the unenviable task of reading a post-surgery statement to the press. 'It came up on the nine o'clock news and I nearly fell out of my chair. You know Gazza is world class and with the transfer to Lazio, it was going to be big news for the next how-many-months.'

The road to recovery was a long and lonely one for Gazza, made even longer after an altercation in a Tyneside nightclub. A fractured kneecap extended the rehabilitation period and nearly scuppered the move to Italy, although after the wait by Lazio, the fee was reduced heavily to just £5.5m. Eventually though, Gascoigne would make his way to Rome and begin a love affair with the fans from the sky-blue half of the capital.

His form was patchy in his first season with the club, having spent over a year out, as he was clearly still shaking off the rust. The media were far from impressed with his antics and post-match comments, but the fans absolutely adored him, even more so after the midfielder had scored an 89th-minute header to equalise against city rivals Roma. He was loved in other parts of Italy too. During a match against Atalanta, their Ultras unravelled a banner of a giant bottle of beer saying 'For you, Gazza'. In three seasons at Lazio, Gascoigne could only muster 43 appearances and six goals, mainly due to a catalogue of injuries, which included a broken leg. He also fell out with head coach, Dino Zoff, which further limited his chances of appearing for the Eagles.

Despite all this, Gazza is still absolutely adored by the fans in the Italian capital. When he returned recently, the crowd held up a banner that said, 'Lionhearted, Headstrong, Pure Talent, Real Man, Still our Hero'. Lazio president Claudio Lotito paraded the English cult hero around the pitch to the delight of the fans. Lotito said, 'Paul represents an important part of the history of our club and it was an obligation on our part to invite him to the stadium. The affection of Lazio people for him has never ceased. He is one of the all-time favourites and still in the hearts of many fans because of his determination, character, and the great games he played.' The club's general manager, Maurizio Manzini, was there in the same role when Gazza signed. 'Paul Gascoigne is a mythical figure for Lazio fans and very popular in general in Italy,' he said.

Gascoigne's time in Italy was over, as Rangers submitted a bid for the midfielder in the region of £4.3m, a club record. With relations at breaking point with the coaching staff, both Lazio and Gascoigne decided a move was for the best. Just like he had done previously with the Lazio supporters, Gazza wasted no time in introducing himself to the Ibrox faithful as he sprinted the full length of the pitch at Celtic Park to get on the end of a Rangers breakaway and inflict the only defeat their Glasgow rivals would face all season. Instant hero status achieved. There were more moments of magic to follow, as his inaugural campaign north of Hadrian's wall brought 19 goals in 42 league and cup appearances.

Rangers clinched the 1995/96 title by beating Aberdeen in the penultimate match of the season. Gascoigne helped himself to a hat-trick as he and Rangers ran wild, including two marvellous solo goals by the Englishman. His first was very similar to his superb goal against Hartlepool, dribbling past two defenders on the left-hand side of the penalty area before lashing the ball past the Dons' keeper. His second was even better. Picking up the ball midway in his own half, Gascoigne set off on a run through the heart of the pitch. Like Moses parting the Red Sea, Gazza just kept going, gliding across the Ibrox turf until he found his way between the two centre-backs and again finished high into the net. His third was a clinical penalty to claim the match ball and seal the title.

A first league championship for the player who had only tasted FA Cup success so far in his career. Rangers also reached the Scottish Cup Final, where they met Heart of Midlothian at Hampden Park. A 5-1 win ensured that Gazza's maiden year in Scotland landed him a league and cup double. There was also a double of personal awards as he walked away with the SFWA Footballer of the Year award, as well as being voted SPFA Players' Player of the Year.

With the midfielder enjoying his football again, it was clear to see that his form had massively improved. This was not only good news for Rangers but also for the Three Lions of England as the European Championship finals of 1996 were about to be held in England. Gascoigne was picked for the squad by his ex-manager Terry Venables, who had taken the national post two years previously. Venables, like Robson before him, loved Gazza. He knew that by pushing the right buttons he could produce the magic needed on the pitch when it counted. Stuart Pearce told talkSPORT:

> Terry Venables was an acute manager. He knew exactly how to handle Gazza. With the likes of Gazza, he almost treated him like a naughty schoolboy at times. There was one incident where Gazza had stepped over the mark and Terry, in front of the group, gave him a bit of verbal, so Gazza pulled his neck in a little bit. Just as Terry turned away, Gazza winked at the rest of the group – it's alright, he's been told, but I still love him – that type of thing.
>
> We knew how important Gazza was to us as a team. Gascoigne, who won 57 caps for England, never received any special treatment from his international team-mates. I wouldn't say we treated him differently, but he was the best player I ever played with. He's the reason why England got to two semi-finals. I'm just lucky that I was around at the same as Paul in our careers. I played the vast majority of my England matches alongside one of the best talents this country has ever had.

The start of the tournament didn't quite go to plan for the hosts as a packed Wembley Stadium could only watch on as England stuttered to a 1-1 draw with Switzerland. Gascoigne, in particular, had been quite poor during the match and there could have been a good reason for the dowdy display. Just a few weeks prior to the kick-off of Euro '96, England headed for China to play a friendly match. Gazza, approaching his 29th birthday, was allowed to go and celebrate with some of his team-mates in town. The drinks began to flow and, before you could say the words 'check-up', Gascoigne and co were being shown a local delicacy, the dentist's chair.

While sitting in the chair, the individual was submitted to the bar staff leaning them back, like a dentist does, but in this case continuously pouring alcoholic drinks straight down their throat. This was a release for the England players, just weeks away from a major tournament. The media at home were apoplectic at the reports and at pictures of established stars strewn across the bar with drink poured all over their clothing. Terry Venables was rightly cross with his players in private, yet in public leapt to the defence of his charges.

Teddy Sheringham recalls how England boss Terry Venables somehow managed to turn it into a positive: 'We know it didn't look very good to the public and Terry wasn't best pleased about it and he let us know in no uncertain terms. But what he did afterwards with the press was pure genius. He said, "Look, I allowed them out; it's on my shoulders." And he protected the players. He defended us and we loved him for it.' Gascoigne being Gascoigne, took the brunt of the criticism and felt a sense of responsibility for his team-mates and the way his birthday drink had spiralled out of control.

With the incident still fresh in the mind of both the manager and the public, Gazza was beginning to panic about being selected for the second group match against the old enemy, Scotland. He was desperate to play, especially as this was against his new club-mates, the country where he was now plying his trade. In the early hours of the morning, anxious and full of doubt, Gascoigne knocked on Venables's hotel room door and begged to be given one more chance. Venables, not exactly pleased at being woken up by an agitated Gascoigne, was very coy about his selection process and sent the bleached-haired midfielder back to bed with a flea in his ear.

Venables was always going to pick Paul, but he wanted his player just to sharpen his mind again. The manager knew that, for England to go far in this tournament, he would need one of his best players on top form. Saturday, 15 June 1996, and Gascoigne's form couldn't have been any better. He was selected to face the Scots and lined up with the rest of his team-mates in the summer sun on the Wembley turf.

The second half ebbed and flowed, but England were struggling to shake off the Switzerland hangover from matchday one. Venables got into the lads at half-time and, soon after the restart, Gary Neville crossed for Alan Shearer to put the Three Lions a goal up. It was so nearly two as a Gascoigne free kick from the left to an unmarked Teddy Sheringham was headed straight at Scotland goalkeeper Andy Goram.

Scotland grew into the match and had chances of their own, with their biggest opportunity coming from 12 yards out. A low cross into the England box was met by Gordon Durie, who was brought down by England skipper, Tony Adams. A mirror image of the Swiss match was beginning to transpire as Gary McAllister placed the ball on the spot. The captain took his run-up and blasted the ball just off centre. Unfortunately for him, David Seaman had stayed big and pushed the ball away to safety.

Moments later came one of the greatest goals ever scored at Wembley, well certainly at the old stadium. Sheringham played the ball out to Darren Anderton on the left. He had spotted the forward run of Gascoigne and played a first-time pass, Gascoigne finding the ball bouncing just inside his left thigh. With Colin Hendry coming across to cover, Gazza flicked the ball over the defender and volleyed the ball past club-mate Goram. Wembley erupted. Gazza had demonstrated to his coach that he was to be trusted in a big match.

As the ball hit the back of the net, Gascoigne headed to the touchline by the goal, where a drinks bottle strategically stood at the side of the pitch. Gazza, quick as a flash, threw himself on his back, while Shearer, Sheringham and Redknapp squirted fluid into his mouth. Genius. A big two fingers up to the press who had vilified the team for their antics in Hong Kong.

Reminiscing about the tournament, Alan Shearer said to 90min.com:

> We were close knit, we had to be. We had to perform because of what had gone on in Hong Kong with the dentist chair! We did perform in the tournament really, I think, and everyone appreciated what we tried to do. We had a great team spirit. I can't remember whether if it was planned just for if Gazza had scored or if anyone had scored, but it all worked out really well – Gazza scored, he was in a dentist chair, we squirted water, the bottle was there. If Gazza had arranged that bottle there then it was perfection like his goal was. And it wouldn't have surprised me if it was vodka in there rather than water!

England and Gascoigne peaked in their final group stage match with another masterclass against the Netherlands, running out 4-1 winners to head into the last 16. A nervy penalty shoot-out win over Spain, with Gascoigne scoring the fourth, meant England would again face Germany in a tournament semi-final, with the Italia '90 wounds still raw. The Three Lions got off to a cracking start with an early Shearer header before Germany hit back ten minutes later through Stefan Kuntz.

It remained 1-1 late into extra time. England surged forward. Sheringham angled a delightful diagonal pass to the far side of the penalty area, where Alan Shearer had pulled away from his marker. Knowing that he couldn't get off a clean shot, Shearer volleyed a first-time ball back across the face of goal. Gascoigne had continued his run into the box but, as Shearer made contact with the ball, Gazza somewhat unwittingly made a split-second hesitation in his run. By the time he realised he could perhaps reach the ball, it was already past him. His outstretched leg missed the ball by the smallest of margins. You probably couldn't have fitted a rizla paper between stud and ball, such was the area of misfortune for England. The match finished in a stalemate and, as was the norm in those days, England crashed out on spot kicks.

Gascoigne had again played brilliantly on the big stage, but it was back to Rangers for his second season. Another league title beckoned in 1996/97 as well as the Scottish League Cup, but his drinking and off-field capers were starting to weigh heavy with the management team of Archie Knox and Walter Smith. With Gazza's third campaign beginning to become a mirror image of his time in Italy, Rangers accepted a bid from Middlesbrough and Gascoigne headed south to team up with ex-team-mate Bryan Robson.

Boro were fighting on two fronts, with a domestic cup and promotion back to the Premier League well within their sights. Gazza's first appearance for the club was in the League Cup final defeat to Chelsea. With matches running out before the end of the season, he was unable to help Boro claim a

Championship title, as Nottingham Forest took that honour. A promotion was there to be celebrated but that was as good as it would get for Gazza, as his omission from the World Cup 1998 squad and well-documented falling out with Glenn Hoddle led to Gascoigne smashing up the England manager's hotel room. This was despite Gazza's sterling performance in Rome, which qualified England to the World Cup finals.

With the midfielder's Three Lions career up in smoke, his drinking and injuries were now beginning to catch up with him. Another move, this time to Everton, where he again linked up with Walter Smith, wasn't enough to reignite the fire inside the playmaker and, by the time the millennium clock struck, Gascoigne was a shadow of his former self. Make no mistake, the end of this tale features a man who had been fighting his own demons for years. His football was a release from his torment of anxiety and antics that followed him wherever he went. Let's not forget that this man brought us some of the best moments in an England shirt during an eight-year period for the Three Lions.

Despite all his woes, Gazza will always be regarded as one of the best players ever to grace the Wembley pitch. But it wasn't just England who marvelled at his genius. Italy and Scotland both had the pleasure of viewing his talents, so much so that Gascoigne was even inducted into Scotland's hall of fame. Team-mate Ally McCoist, who played with Gazza for three years at Rangers, said:

> There's no doubt that Gascoigne has been one of the players to brighten up Scottish football over the last 30 to 40 years. It was an absolute privilege and a pleasure to play with somebody of that talent. I actually think we got the best of Gascoigne when he was at Rangers. And does he deserve his place in

the Scotland Hall of Fame? You're joking, 100 per cent he does.

He'll always be in my hall of fame. Barry Davies, commentating on the FA Cup semi-final victory over Arsenal in 1991, summed him up beautifully as his absolute worldie strike flew into the top right-hand corner: 'Is Gascoigne going to have a crack? He is, you know. Oh, I say ... Brilliant! That is schoolboy's own stuff.' Yes, it was, Barry. Yes, it was.

13

The Final Whistle –
The Man In The Middle

'If you're good enough, the referee doesn't matter.'
– Jock Stein

THE FOOTBALLING landscape is strewn as far as the eye can see with a portfolio of unbelievable players, most notably those that have been mentioned in this book. While we sit in the stands or on the sofa at home watching the drama unfold in front of our very eyes, we also need someone who can keep control of the proceedings on the pitch. The referee is a divisive figure, and a point of constant frustration and often mocked, by at least one set of fans anyway.

Pierluigi Collina was considered one of the greatest referees of all time. The distinctive Italian was renowned for his glistening bald cranium and the steely stare from his laser-like eyes. He was a much respected referee both in his native Italy and all over the globe, officiating at the Olympics, the 1999 Champions League Final, the 2002 World Cup Final and the 2004 UEFA Cup Final. Germany's Oliver Kahn told the *Irish Times*: 'Collina is a world-class referee, there's no doubt about that, but he doesn't bring luck, does he?' While paying the highest of compliments to the man from Bologna, Kahn was referring to the three low points in his career, in which, ironically, Collina was also involved: the 1999 Champions League Final defeat to Manchester United, a 5-1 thrashing at the hands of England in Munich in a 2002 World Cup qualifier, as well as defeat in the 2002 World Cup final itself.

Despite Kahn's misfortune, Collina knew how to handle a match of the uppermost magnitude, as well as the best players in the world. Collina said:

> The role of the referee is to guarantee that the game is played by the rules. You will only get a high-quality match if there are few fouls and few interruptions. On a football pitch, like in business, respecting the rules is a key value. So, the role of the referee could be considered as that of a service provider – for the players or for the game. But sometimes it's more than that, because making important decisions is one part of the referee's job and he can thereby influence the outcome of the match. So, in fact he frequently does become one of the main characters. Contrary to what some people say, I think the best referee is not the one who hides. The best referee is the one who always makes a decision when it's needed.

A man who was concluding his career as Collina was starting out was English referee Keith Hackett. Having spent the early to mid-1970s working his way through the Northern Premier League, Hackett eventually got his break and became a Football League linesman, before making the supplementary list of referees in 1976 at the age of just 32. In 1980, Hackett was given with the FA Cup semi-final between Arsenal and Liverpool. Just 14 months later it was the main event that he was in charge of. The FA Cup Final between Manchester City and Tottenham Hotspur in 1981 meant that, aged 36, Hackett became the youngest referee to officiate an FA Cup Final, until that record was broken by Michael Oliver in 2018.

I was lucky to pick the brains of the man who presided over many matches in three different decades spanning the period from the old First Division to the newly founded Premier League. My questions are in bold.

In your opinion who was the greatest player that you ever saw live while refereeing a match?

I have had the pleasure and honour on many occasions watching several of the world's best players from the best view in the house. Yes, I was chasing them down with a whistle in my hand, officiating games that they were playing in. George Best, who was at the time playing for Fulham on a muddy field at Stoke City but was still able to confuse opponents with his dazzling display of skills. He had an explosive sprint that could catch me out along with his opponents. He lived up to his reputation.

Marco Van Basten was playing for Holland in the World Cup U20 Tournament in Mexico and gave us a demonstration of his talent and what was to come. Carlos Alberto, the World Cup-winning captain, and I shared a cab on our way to Giants Stadium, New York. I watched him close up in a match, New York Cosmos vs Vancouver Whitecaps; he showed his leadership skills that day, calming down Giorgio Chinaglia, who I had earlier in the game issued with a yellow card after an outburst of dissent. After the game, Chinaglia entered my dressing room and requested a signed yellow card and thanked me for my performance.

Gordon Banks, we worked together at a soccer camp in Canada and, in the week, we organised a friendly game. He was between the posts and I was blowing the whistle. I saw how caring and dedicated to the game he was. We later sat in a cinema watching *The Untouchables*. What a player. Graeme Souness, Alan Shearer, Emlyn Hughes, Ian Wright. Paul Gascoigne, Glenn Hoddle, Chris Waddle, Derek Dooley. If I was to select my favourite, it would be Sir Kenny Dalglish, who always gave 100 per cent and possessed brilliant skills.

Was there ever a moment during a game that you wanted to stand and applaud something; if so, what was it?
Yes, chasing after Ricky Villa in the 1981 FA Cup Final when he rounded several of his opponents to score the winning goal. What a moment.

Did you ever look forward to refereeing certain teams/players, so that you could watch their talents from close quarters?
I always enjoyed refereeing Nottingham Forest under the management of Brian Clough. It was a team that contained many great players, including Trevor Francis, the first million-pound player. However, top of my list would be officiating at Anfield. Games where Shankly and Paisley were in control. What a team, what an atmosphere and such knowledgeable fans. The last game I officiated in my career at the professional level was Manchester United vs Liverpool: a good way to end my 23-year career at the top level of the game.

Did you find the bigger matches easier or more difficult to preside over?
A great point and generally the bigger the game, the easier to control. However, I knew that one major error by me would be the headlines the following day.

If you could have officiated in any game in the history of football, what one would you choose?
England vs West Germany, the 1966 World Cup Final. I was only six years into my refereeing career on holiday in Torquay. I watched on television and wondered what it must be like to officiate such a huge game.

Were there ever any players you disliked officiating over for one reason or another?
No, there were difficult players, but for me this was the challenge. How can I keep 22 players on the field?

If a player was on a yellow card and was running the risk of a second yellow, or maybe even a straight red for that matter, would you call them over and calm them down a little? What would you say to them?
I will have gone through what is my step-management process:
1. The quiet word, often delivered by running alongside a player and ensuring that he is aware of your thoughts;
2. Then a more public word, calling the player's captain across. Here it will be a warning with the words 'I want to see an improvement';
3. If a player has committed a red or yellow card offence the card is produced.

You officiated the original 'Battle of Old Trafford'. Were you not tempted to send off Nigel Winterburn for the challenge on Denis Irwin, which prompted the 21-man pile in?
What I saw was a 21-man mass confrontation. I decided that if I sent one player off, it could be fair to send a dozen off. Therefore, I reported the matter in detail to the FA. I attended for the first time a disciplinary hearing where both clubs were deducted points. I thought that outcome was the correct one.

Incidentally, when we reviewed the video at the FA, I pointed out several players who could have received a red card.

For those of you who have never seen the footage, it's still on YouTube. The match in question was on 20 October 1990. Manchester United were at home to Arsenal, a match the Gunners won 1-0. A late tackle on Irwin by Nigel Winterburn caused all bar the Arsenal goalkeeper to pile in on each other. Despite the skirmish between both sets of players, only Nigel Winterburn and Anders Limpar were shown a yellow card. The FA fined both clubs £50,000 for bringing the game into disrepute. Arsenal were docked two points, one more than Manchester United, as they had been involved in a similar brawl against Norwich City in 1989. To this day they remain the only two clubs to have faced a points deduction due to misconduct.

Emma Barrow of *The Daily Telegraph* reported that the match is said to have instigated the rivalry between the two clubs, which continued through the 1990s and 2000s. When asked about the events in later years, perpetrator Winterburn said of the brawl: 'It probably caused a lot of the bad blood between the sides that has lasted for years, but I was just competitive and desperate to win. Does it worry me? Not in the slightest. It was just one of those things that happened and is part of the history of the two clubs.'

It's fair to say that Hackett has seen it all on a football pitch, from the sublime to the outrageous. He's witnessed some of football's eldest statesmen in their pomp and revelled in the company of footballing royalty. At some point in our lives, we've all been a Keith Hackett or a Pierluigi Collina. Sitting on our sofas pointing out where the game has gone wrong or agreeing to disagree about certain decisions for or against our teams. But let's not forget what got us to this point. Some of the most gifted players that have had the pleasure of gracing the game of football. Be it on our screens or in the flesh, football's piano players. We salute you one and all.

Also available at all good book stores

9781801501255

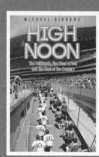

9781785317828

9781801501057

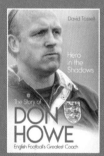

9781801500876

9781801500906

9781801501101

9781801501545

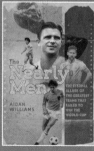

9781801500937

9781801500975